THE DANGEROUS BOOK

*

THE DANGEROUS BOOK

by
JAY RAMSAY

with Martin Palmer

*

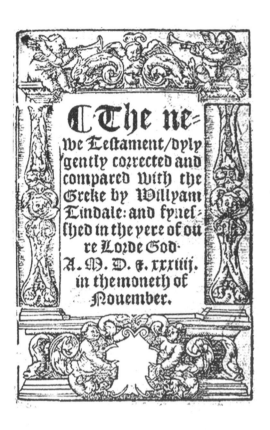

The ne=
we Testament/dyly
gently corrected and
compared with the
Greke by Willyam
Tindale: and fynes=
shed in the yere of ou
re Lorde God·
A. M. D. & . xxxiiij.
in the moneth of
Nouember.

DEDICATION
in memory of William Tyndale,
first translator of the English Bible
strangled & burnt in 1536

First published in a limited edition November 2018
Reprinted January 2019
published by Fitzrovia Press, Somerset

Cover and layout by Ranchor Prime

ISBN 978-0-9570722-4-4

Typeset in Garamond 13pt on 16
Printed in England by Short Run Press Limited, Exeter
on Munken Cream Wove 80gsm
All materials are FSC mix 70%

*

*

But the man who makes me his refuge
will inherit the land
and possess my holy mountain
—*Isaiah, 57:11*

Write the vision and make it plain upon tables
That he may run that readeth it.
For the vision is yet for an appointed time
But at the end, it shall speak and not lie...
—*Habbakuk*

*

IN SEARCH OF THE REAL BIBLE

Introduction by Martin Palmer

O UR MOST IMPORTANT SACRED BOOK has been stolen from us. This is why this book has come into existence.

Its wonder, its depth, its complexity has been ripped away and in the process its power to challenge has been hidden away, buried underneath a simplistic reading which has led many to believe that this Book has nothing to say to them. This most ancient and most contemporary of books has been reduced to a simple formula = 'God wrote it. It is True. We know what it means. Believe what we believe or you are damned.'

This book is a search for the depth and insight of the key stories of the Bible and their mystery, wisdom, threat and consolation. It is a chance to hear again the stories that have shaped us whether we are aware of it or not and which have fed the literary, spiritual and psychological journeys of millions through time and still does today. But why was it necessary to undertake the massive challenge of creating a new poetic version of the Bible?

One day I received a phone call from one of my dearest friends, Jay Ramsay. He and I have worked together since the early 1990s, starting with my translation of the Dao De Jing (Tao Te Ching), the Daoist sacred text, which he helped work into beautiful poetry. Since then he has been poet in residence at events which I, in my role as head of the Alliance of Religions and Conservation (ARC), have hosted around the world as well as poet in residence at St. James, Piccadilly, London.

He was distressed. What I have always loved about Jay's work is his exploration of the Christ story and his delving into the spiritual roots of our culture in order to address where we are today. He had been working with a musician who wanted to set some of his poems to music. This had been going well until he started receiving some quite extraordinary emails telling him that his understanding of Jesus was heretical and so he would be going to hell. Text after text from the Bible was hurled at him denouncing him and his work.

We discussed how this attack is part of a wider problem that the Bible has been stolen from us and turned into a document of disapproval, alienation or even as was happening to Jay, of attack. Those who have stolen the Bible, the Biblical literalists are so often intolerant and feel they have exclusive right to use the Bible. It has led to so much harm. And as we talked we realised Jay could do something about this.

The Bible is a dangerous book. It has inspired, infuriated, perplexed, stimulated and shaped Western culture—and now much of the world. It contains truths and lies and secrets and insights; it is the most contemporary of books, and one of the most ancient.

The idea that the Bible was infallible—for example in saying the world was literally created in six days or that Adam and Eve were truly the parents of all human beings—is modern. By that

I mean is a result of the vast upheaval in Christian thought and communities that was the Reformation of the sixteenth and seventeenth centuries.

Most of the earliest Christians were Greek-speaking denizens of the Roman Empire, heirs to the wisdom, science and understanding of Classical Greece.

They knew perfectly well that the world was of untold antiquity and that we had emerged through a process of evolution, even if they did not then have the strict formula of Darwin. They knew that ideas, myths, legends, stories and philosophy were all brave attempts to explore and comprehend that which lies beyond our language, experience and therefore ultimately our comprehension. Thomas Aquinas, the great Christian philosopher-theologian, who in the thirteenth century brought Classical Greek thought and Christian thought together, referred to this as: 'that which for lack of any better word we call God...'

Until the sixteenth century no-one at any serious intellectual level took the Bible literally. It was always the most marvellous store chest of incredible insights, human weakness, heroes and villains, truths about who we are and why we might be here and the sense of a God reaching out to us. Nor was this exploration of this sacred text done only in the context of Classical Western thought. Throughout the period of the creation of the New Testament there was an exchange programme running between the great university and library of Alexandria in Egypt and the great Buddhist/Hindu university and library at Taxila in what is now northern Pakistan. As a result of Alexander the Great creating Greek kingdoms in what is now Afghanistan and the Punjab in around 330 BC right through until probably the third or even fourth centuries AD, teachers would travel between these two great cultures .

When the theologian Origen studied at Alexandria in the early third century he studied under an Indian philosopher as well as under Greek philosophers. In such a context, ideas about time would have been framed partly in language such as that used by the Rig Veda, namely that this universe has existed for as many years as there are grains of sand upon the banks of the river Ganges. Such a theologian would not take the six days in Genesis as scientific fact. To the early philosophers and theologians of Christianity, the Book of Genesis was a useful source of imagery; a great handbook to understanding human potential and human folly as well as hearing God in response to these issues.

It was not true as data. It was not infallible. It was not right or wrong on issues to do with what we now call science.

These ideas of a struggle between Bible and 'fact' really surged when some people in the mid nineteenth century felt they had to combat scientific discoveries and theories. They used Genesis as a response to Darwin et al, and when that happened something was lost.

What was lost was a sense that the Bible is a dramatic story—indeed a set of different dramatic stories in reality—of an emerging, struggling, complex narrative between a God who begins to explore what divinity and creation, humanity and understanding is and a humanity which responded to the possibilities and opportunities this engagement offers.

So the adventure began. Jay started work, looking again at the key stories, insights and books of the Bible and retelling them as poetry. We would meet every couple of months and go through the background to each of the books he was about to work on. Through these explorations I discovered a great deal I had never fully appreciated before. In particular that in his journey through the books of the Bible, Jay was not just mapping our development—but also God's. Jay does not pull his punches. So for example in the bloody accounts of Judges and Joshua we encounter tribalism at its worst with brief flashes of something greater. But that sense of something greater often gets submerged by the sheer scale of tribalism. Jay traces this through into the New Testament and I will cover it in my second introduction there. Or when Jay tackled Job he delved deeply into the nature of the questions Job confronts. His rendering of the great prophets confronts us with their shocking condemnation of formulaic religion and hurls us into a face to face with the God of Justice.

As we talked, Jay and I also realised that a poetic response to the great stories of the Bible is not new. The English engagement with the Bible has usually been through poetry. In 731 the Venerable Bede told the extraordinary story of Caedmon, an illiterate farm worker who in around 680 joined a monastery in the North East of England late in his life and, when asked to sing, turned the great stories of the Bible into Anglo-Saxon verse. It was said that this gift was given to him in a dream and that before this he could not sing at all. The most famous of the few that we have records for is his version of the Creation. Though as Bede says, this is but a memory of what he sang, and does not do justice to the beauty of the original.

Let us praise the Builder of the very fabric of Heaven,
Praise the glory of his strength and the wisdom that is his.
The handiwork of the Guardian of the world, worker of
    all wonders,
He, the Lord of Glory everlasting,
Who created Heaven as a rooftree for humanity,
Making Middle Earth as our home.

At about the same time, the story of the Crucifixion was written down in Runes by an unknown poet and told through the eyes of the tree on which Christ was crucified. This account, The Dream of the Rood (rood is Anglo-Saxon for tree) opens our understanding of the cosmic, as well as giving a deeply personal significance, to the death and resurrection of Christ, as if told by a voice from nature.

Later William Langland's fourteenth century Piers Plowman intertwines Biblical narrative and imagery with the story of a search for faith, while John Milton's seventeenth century retelling of the Bible in his Paradise poems and Samson Agonistes has dazzled readers ever since, not least because Satan comes through in a most unexpected way. Since then others such as William Blake (in perhaps the most dramatic of language and imagery), Samuel Taylor Coleridge and William Wordsworth have grappled with the Biblical stories in many different ways; later TS Eliot, in his own way Ted Hughes, Mary Palmer, Mary Oliver and Seamus Heaney all play with the Biblical stories to help us understand who we are and where we sit in the Greater Story. And now Jay has taken up the mantle.

So why did we call it the Dangerous Book?

Because the Bible is a Dangerous Book when seized by those who want to define the understanding of God as theirs and theirs only.

It is a Dangerous Book when it is used to justify slavery, sexism, homophobia, the supremacy of some and the right to determine who is saved and who is cast into outer darkness.

It is a Dangerous Book when the God who is found is only the God of Judgment not the God of Love.

It is also a Dangerous Book because through it we encounter both our own attempts to understand God and we encounter God's attempts to understand us.

It is a Dangerous Book because what we find is a mutual process of enlightenment, growing wisdom and deepening relationships which challenges to the core what we thought we knew about God and ourselves, and have in many cases dismissed.

It is a Dangerous Book because it has never ceased to change the world and is going to do so again, and again and again.

And this volume in your hands is a Dangerous Book because it gives us back a story stolen by those who want to keep it locked up in the narrow confines of their worlds and minds. Dangerous not least because this version gives the Book, the stories, back to those who champion in their own ways the insights and truths the Bible has always told about us and our relationships one to another; to our God; to our selves and to our place in the astonishing story of life on earth.

The Bible tells us we are made in the image of God. So let's find out what that image really is and thus who we really are.

So we invite you to enter the dangerous world of God in discourse, engagement and in love with all life, and as a result rediscover that this great book is our own story after all.

Martin Palmer
Bath, September 2018

*

CONTENTS

IN SEARCH OF THE REAL BIBLE
Introduction by Martin Palmer   xi

Note to Reader   xxv

THE OLD TESTAMENT

GENESIS
The Beginning   3
The Fall   7
The Flood   9
Babel   11
Abraham   13
Jacob and Esau   17
Joseph   25

EXODUS
The Birth of a Prophet   30

LEVITICUS   42

DEUTERONOMY   44

JOSHUA
Rahab—A Prostitute   47

JUDGES   50
Gideon   52
Abimalech   55
Samson   56
The Spoils of War   60

SAMUEL 1
The Call   61
The Anointing   63
The Gloaming   65
David and Goliath   66
David and Jonathan   68
Pretender   72
Protector   74
The Medium   77
Death   78

SAMUEL 2
The News   80
Kingship   81
David and Bathsheba   85
Absalom   88

KINGS 1
Erection   94
Youth   96
The Wise   98

The Builders	99
Queen of Sheba	101
But	103
The Yoke	104
Elijah	105

KINGS 2

Elisha	113
The Commission	116
Jehu	125
The Sun and its Shadow	126
Hezekiah and Isaiah	126
The Destroyer	128

NEHEMIAH 130

THE PROPHETS

Amos	132
Hosea	135
Micah	138
Isaiah	142
Habbakuk	148
Jeremiah	153
Ezekiel	160

RUTH 177

THE PSALMS

Psalm 8	180
Psalm 11	181
Psalm 22	182
Psalm 23	183

Psalm 24   184
Psalm 40   185
Psalm 62   186
Psalm 86   187
Psalm 100   188
Psalm 104   189
Psalm 108   191
Psalm 121   192
Psalm 127   193
Psalm 130   194
Psalm 148   194
Psalm 150   195

JOB
The Storyteller   196
Scene 1   200
Scene 2   206
Scene 3   210
Scene 4   214
Scene 5   218

THE SONG OF SONGS
Scene I   224
Scene II   228
Scene III   230
Scene IV   233
Scene V   235
Scene VI   239

WISDOM   242

THE NEW TESTAMENT

INTRODUCTION TO THE
NEW TESTAMENT
by Martin Palmer   259

PAUL
His Own Story   265
Letter to the Church at Rome   275
Letter to the Church at Ephesus   297
Letter to the Church at Colossae   307

THE ONE STORY   317

THE ACTS—CANONICAL
Aftershock   399
Pentecost   400
Family   402
Sanhedrin   403
A Parable   404
Gamaliel   405
The Stoning   406
Not for Sale   407
As the Spirit Moves   408
Cornelius   409
P.S.   410
Peter   411
The Saint   412

THE ACTS—APOCRYPHAL

Thecla	415
Paul and the Lion	418
Andrew to Stratocles	419
Mygdonia	420
Christosophia	423

JAMES — 422

His Letter	424

JOHN 1 (THE FIRST LETTER) — 432

MAGDALENE — 447

REVELATION — 459

GENESIS CODA — 503

Notes — 521

Acknowledgements — 527

NOTE TO READER

Our main texts of reference were *The Bible Designed to Be Read as Literature* (Folio Society, 1957) and *The Jerusalem Bible* (1966)—with reference also to Tyndale's originals in the 1530s, and to the King James version which retains a huge percentage of his work.

Throughout this text, there are brief quotations *in italics* from these older versions designed to give a depth as well as a layering of language and resonance within the poetry.

We encourage you to refer to the original stories, especially in the Old Testament, that are summarised or alluded to here.

Jay Ramsay

*

THE OLD TESTAMENT

*

GENESIS

This is not a re-telling of Genesis: it is a series of meditations and reflections on the stories and symbols we know so well, and which have shaped us so profoundly. At the same time it is a reminder of those stories and for anyone who wants to read them in full. Meanwhile (Jacob and Esau, Joseph) the narrative thread gains momentum as the stories deepen from myth to human reality.

The Old Testament is full of stories, their psychological relevance there to be unearthed as part of the long history of our own nature. This coming into being of parts of our own nature is essentially what happens here, with its echo in subsequent books.

I N THE.
 BEGINNING.
 Darkness.
Formless...
void.
Womb-void
all turned inside.
Darkness over deep.

Sky over sky

But breath.
Then breath
the darkness breathing

Then a great word
a great cry
its echoes written
among nebulae...
star-yolk clusters
'Let there be light!'

And there was light
Light out of darkness,
voice out of silence,
a division bell—a line
between Day and Night.

*

The unknown writer
pauses

breathed through his pen

his eyes, his mind

through the crown of his head.

He writes...and he is
as it is

in darkness unseeing
until there is light

the Word
           that is light

the sun rising

dividing him whole
liquid and solid
left side and right

    *

This is man and woman
made in the image of Creation

forever our human form
so deeply conceived
we can't conceive of it
being ourselves created

as it is

firmament...sky
dry land...grass
the herb-yielding seed

stars...birds
great whales...

and everywhere

and always
it is a Book, and a mirror
a mirror, and a book

a dangerous book
for all our adventure

in the fire and truth
of what it means to be human

a chronicle of grief
seeded

in the long slow ascent
to Love.

*

And God saw that it was good:
what more proof do you need?

A miserable multitude of original sinners

*

Dominion: that crucial, ambivalent word
meaning responsibility, not domination
not centuries of flagrant unconscious abuse
not Man sleepwalking through his evolution—
what Creator could have intended that?

Whatever language the Word breathes in

it's our translation and loss of hearing,
scholarly or ignorant: the same dust
our bones are buried in: priest or pauper,
Pope and prostitute

THE FALL

GOD COMMANDED innocence,
but Man required experience.

Stay forever in the Garden?
Stay anywhere?

Adam his unconscious,
Eve the unconscious of his unconscious
deeper down into the birthing floor
womb, goddess, woman.

God commanded innocence, obedience
but must have known we needed experience.

The Fall of Man is a tripwire:
we were set up to separate and fail, at least
by the God of *our* creation...
                              an afterthought

of our own muddled thinking?

    *

Eve eats the apple

7

and her eyes are opened
Adam eats the apple
and his eyes are opened
this is the beginning of consciousness.

This is the end of the Dream
and the beginning of awakening.

Adam blames Eve
Eve blames the serpent
God curses the serpent
(and Eve, in the name of patriarchy)

But it means they leave the Garden
stopped short of immortality
to make the great pilgrimage of humanity.

God of innocence, God of experience

*

It gets worse, of course it does
because all these things have to come into being
(the Fall that is our only redeeming—)

Eve gives birth to the first murderer
the duality of our destiny:
Cain and Abel, Abel and Cain
and what it means to be either.

Cain was set up, too:
God rejected him

and jealousy was born.
Dark thoughts of separation
from Abel who has it all.

Cain, Cain, unbearable pain
picks up his cleaver of bone.

Cain is cursed
and yet preserved
his forehead mark singles him out
forever in the land of Nod.

Original sinner.

(And for a later fingertip
touch in time—
with its cross of Ash Wednesday ash...)

God could simply have wiped him
from the face of the earth.

We would have done, and we have
without a cunning plan

without the Serpent's Genesis
that has never been written in words.

THE FLOOD

GIANTS IN the earth:
an amused smile, echoing down the years

until a tooth discovered in Hong Kong
and DNA tested in 3D
suggests a man at least nine feet tall...

Meanwhile God seems unsure
of how long any of us should be living,
there is only infantile rage at His Creation!

Saving the best is what Noah was born for,
as God pours water all over his own painting.

Either that, or the first tsunami
in pre-recorded history
was framed within the story.

However hard it gets, God will not destroy humanity
afloat in the ark of our faith—
signalled by raven and dove.

God promises not to do it again,
requiring the blood of our lives.
His Covenant.

His bow set in the cloud,
his burning rainbow of gold,
his everyday rainbow after rain.

*

Noah gets drunk
his sons discover him
naked in his tent.

Ham is cursed for shaming him
Shem and Japheth exonerated
walking backwards to cover him with a cloth.

Noah blames his son
rather than his own cosmic loneliness.

The echo is familiar.

Still he makes it to nine hundred and fifty,
a little mirror of his own Maker.

BABEL

THE PICTURE of it
like Pisa
vaulting up into the dream of the sky
impossibly high
as the builders
strained to reach the sun
like Icarus
before his wings were born.

And our language was one
and God didn't like it
so he confounded us—

our tongues suddenly
twisted
into all their different sounds

to the left, and the right
and all around
as we climbed down...

What was it?
Another taste of what wasn't for us
and yet in all time
we've been building that tower
ascending through the centuries
from invention to equation
as near gods as we could be
but always fallen

and always fighting
refusing to listen
Babel became our babbling
exile in difference

Now we long again for union
under an empty sky

        *

God behind 'God,' surely...

Disobedience comes into being
jealousy comes into being
murder comes into being
incest comes into being

while God remains innocent
of the condition He has himself created?

ABRAHAM

ABRAHAM LIES to save his skin
Sarai passed off as his sister
as Pharaoh takes her in.
Sheep, oxen, he-asses
manservants and maidservants
she-asses and camels.
Pharaoh is taken in.
The plagues descend on him.

*

Separation comes into being
Abraham dwells in Caanan—
Lot on the cities of the plain;
the land could not sustain them.

*

Too many kings, all of whom
smote each other *astheirnamesruntogether*
like blood outside of their hearing...

only Abraham keeps faith with the altar of his listening
and Lot, beloved brother

*

Tricky business with the mistress
promoted by her mistress
to conceive the child she could not

13

—then looks down her nose at her.
Female shadow comes into being:
Sarai kicks her out!

God finds her in the wilderness.
Her name is Hagar.
Commands her to go back
but promises her Ishmael,
a wild man full of anger.

*

Circumcision comes into being
Abraham 90, Ishmael 13
the mark of specialness
for a father of many nations

under God of Babel and the Penis.

*

Three strangers promise Sarai she will have a son,
laughter comes into being! —
(Sarah is forty years past her menopause)
but in God all things are possible,
as he takes pains to tell her.

No joking matter
for a woman to laugh at a man.

*

However, compassion comes into being
in this God of Unravelling
as Abraham asks mercy for Sodom.

First direct challenge to God:
Abraham bargains...*chutzpah!*

This is a God who can also get it wrong
Abraham bargains by degrees
counted in human lives.

Meanwhile two angels visit Lot
and he'd rather give up his daughters for rape
than any harm come to these strangers
(as custom dictates...)

The angels strike them with blindness,
and God prepares the firestorm.

*

Don't look back
the past is dead
don't linger
on the burning ground

face forward for your life
or you are a monument
—your wife turned into a pillar of salt
dried of all moisture.

*

15

Lot's daughters loved him so much
they were willing to sleep with him to preserve his seed
'Come on, let's get the old man drunk—'

God refrains to comment.
Moabites and Ammonites come into being.

*

Isaac comes into being
and Sarai's laughter is sanctified.

But Hagar, her son mocking,
is sent into the wilderness again.

God saves them with water,
then turns to test Abraham
to sacrifice *an idea.*

This God behind God
is a complex Being.

He wants total obedience.

Abraham is led like a lamb,
Isaac trots beside him.

Blind faith comes into being—

and the ram is snagged in a thicket.

But Isaac is traumatised:

he wants nothing to do with this God,
only his wife Rebecca, who heals him.

*

Abraham insists he himself pays for the land,
honouring comes into being.
He buries Sarai in a cave
and the land is his.

400 shekels, Ephron: we are worth it.

JACOB AND ESAU

c. 1800 B.C.

THE RIVALRY of twins comes into being,
the light one and the shadow one
the smooth one and the hairy one
Jacob and Esau: and all the struggle between them.

Jacob wants to be Esau without being him
the firstborn for his father's blessing
so he cons him out of his birthright
for a mess of red pottage—his vitality...

Then pretends to be him, donning a hairy skin
bringing the venison old Isaac is requesting
so when Esau comes, he gets nothing
but confirmation of second place

until he breaks the yoke from around his neck.

*

You don't have to be pure to have a vision:
Jacob wanders out from Beersheba
on the advice of his mother (Esau wants to kill him)
and finding a place for the night, sleeps on stones,
then dreams the most famous of dreams:

a ladder rising from earth to heaven
all the angels ascending & descending in between
and God above blessing him
with all he could ever hope to be.

It's only a dream, or how he wants to feel;
the chosen twin. But God shows him
that you can go *up* and you can go *down*,
heaven's gate is your reckoning.

Jacob turns his bedding into a pillar;
pours oil over it, as if he knows
even as he knows nothing.

*

But he knows love when he sees it.
And even before that moment, as if in a dream
he rolls the huge stone from the well's mouth
to water the sheep.

Then she comes with her father's flock,

18

and kissing comes into being.
And Jacob *lifted up his voice, and wept*
we may imagine him
the stone rolled from his heart
watering his cheeks

as Laban, the father, comes out to greet him.

Seven years he stays with her father, for her
and they seemed unto him but a few days
before he can make love with her.

Engagement comes into being
like a rock, a foundation.

Jacob is grounded in love
and love's labours.

   *

Then something strange happens:
custom demands the firstborn
must be married first—
so Jacob has Leah 'for a week'

but then has to serve another seven years
to get Rachel!

Meanwhile, he has two of Leah's children
—she hoping this will turn him to her.

And Rachel can't conceive

suggests her maid instead,
and Jacob went in unto her.

Rachel's maid conceives twice,
so Rachel herself is satisfied.
(Leah and Rachel like competing twins)

Then Leah gives Jacob *her* maid.
Two more children.

Is Jacob having a good time?
Where is his heart in all of this?

    *

He shall lie with thee tonight for thy son's mandrakes
says Rachel

so Leah comes out to meet him,
as he comes in from the fields.

We may imagine him
between two potent females,
turned on to his seed.

Leah conceives, his fifth son
she reasons it's because
she gave him her maid,
so God is pleased.
She conceives again!
And again...a daughter, finally

God remembers Rachel, then
and gives her Joseph.

Jacob wants to leave and go home, now
wives and children in tow
but Laban doesn't want to let him go.

*

The Lord has blessed me for thy sake.

Jacob offers to take from his flock
all the speckled and spotted ones
if he will only let him go.

Jacob peels the rods of green poplar
hazel and chestnut
so that his flock will conceive,
leaving the weaker ones to Laban.

Then the Lord tells him to go home
and he speaks to the women—
sitting them, and his sons, on camels.

He's no prodigal
it's time for him to go—
taking his own strength with him.

He crosses the river towards Gilead.

Laban pursues him.
And remonstrates—

(Jacob has done a runner,
his girls have gone with no farewell
he wanted to see him off with tabret and harp!)

Meanwhile Rachel has stolen the images
sits in her tent with them under her...
telling him it's the time of the month.

Laban finds nothing, and Jacob explodes.

They set up a pillar of stone between them.

In the morning, Laban finally lets go.

*

Jacob returning home
sees the host of the air around him,
angels of the Lord. Sends messengers ahead, to Esau.

News comes back. He's coming, with 400 men.
Jacob blanches, divides his caravan.

Jacob prays, in confusion.

Love is coming to meet hate
that has festered, unresolved.

Jacob, left alone
wrestles with an angel deep into the night
—until his thigh is out of joint—
this stranger will not let him go,

until he blesses him...

In the morning, he's re-named ISRAEL
(meaning: one who wrestles with God)

And he calls the place Peniel
for I have seen God face to face, and my life is preserved.

Then Esau comes, with all his men
and forgiveness comes into being,
he runs to him and embraces him;
the two brothers weeping.

Jacob begs him to accept his blessing.

*

Rape comes into being,
Dinah is taken by Schechem in her tent
and yet *his soul cleaved unto her.*
Not merely rape, then.
But it's not how her brothers see it.
Meanwhile, she is silent.

The brothers come up with a plan
circumcision for all; one people—
but it's a deceit.

Deceit comes into being,
the snake slides into their minds
out of Eden...long left behind.

While the men are still sore
Jacob's sons steal into the city
with their drawn swords
and steal their animals, children, wives.
It is not dignified.

Tribal war comes into being,
not Jacob and Esau.

Their excuse? The love that is limited
that is only for our own
like the God we believe in that is only for us.

Meanwhile, she is silent
as the centuries which have no voice.

Tribal stupidity is born.
Her lover lies slashed by a sword
that has never solved anything.

Jacob returns to the pillar.

Rachel dies in labour.

Isaac gives up the ghost.

All funerals lead to Home.

JOSEPH

JOSEPH is a dreamer just like his Dad,
the rock musician of dreamers
with his rainbow dreamcoat, made by his Dad.

Joseph is narcissistic, a naïve young man
imagining his brothers as sheaves
all bowing down to him.

I mean, because he tells them so.
Joseph is hated for his dreams.
Even his father berates him.

'Sun, moon and stars all obedient to you?'
he sends him wisely away.
His brothers go after him

to cast him into a pit
with no water, or anything in it.
No blood on their hands!

Then the Ishmaelites come by.

Joseph sold for twenty pieces of silver
his coat dipped in goat's blood returned to his father.
That's what you get for being special.

Jacob distraught, his dreams all gone.

*

25

But the dreamer lives on,
finds favour with Potiphar, his Egyptian master
promoted to be his house's overseer.

Tested by Potiphar's wife, he overcomes
temptation like a chivalrous knight
—even as she keeps trying.

Scorned, she tries to frame him:
his master throws him into prison.
But still he rises. The Lord is with him.

Butler and baker both come to him
and tell him their dreams. He's listening, awake.

Clairvoyance come into being:
baker will be spared, but butler damned
the eye of destiny is open—

Joseph can see it.

Then Pharaoh has his dreams:
seven years harvest, seven years famine.
Joseph sees everything

and is put in charge of all Egypt
wearing Pharaoh's ring on his hand,
with a temple priest's daughter in his bed.

  *

Thirty years to heaven, the book says

and Joseph is a master of disguise.
Famine in Caanan. His brothers come down
to buy corn, not realising it's him
—accusing them of being spies—
the deal, their younger brother Benjamin.

They must bring him, or die.
Meanwhile he detains Simeon,
and as they open their sacks on the road
their money's been returned to them!
Joseph is teaching them a lesson, and
his dream will be a prophecy.

＊

The food runs out, they have to go back.
Jacob is bemused, too: he's part of it.
These selfish brothers to be stretched the extra mile
into the theatre of their awakening.
Joseph bides his time, like Prospero
as the love builds slowly up inside him.

Meanwhile, they bow before him
until he can begin to bear it no more
his secret tears, his forgiveness;
love stronger than them all.
But one last bit of magic left to enact,
his silver cup hidden in Benjamin's sack

will look like an arrant theft.
It does. Joseph's steward arrives—
they all go back to Egypt in shreds

of boiling anxiety, their dross on fire.
Joseph, alchemist, holds his cool:
their begging is purification.

          *

And the love is bigger than Joseph
as he orders everyone to leave the room
except his brothers: then it bursts open
his tears, his truth, his disciples dumbfounded
God sent me before you, he tells them
God the playwright, its director and dreamer

in a love that's only just beginning
Genesis, the beginning of everything
good and bad and beyond—
in a field where He is waiting...
as he asks them to bring their father Jacob to him,
sending them finally on their way.

Jacob's heart faints: his son redeems him,
the dream that seems insane is accomplished
the dreamer grown beyond his dream
in obedience to a love that is beyond him.

This will be the way, when Jesus
comes for the tribe that is humanity.

Jacob speaks into the last days,
in the eye of crystal: his soul transparent
as their destiny: only Joseph is truly blessed
his tribe among the twelve the golden thread,

Revelation, the beginning and the end:
Joseph's dying words: the road out of Egypt.

EXODUS

Exodus begins with a key story: the story of Moses. Moses is our first prophet; his daimon, his destiny, his huge task to lead his people out of the bondage that is Egypt with its spiritual materialism. But it also debates the nature of an angry God—a jealous God—and a tribal God defining 'us and them' that will be transcended.

THE BIRTH OF A PROPHET

1

THERE IN THE BULLRUSHES, with death all around him
and only the sky above him: the women waiting
till Pharaoh's daughter comes out and her heart opens,
long before God has spoken.

He is chosen as naked, on the edge of time
and in every living moment.
God the Mother must have been there,
Her Name unspoken.

2

Young Moses goes out among his brothers,
sees an Egyptian beating one—
and his heart ignites...
the raw burning is inside him.

Looks round, this way and that
then kills him, and hides him in the sand.

Who made thee a prince and judge over us? they ask him.

Moses has no answer: flees for his life,
and sits down by a well.

Is he wrong or right?
The fire is inside him.

The daughters come. He helps them water the sheep,
their father gives him Zipporah
and she gives him a son
Gershom: because he's been
a stranger in a strange land.

Somewhere between sane and mad
with only his heart to guide him.

3

Then You came to him in the desert
flaming out of the heart of a bush

that was his own heart answered—
and the bush not burning—

and the voice calling him by name

and his voice answering
to his Father telling him
to take off his shoes.

Sacred ground
there is no escaping
a place
       where there is no hiding

the Presence
       there is no denying

the eye of the needle
where only the I AM can survive.

Who am I? asks Moses
not yet understanding
this Being that is with him
(no man can)

4

So You hand him a rod
that is a wand
commanding him
to cast it on the ground

as it becomes
a snake—he starts away...
then takes it by the tail:
a wand, a rod again.

Magic comes into being
like his own hand
become a leper's hand—
then his own again

And the Nile water
become blood on the land.

5

Moses protests
(still not understanding)
being of slow tongue

And You tell him
I am your mouth.

Still he needs Aaron
(this is too much!)

You between them, as one
to tell Pharaoh
'Let my people go.'

Again, again, and again.

6

What does it take?
Rivers of blood.
Frogs. Lice. Flies. Dead cattle.
Hail, fire, locusts, darkness
strength beyond strength

until Pharaoh's hardened heart is broken
and Moses becomes Moses
made by magic with the grace of the Lord,
made by the Arch Magus of us all.

The Israelites, who once had to forage for straw
leave with silver and gold.

Moses carries the bones of Joseph with him,
who saw this world come to pass:
a prophet bearing his ancestry.

7

A pillar of cloud by day
a pillar of fire by night
across the Sinai wastes
the pathless land unchanged,
that once was under the sea.

Strange rocky shapes: cliffs, gulleys
asteroid fragments...like a dream.

Strength beyond strength
for the whole people, then
as Pharaoh's chariots come after them,
and they falter.

And Moses says *Fear not. Stand still*—
This is the end of the beginning.
Cloud covers the Egyptians,
and the Red Sea parts.

Pure magic prevails;
the sea walls crash back in.

The Egyptians see the Lord before they die.
The Israelites see the Lord as they live

led out of bondage by prophecy,
the trance where it all begins.

INTERLUDE = THE SONG OF MOSES

THERE'S only one problem
that still lives mightily in all of us.
Moses, or rather his writer
sees the Lord of Hosts as a War Fiend
whose morality is only satisfied by revenge.

Anthropomorphism comes into being,
conceiving God as we are, not as He is
or else, we may say: He has been through this
evolving into a very different Being

while His Creation still labours under the illusion
that he sanctifies our killing.
No wonder we had to kill Him—
or keep him alive as the deluded jihadist
He never was

champion of our own ignorance,
our own Red Sea uncrossed...
littered with bodies and refugees

Israel, Syria, Yemen:
one insanity.

Deus absconditus:
Korea, Vietnam. Wouldn't you?

'*I will live in the silence
of humanity's heart*

*the one place they will never look
until it's almost too late...*'

But let's get back to Moses
and the Land he was promised
beyond slavery and fate.

8

No water.
And the waters of Marah bitter,
but when a tree is thrown in

it tastes sweet.

You again.

And Moses speaks as if he is You,
You speaking through him.
Prophet, priest, king.

And at Elim, all the water they need;
before the Wilderness of Sin.

And again, they don't believe him.
Sinai after Egypt: a dread transition,
the past still clutching, calling

then manna from heaven
out of evaporating dew...
(they called it 'manna'
because they knew not)

...like coriander laced with honey
white in the sand.

Manna to be eaten now
or it breeds worms

manna of this moment
not to be missed

The present moment comes into being
beyond history and expectation—
the miracle of what is.

And Saturday's bread sacrosanct.

And for forty years out of time.

And again, no water
until they're almost ready
to stone him.

His rod again,
whacking the rock
for their disbelief in him.

Water of a Living God
(in whom all things are possible)

Moses raises the rod
and Amalek falters—
all day he has to keep it up
beyond weariness...

Aaron and Hur either side of him
our prophet sitting on a stone
till the going down of the sun.

Alignment comes into being
not losing the connection
until the thing is done.

9

Jethro to Moses: supervision
'You can't do this all by yourself
or it will wear you out
with people all day
from morning to evening.'

Moses listens. 'The thing is too heavy
(like the stone he's sitting on)
the people need laws.
The people need leaders, too
not just you.'

Jethro saves him: job done
goes his way home. His gift to Moses,
wife and family.

No one can live by God alone
(prophets and philosophers
          will go mad when they try)

10

You're an angry parent:
You come down in fire
on Your Untouchable Mountain.

You are a Jealous God—You say so,
You can't be taken in vain.

Oh lonely magnificence
in your Cloudy Tower!

O absence of relationship
there being just one of You!

These myriads of moons later
we sift the wheat from the chaff,

the manna from the broken stone.

Even Moses has to remonstrate with You,
human as you also seem to be,
great tribal deity.

Your anger becomes his,
passionate, operatic.

He breaks the tablets.
He decimates the Calf of Gold in fury.

He is a jealous demi-god
ordering butchery.

Chaos, insanity.

Meanwhile You can't be seen
even as You pass on by
there's only a glimpse from behind.

Your rage passes, a storm.
You replace the tablets

in the calm light of morning.
Moses comes down
the skin of his face shining

not as gold, but a light
emanating from inside him

born out of the flame;
like its secret name to come.

LEVITICUS

*Both Leviticus and Deuteronomy signal limitation, even with the
promise of a more enlightened view ('and thou shalt love thy
neighbour as thyself'). They are, after all, the oldest parts of The
Bible, books of the law that seem to be outmoded. Deuteronomy—
with its immortal phrase 'underneath are the everlasting arms'—is
also a complaint against this kind of deity and its unfortunate
proximity to dictatorship. But the seed of transformation is here in
the power of blessing.*

O UT OF THE DEPTHS of time
  out of the tablets of stone
comes the timeless that is Now
the fulfilment still to come:

leaving a corner of your field
for the poor and the passing stranger,
your vineyard also...

and thou shalt love thy neighbour as thyself.

LEVITICUS

Your heart leaps up until you read
of the woman about to be whipped
while the man gets off with a ram
who scapegoats his infidelity for him.

Broken stone in the rain: a necropolis
of outdated codes leading to the Vatican

adultery, beard trimming, piercing, tattoos
are yet to be in fashion
—as is racial inclusion.

Weights and measures fill with the rain
until one comes who will utterly tip the balance
(like the tables in the temple—)
and recycle the Leviticus Newspaper forever.

DEUTERONOMY

POOR CHILDREN of Israel
left wandering in the desert: hot, cold
hungry, thirsty, human, complaining
only to have rage constantly thrown against them

without empathy, gentleness, tenderness
without the Mother: a crotchety old man
ranting in the attic of the sky
hurling fire, plagues, judgement.

You stupid old dictator
template for all future dictators
get yourself a wife: find some friends
deal with your metaphysical insecurity
I am weary of your humourless affliction.

What kind of God is this
tribal vengeful superpower?
No Father of mine, or the future.

*

But when Moses blesses, the future is born
from his mouth and his human heart
the blood on his hands as if washed clean

the thousand saints in his inner eye
his prayer for Reuben and Judah
the love of the Lord that can be
in Benjamin, wrapped round him like a cloak
breathing between his shoulders

and for Joseph blessing his land, blessing Creation
the dew, the fruits of sun and moon
the mountains and the hills, the flowers, the bush
and the blessing on the crown of his head
that is his hair, his skin exposed, open
no earthly crown of gold or a king
but a white infinity opening
into the heart of spirit

his glory a man's, an animal's
and the rarest of horses, a unicorn's
to bring the people together—

This is blessing
for Zebulun in his going out
and Issachar in her coming in
this is the abundance of the sea
like a breast for humanity
and hidden treasure in the sand

Gad the lion, Dan the lion's whelp
Napthali, also blessed: and Asher
where the true God is his refuge
and beneath him, the everlasting arms.

Moses dreams of Israel before he dies,
from the top of a mountain: looking down
to the south and the sea across the plains.
He is shown it, but cannot go there
because it is the future, and his time has come
but I have seen what I have seen.

His burial place in Moab a mystery,
no one has ever found it.

He dies like a dream into a dream
the way he'd floated, among the bullrushes
with only the sky to answer him.

And he'll become that sky and a future son
who will find the Father inside him.

JOSHUA

Joshua: we pass on to the first of many stories about or including strong women. We may be surprised by how strongly the feminine is represented here, perhaps because we are used to seeing women in the past portrayed as secondary. Rahab here speaks in her own voice directly.

RAHAB—A PROSTITUTE

THEY'D BEEN sent out to spy,
   but I knew who they were
those children of Israel.
We'd heard all about them
and their mighty God of Fire
(I know a God like that
in the anger inside every man.
I know how it softens, too).
So they came in under my roof.

Clean enough men, burnt bright by the desert—
but they had their own business.
I liked them though, and more
than our jumped-up Jericho king who thought
I was always here to do his bidding.
I've always been my own woman.
So I took them up to the roof
and hid them under the piled flax
as they questioned me at my door.
I let them go by—'quickly, that way!'
I feigned urgency. I know how to pretend, to men.
Then I told them (come back down) all I knew
the Red Sea, the Amorites, Jordan, all of it
to make a pledge, a promise with them.
As I said: I liked them: they were different.
Their God had somehow spoken to me.
Our life for yours, they agreed.

I let them down on a cord by the window;
I told them, wait three days in the mountains.
And they said: *hang this scarlet thread*
in this same window, then we will know.
I still have it, coiled here in my hand.

I heard they'd surrounded us.
The Jericho men jeered at them
with their covenant like a sedan chair.
Then we heard the trumpets—shrill, blasting
around and around like a spell
and then what we thought could never happen—
the whole front city wall fell down.

JOSHUA

I stayed in my house. It was terrible.
The sound of their swords was everywhere,
the cries of our people: of pleasure turned pain
a devil inside every man, woman and child.
They even killed the animals. Everything.

I watched the scarlet thread dangle,
with their blood.

My heart wept: I had betrayed them.
For what? for something new, I thought.
I can't explain. I chose it, in spite of me.

When they came for me, I was ready
—all of us, my whole family—
but all I felt inside was confusion, shame.
They have taken us to be with them,
with all the city's treasures,
all that was left, and this scarlet thread.

My gate is shut: I will never touch
a strange man again.

JUDGES

Judges continues the theme of 'judgement': meanwhile human expression if our nature is opportunist, visceral, violent—and not specific to men or women either. But out of this amoral situation heroism can emerge beside the lesser evil of men like Gideon and Abimalech. This is also the paradox of Samson, bound to his body (and emotions), pushed into his spirit. Meanwhile the spirit of woman is also oppressed and suffering: 'The Spoils of War' imagines a line being drawn.

I NTERESTING CONCEPT: God's next move
to set up judges against his errant children,
in the form of their oppressors, while they go *a-whoring*
after other gods...more golden calves.

Possessive father, mystical patriarch
brings on Eglon, king of the Moabites
a mini-pharaoh they are bound to for eighteen years;

but also brings on Ehud, a left-handed man

50

who does a very left-handed thing—
the bearer of a gift hidden along his right thigh
—a double-sided sharpness.

Poor fat Eglon sitting in his summerhouse
is duly deceived, and receives the gift
up to the hilt in his swollen gut
as all the shit pours out.

A shady business, no doubt.

Elud escapes and trumpets his success
on the mountain, as he leads them down
to slaughter ten thousand Moabites in a day.

Apparently, a good result.

*

Rebellion continues. Enter Deborah, a prophetess:
Israel has a female judge.

She presides under a palm tree that bears her name.

The Children now bound to the Caananites
with their nine hundred iron chariots,
commanded by Sisera.

And she prophesies their deliverance
on Mount Tabor
Sisera delivered *into the hands of a woman.*
How can that be?

51

(More left-handed stuff, for sure)

Sisera fleeing with his routed troop
finds himself outside a friendly tent
(or so he thinks—) as Jael invites him in,
with soothing words for his weariness
and a drink of milk for him.

How can he refuse?

She tucks him up like a mother, a lover.

Then as soon as he's peacefully sleeping
she takes a tent peg with her left hand
and hammers it into his temple—
fixing his head to the ground.

Job done.
   God alone
can take a righteous fork in the road.

GIDEON

STILL it continues. The Children bound this time
into the hand of Midian.

Meanwhile arises Gideon
while the children are hiding in caves
in the mountains; left no food
their enemies swarming like grasshoppers,
they and their camels without number.

Gideon, an ordinary kind of guy
is found threshing wheat by a winepress
to hide it from the Midianites,
as the angel of the Lord appears.

He speaks to him in his own language: *food*.
Asks him for a sign.

The rod strikes the rock again
and the whole picnic is consumed!

He deconstructs his father's altar to Baal,
and the grove of trees all around it.

The price should be his life.

But Gideon blows his trumpet
to awaken Israel all around him,
then asks for a second sign...
a fleece of wool left out overnight
full of dew, the earth dry beside it.

And it is so.

And again, literal proof: dry fleece this time,
wet ground all around. It is so.

But now it's Your call
to number the faithful who will not think
they've gained victory simply by their own will.

In the end only 300 remain out of thousands,

drinking by hand from the river.

It seems random, it cries disaster
but he will prove Your Power.

Even one of the men dreams
a bread loaf crushing the enemy host,
like a falling rock rolling from tent to tent.

Gideon is satisfied.

Divides his company: it's a night op
with trumpets, pitchers and lamps.

It's a pantomime haunting—a nightmare!
the host wakes up screaming—and de-camps.

Gideon in hot pursuit.

Succoth and Penmel deny him bread,
Gideon will revenge
their lack of faith with unholy rage—
he becomes what he's been told, a burning story.

There's no stopping him: no mercy
he's no prophet, or saint to come
he's a root and branch killer, and his karma
is to be entirely forgotten:
dust with his father, sand in the wind.

How many others like him?

ABIMALECH

ABIMALECH: the prototype of ambition
extends his father's curse: thinks nothing
of murdering all his brothers
to gain his position, or worse

(Abimalech, the bastard son
of Gideon's fling with a maidservant).

His younger brother survives
to prophecy the worst:
a tree ruled by brambles.

The bad seed already sown,
evil breathes easily in
among the men of Schechem
turning our anti-hero against them.

Deception follows deception
with two-faced Zebul.
Abimalech destroys the city,
and turns its whole ground barren.

Moves on to Thebez, his hour nearly come.
The men and women hiding in a high tower
as he hacks at its foundations,
tries to burn it down—

until a woman (a woman!) drops
a section of millstone exactly on his skull
his judge in heaven...and with his dying breath,

(because his ego just can't stand it—)
he gets his armour bearer to finish him off.

Irony has come into being, that is
all that happens without the spirit,
guided by the spirit—

our own judgement, and damnation
The Fall of Man falling still
down the corridors of history and time
crammed with their travesty of men.

SAMSON

SAMSON, superman
born of barren woman
purified, pseudo-virgin
immaculate conception—
a Nazarite (not Nazarene) unto God,
in the land bound to the Philistines.

The angel of the Lord arrives like a man,
vanishing upwards in the sacrificial flame.

Prophetic detail.

Samson superman sacrifice
tragic hero prototype—
exulting in the God of his own body
but all balls, brass: no reflection.

He's just not very bright
(but he will get you through a graveyard at night).

Desires a wife, a Philistine.
No talking him down. His parents try.
It's clearly not a great idea.

Samson, body-building muscle man
wrenches open the jaws of a young lion
on the way to her—

Samson, a lion of a man
takes his brawn from its body
its swarm of bees, its honey.

Samson, neanderthal shaman.
Wild man.

Puts his riddle to the Philistines
(we sense this will not go well—)
who, after a week, threaten his wife.

It ruins their wedding feast.
Finally he tells her, and she them

They guess it, then: *lion.*

Samson leaps leonine to the wrong conclusion
that someone must have *plowed with my heifer*
(his suffering wife) for the answer.

Tragic flaw—

slaughters thirty of them
to keep his side of the bargain;
and meanwhile estranges his woman.

Samson, jealous man
ties firebrands to the tails of three hundred foxes
then sets them loose in Philistine corn
as well as their vineyards, and their olives.

(More poetic licence we must assume,
the tale swollen, phallic in the telling—).

Samson very angry man.
They torch his father-in-law and his wife.

Samson rampaging man
kills as many of them as he can
(those bastard Philistines).

So they come to bind him.
He springs loose, of course—
powered as they are not
grabbing the jaw bone of an ass.

Raging, boundless ego man
bumps off a thousand of them, and trumpets it.

Warrior man, triathlon man
catch him, catch him, if you can.

Goes down to Gaza, sees a harlot;
hefts the doors of the city gate away with him.

Samson, unstoppable man.
Loose cannon of cannons.

Enter Delilah: the very subtle and different
sinuous strength of a womanly woman.

We know now what must happen.

He plays with her, but his will ebbs
he can't resist her invitation.

It's an outbreath, a moment of rest
his own secret longing to be loved and taken.

(He's a pussycat, he tells her everything)

The seven locks of his head...shaven.

Eyeless in Gaza, bound with brass
our tragic hero a slave—
reduced to party entertainment
set between the pillars in chains.

Samson, pure strong will man
only his strength can save him.

Prays one last time

to die as he has been made:
a burnt-out offering,
no one's judge but his own.

Mount Olympus, witness this:

watch it all come crashing down.

THE SPOILS OF WAR

EXPENDABLE woman,
taken all night by the Benjamites...
until she crawls back to her lord's lodgings
reaches the doorstep, and dies.

Lifted by him, put on to a donkey
ferried home: and then cut
into twelve pieces like so much meat
to be sent out into Israel—

What price can be paid for you?
Not this warring of men, bent on revenge
surrounding Gibeah: not this tribal ruling either,
even as the daughters of Shiloh come out to dance

you're forgotten. The Benjamites have wives again;
your sacrifice to the tribes, the silence of your flesh
in the suffering of every woman, centuries hence
before She rises up and says: *No More.*

SAMUEL 1

With Samuel a very different man comes into being, becoming a meditation of what true kingship might mean: the serving of a power higher and greater than ourselves symbolised by 'anointing.'

This brings us towards the first recognisably modern character in The Bible in all his complexity: David who becomes King David, juxtaposed with the obsessive Saul who may be secretly in love with him...he can't leave him alone.

THE CALL

1

THE PRESENCE of the mother
and the innocence of the child.
Eli gets it wrong:
he thinks Hannah is drunk,
when she's pouring out her heart to You.

In her humility

is her conception
that is Samuel.

What does it mean to hear the call?
Maybe it means to pray first,
and then listen...

In both, the yielding
in both, the conceiving
only known to woman.

But Samuel hears it too
(and so may you)
It startles him.
He thinks it's Eli calling, but it's You.

Three times he wakes him
(his eyes *waxed dim,*
his sons betraying him...)

then he sees it is the Lord:
the call passed over him, to a child
like gossamer in the wind.

Samuel hears it. Is afraid
but tells him *every whit*—all of it.

Purity knows no hiding,
and Eli surrenders:

only his own death to come,
his redemption.

2

The voice she calls on
calls her son

Mother and child
shall be divine: as One

Out of misused flesh
comes a pearl of reckoning

His words will not fall to the ground.

THE ANOINTING

SAMUEL HAS TO LISTEN to the people, too
as his sons go astray.
The glory is departed.
They want a king.

Samuel: you must be joking!
But they want their glory restored to them
(having forsaken You).

Saul is found wandering
in search of his father's asses,
a shepherd of donkeys.

They lead him a merry dance,
Shelista to Shalim and Zuph
where his servant tells him

about a Man of God.

This brings him to Samuel
with a fourth of a silver shekel
(Saul listens to him).

Samuel, the seer, sees him
as the Lord has told him, in his ear
Behold the man.

Saul modestly demurs
born of the least of the least
of Israel's tribes:

Samuel takes him to the high place
to feast...
                    and then commune.

In the morning, he sends his servant on
as they stand near the end of the city.
The moment has come.
He lifts a vial of oil above his head
and as it pours down, Samuel's words pour
into the hours ahead he is seeing
where he's *turned into another man;*
a baptism and a birth that pours
on into a woman's hands
over the head of her king
whose kingdom is not of this world.

And as many kings as years
shall rise, fall and be gone

before royalty attains
its true anointing.

'God save the king!' their voices resound.

THE GLOAMING

1

HERE WE HAVE something
never before seen
and it's only a mention, a sentence
like a whisper in a dream.

Music comes into being,
music after love. Prophets, kings, soldiers
have been angry unto death, raging
has been the norm, revenge
the order of the day.

An eye for an eye
like the sun at midnight.

Saul is no exception, until
his heart is strangely touched—
he sends word to Jesse: bring me your son.

Young David takes up the harp
till Saul was refreshed, and was well
and the evil spirit departed from him.

2

An Aeolian harp left by an open window
its strings brushed by invisible fingers
in the heaven that is our future, our becoming.

3

Saul becomes soul
as his namesake, Paul
loosened from his ego
for one twilight moment

by the Love that knows it all.

DAVID AND GOLIATH

SAMSON RE-INCARNATED
on the other side of the fence now
Goliath of Gath: inflated warrior man.

His height, his helmet, his breadth
the staff of his spear, the brass on his legs,
his shield-bearer out before him.

We all know this story:
the slingshot that brings down the giant,
the new world—the old.

Let's hear it again.
David is the youngest son
sent to run an errand
of food for his brothers and men.

He arrives. Shouts!

Goliath steps forward.
Everybody freezes.
David hears the prize
for outrageous courage

his question answered.

Eliah, his brother, jealous
puts him down
but David won't be put down.
Saul tells him it's impossible
(the old world cannot change)
—David tells him otherwise.

His harper's hands have the strength of an animal.

He heaves on Saul's armour
and then: he takes it all off!

Five smooth stones from the brook
his bag, staff and sling is all he has!

With his ruddy face and fair hair: a homespun,
he's a Fool, a zero card, something totally new.

Goliath laughs,
David speaks
the language of the brag
the Word against strength.

The battle is on. Till the end.

David runs. His first strike rings true
as a harp string tuned—

the stone sinks into Goliath's huge forehead,
his other eye...instant death.

No sword in his hand, you understand.
Severs his head, killed—

the old world is dead.
The new is born of faith
                    and sophisticated skill.

DAVID AND JONATHAN

THE LOVE of a man for another man,
and that love comes into being.
Jonathan's soul *knit with the soul of David,*
and Jonathan loved him as his own soul.
No word for it—but we know (if we do)
a love that is new
in a world that still refuses it.

68

Soul to soul, no tribal convenience
of fathers giving their daughters away.
No dowry, ahead of time.
They make a covenant instead,
and a covenant is divine.

Saul gets paranoid
(his evil spirit in a nutshell)
hating David's glory
ten thousand beside his thousand.

He really doesn't like it
(the ego hates what denies it)
behaves like a jilted lover;
but Saul is incapable of love.

He's had his chance,
soothed by his angel's harp.

Tries to marry him off to Marab.
David sees the plan.
Then he tries it with Michal;
David's put on the spot.

Saul thinks he's set him up
to be dealt with by the Philistines
no blood on his hands—
(already red with blood).

David only seems to oblige
taking Michal as his wife
(his soul already in paradise).

Saul only gets more anxious.
Jonathan, of course, tells him all.
Advises him to hide.
Speaks to his father, then

tells him like it is
Wherefore will thou sin against innocent blood?
David has done nothing wrong.

Nothing but killed the most dangerous enemy warrior
for all of Israel and its king—
Saul must be crazy. And he is.

He agrees, just like Pharaoh
with a promise as easily broken.
Two-faced politician,
sits with javelin in hand

as David plays on,
—then hurls it at the wall.
David already gone.

Michal lets him down out of a window,
an innocent man on the run.
She covers for him, like a son.

Saul sends messengers after him
into the aura of Samuel
and even they start to prophesy !

Samuel and David in Naioth:
Samuel the kingmaker.

Even Saul is touched
to take off all his clothes
in all that presence.

David appeals to Jonathan:
for God's sake, what have I done?

His crime in a twisted imagination
where the father tries to kill the son
because he knows he's outclassed.

David: *there is but a step between me and death.*
Jonathan prays aloud.

David hides by the stone of Ezel
waiting to see which side the arrows land...

Saul lashes out at Jonathan
for loving this son of Jesse
unto the confusion of thy mother's nakedness
arguing him out of his inheritance.

But Jonathan will not be swayed
even by a murderous, bullying rage.

The arrows fall. David must go.
He falls to his face on the ground,
then bows three times
and they kissed one another
and wept with one another,
until David exceeded.

Their bond only stronger, as true love is
threatened with its destruction.

A love that not even death can touch
that is the Lord's dominion,

and ever more shall be.

PRETENDER

'SILENCE, exile and cunning'
as it was later named—
David could have invented the phrase.

Feigns royal business to Ahimalech
to get some bread.
Purloins Goliath's old sword.
Flies on that day *for fear of Saul*
his hound of heaven from hell.

Reaches Achish, king of Gath
and feigns madness
scrabbling on the door of the gate,
letting his saliva dribble on his beard
(Achish is not impressed!)

Escapes to the cave of Adulam
and is joined by four hundred men
who hate the Saul Government.

Saul makes a self-pitying speech:

no one feels sorry for him.

Doeg grasses on David,
Saul sends for Ahimalech
who bravely speaks the truth,
threatened unto death.

Saul's footmen won't follow through,
but Doeg does. In every moment
we make our choice:

Doeg chooses sacrilege, the dog.

David, to go to Keilhah
against more Philistines
saving the city.

Saul thinks he has him, this time
finally surrounded.

And Saul sought him every day
but God delivered him not into his hand.

The Zophites come to Saul:
more self-indulgent speech
(Saul has no friends, really).

David is fleet of foot in the wilderness of Maon,
and then En-gedi, among the wild goats.

Saul goes into the cave where he is,
hiding at the sides. This is David's chance—

then he does a wonderful thing...
he slices off a piece of Saul's robe in the dark!

But in his heart, it doesn't feel right.

He follows Saul out of the cave
calling him by name. Declares everything,
likens himself to a dead dog or a flea.

Saul, blinded by his shadow
finds his heart missing a beat.
David is the prodigal. Saul weeps.
And confesses. David is the better man,
and he is.

PROTECTOR

NABAL AND his beautiful wife Abigail
like Beauty and the Beast.

Nabal is a thug-shepherd
shearing his sheep.

David seeks a barter with him,
Nabal doesn't know who he is.

One of his young men tells Abigail the situation.
Her response? The complete opposite
she sends bread, wine, sheep, corn,

raisins and figs, enough for all of them.

Bountiful woman,
rides in on a donkey.
And bows to him.

She's a woman ahead of time.

David blesses her
a true man, her true protector;
she goes in peace.

Nabal's heart *died within him*
and he became as a stone.
Ten days later, he's dead
his evil returned on his head.

Beauty goes to David,
with five bridesmaids on asses.

(Still, David takes another wife as well)

Saul meanwhile remains Saul
seeks David again in the wilderness of Zoph;
he's obsessed, he can't leave him alone.

Saul asleep in a trench,
spear stuck in the ground by his bed—
David has another chance.

Again, he refuses it
(who can kill the Lord's anointed?

Only the Lord himself).

But takes his spear, and his water!

Cries out to Abner. Saul awakens.
Again David asks him...same question,
a partridge hunted in the mountains.

Saul confesses again,
this time a little more fully
fool that he is—
(and not of innocence, but experience).

David doesn't believe him,
he's heard all this already before
it's just Saul in his abusive cycle.

David knows protection when he sees it,
goes to Achish: sane as the day
men, household, and wives—everything.

Achish gives him Ziklag
safe in the land of the Philistines
for all their wars against them.

Nothing (when you've had nothing)
is to be despised.

THE MEDIUM

SAUL is desperate.
He's thrown out all the psychics
and magician-healers from the land
but now he's surrounded by Philistines again.
And God won't speak to him
neither by dreams, or Urim, or prophets.
He is alone.

But hears there is a witch at En-dor,
exactly the rejected kind.
Disguises himself, goes by night
pretending to be what he's not.
The woman, of course, smells a rat
(she knows what Saul has done).

He asks her for Samuel: up his spirit comes
*Why has thou disquieted me...*he asks
Why are you asking me?
It is the moment of truth.
It is all bad news.

Saul collapses, the energy gone out of him;
he's had no food either.
And she, in her womanly compassion,
offers some to him. He refuses.

His servants implore him: finally he agrees.
How desperate do you have to be
before you can begin to listen?

Saul in a daze sits on the edge of her bed
while she does the cooking.

O great king
humbled by a woman.

How many men like him?
No need to ask.

And how many women
who have always had God in their hearts,
knowing the false from the true

and the life beyond the grave
there is no hiding?

DEATH

SAUL has lost everything:
Jonathan and his other sons.
The arrows rain down.
Picture him. Where once was oil
arrows shafts, piercing.
Tragic king.

He asks his armour bearer to kill him
who refuses, as *sore afraid*.
Nothing else remains.

He takes his sword, fingers the upturned blade
for a moment long or short
his whole failure in his hands—
then falls on it.

Cue armour bearer, who follows suit
faithful as an Indian wife.

'Those who live by the sword
shall die by it...' the unspeaking air
is the first to coin the phrase.

Head removed, armour stripped
his body tied to the wall of Beshan with his sons;

rescued by night, but for burning—
their bones buried *under a tree at Jabesh*
slowly turned into its sap.

SAMUEL 2

Jonathan is dead, David becomes king. The story continues. David's tears for Jonathan are repeated in his grief for his son Absalom who betrays him.

THE NEWS

THE MESSENGER arrives, a young Amalekite
his clothes torn, earth on his head
as David asks him for the news.

In one word, *Jonathan* is dead.
Imagine him: stunned.
Beyond pain.

He asks again.

No words then. He tears his own clothes, weeping.
Only rage holds him above grief, from drowning.

This boastful son of a stranger has to pay
for a truth that can't be named
that is breaking his heart,
as he turns away

to poetry, flung in the air—
like the finest spear, dissolving.
How are the mighty fallen!

The young man dead at his feet, like Jonathan.

Thy love for me was wonderful
passing the love of woman.

KINGSHIP

TROUBLE almost from the beginning:
David is crowned in Hebron
—but the kingdom is divided.
Saul's surviving son rules Israel,
Abner the kingmaker.

Disaster by the pool of Gibeon:
young men from both sides
meet in a weird dance of death,
the result—apartheid.

Abner in flight, routed
pursued by Asahel
as light of foot as a wild roe.

Abner tries to distract him
shouting back over his shoulder
'Hey, take that armour!'

Tries another tack:
'How would I face your brother?'

Then spears him under the ribs.

Joab takes up the pursuit.

Abner calls back with immortal words
Shall the sword devour forever,
Knowest thou not it will be bitterness
in the latter end?

—his cry reaching us now.

Joab blows a trumpet;
everything stops.
Everyone stands still.

The moment reaching us now.

But the war of the houses continues
like York and Lancaster.

Abner is sleeping with Saul's old mistress,
Saul's son doesn't like it—
(it's just too close to the bone).
Abner is furious after all he's done,
threatens to make union—in David's favour.

That shuts him up.

But Abner is serious: approaches David,
who barters for the return of Michal
his Saul-given wife...perhaps
his last link to the past.

It's hard on her, and her husband
it seems cruel and sentimental
but David's plan is union.

The deal is done.
But Joab wants revenge,
slanders Abner behind his back
brings him back from the well at Shirah

then taking him aside, as if in conversation
knifes him just like he did his brother.

David makes the judgement
Let it rest on the head of Joab.

David commands they mourn before his grave,
and David has the union.

And again: when Saul's son is murdered in his bed
as if to avenge him—his verdict is the same:
they hang over the pool in Hebron.

The ark of God is dusted off
and set proud on a new cart:
the celebration is a festival

of music *on all manner of instruments*
harps, psalteries, timbrels, cornets, cymbals.
And David is a dancer in his linen ephod
as they shout with the sound of the trumpets,
the cart entering Jerusalem

—and he dances, he dances

while Michal gazes horrified
from a window somewhere above.

David blesses everyone
with gifts of bread, meat and wine.
They're all having a good time.

Then he comes home,
and she's at him—embarrassed!
But he won't be shamed
his passion ignited—
it's a greater love he's dancing for,
'*It was before the Lord...*'

but she misses the point,
remaining childless all her life.

Unhappy wife.
(Did David really fancy her anyway?)

Meanwhile is Jonathan still in his mind?
He must be—their covenant
in all its secret divinity.
So when Ziba tells him Jonathan had a son

David sends for him immediately
lame as he is and bemused
by a king bowing to *him*
(David and Saul have changed places).

David gives him everything
he couldn't give his father
He shall eat bread always at my table
—and as his own son; with his son, too
his kingly heart generous,
after his own truth.

DAVID AND BATHSHEBA

DAVID's shadow has the pick of them
walking high up on the roof of his house.

Early one evening, spies Bathsheba
washing herself down there...

David-Lothario likes what he sees
her falling hair, hands soaping her breasts
give him the idea.

Sends messengers, and takes her.
Simple as that. Kingly prerogative,
to a man. No need to think it out,
or the possible repercussions of his must-lust.

However, there are some.
(More than a man ever bargains for).

She gets pregnant, for a start; and she's married
to Uriah the Hittite.

Damn.

Sends messengers for him.
Enquires after the war.
Tells him to go home and 'wash his feet'
(i.e. sleep with his wife)

Uriah does not, despite the gift of meat
sent after him (to appease him).
He sleeps outside David's door instead!
This could become embarassing.

Uriah's logic is impeccable
showing David up for what he is.
Not even drunkenness can shift him.
Then David writes to Joab

'See you put Uriah on the front line'
(then we'll hear no more about him).

David, you little shocker:
a better man than you has died.

He rationalises it to the messenger
for the sword devoureth one as well as another,
i.e. 'whatever'...while Bathsheba cries.

Then takes her back in, and has her again—
but not in Your Eyes.

Nathan intervenes: here's a parable for the king.
Two men in a city: one rich, one poor.
The rich man has everything, flocks, herds;
the poor man only has one lamb
which he loves like his own daughter.

But when a traveller comes, the rich man
gives absolutely nothing of himself—
he takes the poor man's lamb instead.
My Lord, what do you make of that?

David explodes, telling him
the man should restore the lamb fourfold.
Nathan the prophet tells him
what he already secretly knows:
Thou art the man.

He reads him the riot act, fearlessly
the bravest man we have—
sparing him nothing
(not even his other wives).

A new sun shines.
Time for my lord to eat humble pie.
He does it,

and his illegitimate progeny is the price.
The child falls sick. The king fasts,
lies down all night on the ground.
Not even the elders can get him up.
A week later, the little boy is dead.

What an absolute mess.

David gets up again: washes, changes
his clothes, prays; then eats again
but this is no resurrection.
His servants are enraged.

David: I can't bring him back again,
so what's the point in mithering?

He's wrong and he's right
and somewhere in between
Bathsheba conceives again
—a substitute son—

who's name is Solomon,
born of darkness and light.

ABSALOM

IT BEGINS with incest,
with a wrong that can't be righted.
Absalom's brother Amron
fancies their sister Tamar
and won't take no for an answer.
She begs him: he sticks it in anyway
(like father, like son?)
Hates her afterwards, rather than himself
little bastard.

She wears a robe of many colours

(like all the king's virgin daughters)
which she's tearing in as many shreds,
ash on her head.

Absalom is no help either
'Hey, he's only your brother...'
Tamar is desolate. David, his father, furious.
Absalom will have revenge:
gets his brother drunk, it's easy
as fucking.

But it escalates. The other brothers fly,
word comes back that they're all dead.

David torn to pieces
Joanadab comforts him: it's only Amnon,
but Absalom doesn't return.

David misses him, longs for him
as only a father can in his heart
(a heart that will be broken again).

Joab gets a wise woman from Tekoah
to tell the king a parallel story
quickening his heart to action.

She does it beautifully, even
as David sees through it.

He sends for his son Absalom
to come back to Jerusalem
but will not actually see him

(after all, he's murdered his own brother)

Absalom's a good looking guy
his hair alone is worth its weight
but David still won't see his face
—and Joab can't help him now.

So he sets Joab's barley fields on fire!
Demands a meeting!

David absolves him with a kiss,
but a kiss is still not enough.

Absalom sets himself up as judge
by the city gate: he wants his place:
rebel prince in waiting.

Goes to Hebron as if to serve the Lord
but actually to stake his claim
taking all his men with him,
and they knew not anything.

And the conspiracy was strong.
Wind of it reaches the king.
He's ready to leave at once
leaving ten concubines to keep the house.

Heads for the wilderness
(just like old times).

David sends Hushai as if in homage
to confuse the counsel of Ahithopel,

and of course to report back everything.

Meanwhile Absalom reaches Jerusalem.

A servant of Jonathan's son
happens by with abundance:
bread and grapes for everyone.

But Shimei also comes to curse him
and David lets him curse on:
behold, thou art taken in thy mischief
because thou art a bloody man.

David's Nemesis has come:
he knows it's the Lord speaking;
Shimei raves on.

Besides, it's nothing:
his own son wants to kill him!

Shimei throwing stones and dust.

Hushai reaches Absalom,
delivers his winning speech.
Absalom turns for counsel,
which is to sleep with the ten women
in the sight of all Israel!

He also offers to kill David,
and bring all his men back with him.

Then Absalom turns to Hushai

who persuasively disagrees
advising him to go out and fight
(God's hand, they say, was in this).

Hushai: quick, go tell David
and tell him not to linger.

The messengers hide in a well
covered with a cloth and ground corn
by another good woman...
Absalom's men pass on.

David crosses the Jordan.

Ahithopel goes home and hangs himself,
knowing his day is done.

David organises his army:
I will surely go forth with you myself also
but his men won't dream of it
Thou art worth ten thousand of us...
He hears them. Stands by the gate,

wishing no harm to his son
(but it's a dream: it's already too late).

Twenty thousand men die that day
and Absalom, riding under an oak,
is caught up in its branches by his throat
as his mule gallops on away.

How can we kill the king's son?

Joab knows the answer:
three darts to his heart—
ten young men to finish him.

Joab blows the trumpet again,
but silences the messenger. Not yet!

Tomorrow is the day.

Two men run.

David sits between the city gates;
the watchman sees them coming.

David hopes for the best.
'All is well,' pants Ahimaaz,
delivering the worst—

Cushi arrives, and completes it.
Two darts to David's heart
in the chamber above the gate
where a king weeps alone
as his heart breaks...

Would God I had died for thee
O Absalom, my son, my son...!

KINGS 1

We come to the Book of Kings and to the character of Solomon, David's successor and (womanising apart) a very different character, more idealised than real because it looked good for Israel in what was also a rare time of peace.

So in some ways Solomon is a PR job; but scratch the surface, and who he is can also be seen. The Queen of Sheba would agree.

ERECTION

DAVID SO OLD and cold
they cover him with layers,
but he can't get warm for the life of him.

Someone has a bright idea
that a young woman could accomplish it!

Abishag: she tries
'cherishing' and 'ministering'
but he can't get it up.

But he can for his son
and surely, this is the story.

When Adonijah fancies himself king
instead of Solomon,
Nathan and Bathsheba hurry to intervene.

David rises to the occasion,
kingly will is his being,
it's stronger than sex.

David sees it all as it should be
Solomon on his mount;
Solomon anointed.

The people shout.

Adonijah hears it in his last mouthful
as all his guests abandon the table.
No speech. The party's over.

He grabs the horns of the altar in fear;
prays to be spared.

And Solomon forgives him
—he sees it's punishment enough
he's more than worthy as David's son.

Father and son, both standing
kingly at the beginning and the end.

David prepares him for his death

'*I go the way of the earth...*'
he doesn't say 'to heaven'

only to *keep the charge of the Lord thy God*
as he's done (and also not done)
but above all.

Do therefore according to thy wisdom
even as he leaves him his legacy
of memory and all that's incomplete.

And more than that, he blesses him
with respect: a father can do no more
but for a son, that lasts forever
while he walks on in this world,
where he can also walk tall.

YOUTH

SOLOMON the wise? Not in the beginning,
he's nervous, knee-jerking, fearful, alone.
Adonijah wants Abishag for a wife
asking Bathsheba to intercede for him—
and Solomon thinks it means the kingdom;
Adonijah loses his woman *and* his life.

Abiathar the priest exiles Anathoth,
it's not even clear why. And Joab,
running for sanctuary to the tabernacle
called out by the young king's hit man
to be a sacrifice for all his sins

committed in fidelity...

Shimei, his father's Nemesis, bound to stay
as if under house arrest in the city.
Three years later, pursuing two servants
he breaks his curfew on his ass:
Young Solomon returns his cursing to him,
even as David condoned it.

Thank God he goes to Gibeon and has a dream.
God appears, asks what he wants from him:
and if 'God' means his own wiser part
this is how he answers:
he asks for *an understanding heart*
that I may discern between good and bad

confessing his youth, his ineptitude
and You approve—this is the turning.

Neither long life, riches, or his enemies
but what understanding means is
he can have *both* wisdom *and* abundance
and a reputation no king has ever had,
more gold than a Pharaoh could imagine,
and long life too—

will he be worthy?
He wakes from his dream.

He has everything to do.

THE WISE

TWO WOMEN come to him, both claiming a child.
Both gave birth within hours of each other,
but one baby dies...one remains
stolen by the other woman, or so she says.

Solomon listens into his wisdom.
It's an impasse. One of them is lying,
but which?

Wisdom is another way between,
an edge transcending: a third body and being.

Then it comes to him.
'Bring me a sword.
Why not cut the baby in two,
one half to you, the other half to you?'

It has the desired effect.

The honest woman speaks up immediately
'Oh let her keep it, please don't kill it!'

The lying one agrees: divide it.

The difference is plain to see
—it's easy to intervene.

Solomon gets it right this time,
and the story's on everyone's lips.

THE BUILDERS

THE KINGDOM is his,
and the kingdom is at peace.
Your promise is fulfilled:
they bring him gifts.

His heart grows with the abundance,
more begets more
even as the sand that is on the sea shore.

You are in him,
You speak three thousand proverbs
and sing a thousand and five songs,
Creator God.

Creativity comes into being
and Hiram, King of Tyre, becomes a friend.
And Solomon knows: it is given *to be given*
which means to give it back.

It becomes the House of God:
to be builders, not destroyers
—this is the story.

Cedars out of Lebanon!
Fir trees, too.
Wheat and oil for Hiram in return.
An army of builders, not soldiers
bringing stones to lay for the foundations.

Four hundred and eighty years after Egypt

in the month called Zif (which is February)
the children become builders.

It's a coming of age: not a tent or a camp,
but a great house.

This is the story, and all its measurements
with its *chambers round about.*

And the house free-standing
                                                built in silence

the materials already all prepared—

No ordinary house
with its boards of cedar
and carvings of knops and open flowers

—all ready to be overlaid with gold.

And the house full of angels, wings spread
from wall to wall, with its olive doors
and carved palm trees: all coated with gold.

Seven years to its completion
in the month called Bul (which is August).

Solomon builds his own house, too
(some say, as vaingloriously)
and one in the forest of Lebanon
and one for Pharaoh's daughter, his wife now
where the inner court is also the Lord's:

sanctum, and surround.

Make God the centre of your house
the story says: your dream house
and your simple living altar

where you sit and remember,
and it shall be as gold.

But hush, a woman is coming...
with some *hard questions.*

QUEEN OF SHEBA

SHE'D HEARD of his fame
but why should she believe in it?
Another egotistical king?

How does a woman believe in a man?
She tests him.

And since she's a queen, she arrives
with a very great train
camels, spices, gold, precious stones
she brings everything she is.

If we could only hear her questions!
We're only told
she communed with him of all that was in her heart.

She tells him all: he listens,

and his listening is all.
Ask any woman.

He answers too, or You
answer from within him.

He is a man who can listen,
hiding nothing of what he's given.

Consider the air, transparent between them.

She surveys everything too, to see it's real
his house, his servants, his food, his ministers
—she checks him out!
(Ask any woman).

She watches him ascend to the house of the Lord
and there was no more spirit in her

no more fight, at least for now...
only something that has not been before.

And so she gifts him with what she's brought
her abundance, her heart warmed—
and he denies her nothing in return

of what can be between a man and a woman.

And what does she ask of him?
We can only imagine.

BUT

But King Solomon loved many strange women
like father, like son—his shadow
Solomon on a dating site wants them all
Moabites, Ammonites, Edomites, Sidonians, Hittites
specifically against good advice which is
they will turn your heart away after other gods.
Solomon turns, and turns.

She with the dark hair, she with the bright eyes
the red hair, and the smile between her thighs...
his Egyptian wife is not enough
Solomon cleaved unto these in love.

Sex or love: is it either
(soul friends, one or both, or neither)
seven hundred wives, three hundred concubines,
Solomon-Casanova: no exaggeration
his building matched by his desire.

But they turn his heart away: it is said
where is his heart after so many nights?

Is it in his own chest, or in the dream with them
one after another, then another?

If you are a jealous God, you are angry
as any other woman might be:
if you are Love, You say sadly
'your kingdom cannot be inherited'

Ashtoreth, Chemosh, Milam
the incense rises

Ahijah rips Jeraboam's garment—
the kingdom will be divided

His prowess reduced to one tribe...

How many women does a man have to love
before he comes to Love—his heart's Magdalene?

THE YOKE

REHABOAM misses a trick,
the anti-Solomon (his son).

Jeraboam gives him his chance:
lighten our yoke—an olive branch.

The old men advise him:
serve your people, then they will serve you.

But he refuses.
He listens to un-wisdom,
rule by fear and oppression.

It reads like a curse.

It goes nowhere but into division,
and Adoram (an innocent man) stoned.

If un-wisdom becomes history
ignoring its elders, and all we've learnt,
it becomes what it still is—the worst.

The yoke on us—automatons.

ELIJAH

WILD MAN of God—
with a prophet's fearless tongue
no king's fool, or anyone's.

King Ahab has been worshipping Baal
and taking all the children that way
under the sway of Jezebel.

Elijah says it will not rain—
then has to run for his life
obedient to the Lord in his ear.

(He's obedient, and he's wild—that's Elijah).

Ravens come and feed him,
morning and evening
bringing him bread and meat.

But then the stream dries up.
What now?

Arise, get thee to Zarephath
where a widowed woman is waiting

at her wits' end...in grief.

Elijah follows the guidance
and there she is.

And he's one with her, a beggar
for a morsel of bread and water
it's all she has left.

Her heart is longing for death.

Elijah's need saves her
his promise sustains her,
The barrel of meal shall not waste...

But the widow woman needs more than one
miracle of faith.

Her son falls sick. She turns on him.
Elijah tells her *Give me thy son*

Lifts him up into the heaven of the house,
lies him down on his bed
and cries aloud

his prayer sounding from his chest
as he leans down over the child.
Three times—
let this child's soul come into him again.

And, Lazarus-like before time
the child revives;

his mother is satisfied.

Elijah brings Life.

Meanwhile, the land is dry.
Ahab stirs. Sends Obadiah
to find grass to save the horses...

and out there he meets our man,
falling on his face in front of him.

Elijah, fearless: tell Ahab I'm here
Obadiah, shit scared: you must be joking,
I will die.

Elijah stands firm. Obadiah is fine.
Ahab comes out to meet him:
Art thou he that troubleth Israel?

Elijah turns the tables on him:
It's you, Ahab, that's the problem
because you've lost your way...

Elijah's idea descends from on high
gather to me all Israel unto Mount Carmel
—only a king can command it.

And bring all the prophets of Baal
while you're at it...and all the others
who dine at your wife's table.

Ahab is obedient.

What else can he do?

Elijah addresses them all: in truth
is it God you serve, or Baal?
(it can't be both)

They are silent. They know.

It's four hundred and fifty to one,
Elijah the last man left.

Elijah's last stand.

It will take a miracle. He knows.

And You are its flame.

The Baal-ites prepare their altar
and bullock steak
but put no fire under.

Then they chant his name over and over,
from morning until noon—
and absolutely nothing happens.

Not even their cries, or self-harming
with knives and lancets
make a jot of difference. Only blood.

Elijah reckons Baal must be sleeping
after a night out on the town.

And by evening, still nothing.

Elijah's turn now.

He repairs the broken altar,
taking twelve symbolic stones
(one for each tribe)

Digs a trench around it,
prepares the sacrifice...then orders
water to be poured all over it,
once, twice, three times!

He's some director.

Then he lifts his voice again,
this time for the people

and the Fire Descends.

And they all fall down
like Obadiah, to a man.

Game over.

Elijah to Ahab: now for the rain.
Tells his servant: look seawards,
and Ahab to come down.

A little cloud out of the sea, like a man's hand

The sky black. Clouds. Wind.

Ahab runs back to his wife,
tells her all Elijah's done—

Jezebel: it will be his life, or mine!

Elijah, back in the wilderness
sits down under a juniper tree
utterly exhausted:
prays in all humility

take this cup away from me
for I am not better than my fathers.

But the angel says 'Arise, eat'
And a cake appears in the fire,
a cruse of water by his head

Arise and eat, because the journey is too great for thee,
world-weary one.

Reaches a cave alone,
to go in for peace of mind

and the wind comes to the mountains,
a gale—then a rock-breaking storm
but You are not in the wind

or in the earthquake which follows it
nor the fire after the earth has moved,
but You

are a still small voice

small enough to sit inside him
at the very centre of his heart and mind.

Elijah wraps his face in his cloak,
stands at the cave's mouth

and You speak to him,
asking him by name

then, again, telling him.

Elijah, obedient to the letter
throws his cloak to Elisha
who can only follow him
because he is true.

Meanwhile Ahab wants Naboth's vineyard,
but Naboth honours his inheritance.
Ahab sulks.

Jezebel (his wife): 'Man up,
I'll sort it for you like I always have.'

So she forges letters in his name,
to frame him—
so poor old Naboth will be stoned away.

Ahab gets what he wants, on a plate.

Word comes to Elijah,
just as Ahab asks him
Hast thou found me, O mine enemy?

Ahab knows it's true,
Elijah's curse is a stone
not even Jezebel can avert.

The dogs will eat her,
nothing could be worse.

Ahab, ashen, fasts, in sackcloth
his only hope of surviving

A man that gives his power away
knows no thriving...

Bad luck waits for his house.

KINGS 2

Meanwhile Elijah and Elisha take us further down the road of purity and prophecy and what being kingly really means in anticipation of 'my kingdom is not of this world,' Jesus' famous statement.

At the same time the shadow is ever present (Rehaboam, Jehu) where the son by no means follows the father. But still good men like Nehemiah keep coming, promising redemption.

ELISHA

Guru and disciple
Elisha won't leave him,
Elijah's shadow as he will also be.

Bethel, Jericho and Jordan
he follows him like the sun
or as a man's shadow walks everywhere
with him when he walks in the sun.

He wants to be one with him,

to be as him:
he wants a double portion of his spirit.

Elijah: *thou has asked a hard thing...*
as hard as our understanding of it,
and it's in Your Hands.

Then the chariot comes, all fire
dividing the man from his shadow,
dividing Elisha from his master,
and taking the pure man up to heaven
to the highest air of wind...

Fire as sudden as an eagle's descent
knowing its prey...and then silence.

Elisha is left alone, crying out
My father, my father...

as close to You as he can get.

And he saw him no more.
He picks up his cloak
and brings it down on the river

'Where is the Lord God of Elijah?'

His question answered:
the waters part—
the prophet's witnessing
says he got what he asked for.

But they don't understand where Elijah has gone,
they want to send out a search party
in case he's landed somewhere in the mountains!

Elisha agrees, reluctantly.
And of course, nothing.
Elisha: I told you so
(inwardly grieving).

Meanwhile they ask him to heal the waters.
He throws salt into them; speaks the Word
—and it is so.

Thy Will shall be done.

And the sun has its shadow
when the little children come
and tease his bald head:
he curses them.

He curses them, and two she-bears
emerge from the wood...
slaughtering forty two of them.

Suffer the little children to come unto me?
We're not there yet...

We're not even in sight of it,
or where Elijah has gone.

THE COMMISSION

RELUCTANT miracle-worker in a divided kingdom
confronted by three slippery kings
begging a favour against Moab.

Only Jehoshapat is credible to him.
He wishes the rest back to the Source
to the prophets of thy father and thy mother.

It's true these political animals are hard to deal with,
harder than bears or camels or asses.

But he agrees. They're desperate for water.
He calls on a minstrel: then an inspiration comes
Make this valley full of ditches.

By morning, they're full up.

Meanwhile the morning sun on the water
to the Moabites looks like blood
so they think the kings are dead—
but it's only a trick of the sun

that means their hour has come.

And this is but a light thing in the sight of the Lord
says Elisha

and he's right,
a miracle for all time
          is something completely other.

*

A grieving woman comes to him:
she's just lost her husband
and the bailiffs are at her door
wanting her sons for payment.

What can Elisha do?
(What *can* I do, he thinks...)
Asking her: what have you got in your house?

'Only a pot of oil' she replies.
Elisha improvises: ok, go and borrow
as many vessels as you can from everyone,
borrow not a few: and when you're done
lock yourself in with your sons.

Then pour out the oil you have,
and keep pouring.

She does: and it fills all the vessels,
and more. Her cup runneth over.

Elisha: now sell the oil, repay the debt
and live freely off the rest...

his own heart oiled into warmth.

*

Then his heart takes him further.

117

In Shunem, a woman befriends him
giving him bread every time he passes;
then she makes space for him inside
a little chamber...on the wall.

Elisha rests there with his servant,
revered as a holy man, and loved.

What can Elisha do for her?
She doesn't want to be spoken for to the king
or the captain of the army—
she's a woman without a child
and her husband is old.

Elisha tells her she will have a son.
She believes him not.
Then conceives...miraculously.

The child grows, but then falls one day
running out to his old father
'My head—my head!'

He dies in his mother's lap.

She takes him to Elisha's bed.
Then makes all haste to find him
beyond the logic of her husband's advice.

She comes to Mt. Carmel:
Elisha instantly recognises her
'Gehazi, go and ask if she is well—'

She kneels and grabs at his feet
unrestrainable. Gehazi tries—

Let her alone, for her soul is vexed within her...

'Was your promise an illusion?' she cries.
He meets her eyes.

Then hands Gehazi his staff
commanding him to go to the child,
and lay it on his face.

Mother goes with him, straight away.

But it doesn't work.

It needs Elisha in person.

It needs his mouth, his hands and his eyes
his whole body...for the child's life
as he slowly stirs, and sneezes seven times.

It needs his whole heart, like a sacrifice
with its gift in return: *of Life.*

*

'There's death in the pot,' they cry
with its poison of wild gourds
like the unconscious mind—

But Elisha sprinkles meal, manna

119

in the soup: the pot is sanctified.
And it feeds them.

Take, eat; this is my metaphor,
ahead of time.

*

Miracle worker and judge:
Naaman comes to him from Syria
a great man, but a leper
and led by a little child.

The king of Syria sends a letter,
the king of Israel is dumbfounded
assuming he's trying to wind him up
'Heal this man of leprosy?
Who does he think I am!'

Enter Elisha. It's not a king's job,
and he knows it. Calms him down.

So Naaman arrives at Elisha's house
full retinue in tow, full ego.

Elisha sends out a messenger:
go and wash yourself in the Jordan seven times.

Naaman is mightily offended!
He didn't even come out to meet me!
And anyway, *our* rivers are much cleaner than this.
What does he think he's playing at?

His servants have to calm him down, too.
'He's a prophet. So why aren't you listening
to what he's asking you to do?'

Naaman acquiesces: goes down to the river
washing himself of his pride,
comes out with the skin of a child.

Chastened, offers Elisha a blessing
—which he refuses.

Offers him gifts: the same
—but bids him *Go in peace.*

However, Gehazi gets wind of it
liking the idea of a bit of silver
and a change of clothes: why not?

Follows after him.
Naaman, in the giving mood
hands him twice what he's asked for.

Comes back well pleased, as we may imagine.

Elisha is furious:
Gehazi blanches, lies to him.
His gift then? Naaman's leprosy,
whiter than snow.

*

'This place is too small. Come and live with us—'

they say to him, each man carrying a beam of wood.

But when they come to the river to cut down more,
accident: the axe falls into the water...!
(And it's not their own)

Where? asks Elisha. Then throws in a stick,
and the axe floats to the surface

as if it was made of air.
(which it is)

    *

Elisha has the power. He is all eye
and ear, and heart, heart-sensing...

Sees what the king of Syria is thinking,
sees where he is: warns Israel
and saves the king *not once or twice.*

The Syrian king despairing, told
the words thou speakest in thy bedchamber
are audible to Elisha!

So he sends his horses and chariots
to Dothan, to surround him.

'Alas my master! How shall we do?'
his servant asks him.
Elisha calms him,
asking You to help him visualise

the mountain full of chariots and horses
surrounding *him!*

And then he blinds the enemy.

Then leads them away
out into Samaria, naked as the day.

And opens their eyes.

The Israel king, excitedly:
shall I smite them, shall I smite them?

Elisha sees beyond: commanding him
set bread and water before them.

Thou shalt not kill.

The air hangs still.
Forgiveness comes into being,
closer than the sun. It hovers in the stillness,
it breathes, it rains feather-light down.

The captive army entranced
eat and drink all they need, then leave
(still dazed, smiling, even laughing)

never to return again.

*

Then Elisha goes to Syria—Damascus,

123

where the king is sick and ailing.
He hears he's come.

Sends Hazael out with gifts to greet him,
every good thing there is from the city
with as great a question
(*Shall I live?*)

Hazael asks him.
Elisha sees all.
That the king will die
and more, so much more
and worse, as he begins weeping.

'*Why weepeth my lord?*'

And what can he say?
He sees all Hazael will do,
and tells him.

Hazael protests, of course: but it's true.
His destiny awaits him.

He goes back to the king, and lies
with a half-truth to conceal his disgrace.

The next day the king takes a wet cloth
and covers his own face.

Hazael reigns.

JEHU

But then Elisha has a strange idea
coming more from his own brain than God;
Take up this box of oil in thine hand.

He knows Jehoshapat: but Jehu's a blind date
to be anointed king of Israel just like that—
in fact, they think it's mad.

Jehu likes it, though
(whatever he secretly knows)
Hmm, a king: I'll take it...
and his commission is revenge
to decimate the house of Ahab,
to be a mere instrument of slaughter.

Jehu, the anti-Elisha
unwittingly loosed, like his shadow
to blot out the work of the sun.

Everyone asks him 'Is it peace?'
But how can it be? His chariot is driven.
Behold the man, driven
                              by false prophecy.

Behold his irate travesty,
ranting with self-righteousness.

Even Jezebel asks him
'Had Zimri peace, who slew his master?'
She paints her face. Her hour has come.

The eunuchs throw her down.

Jehu is nobody's saviour,
his memory eaten by dogs.

THE SUN AND ITS SHADOW

ELISHA, sick now, dying
tended by Jehu's grandson
echoing the words he cried aloud
when Elijah ascended beyond the clouds.

Elisha: *'Take bow and arrows.'*
Joash opens the window to the east
and looses it as he's been told to—
towards Syria.

Elisha, prophet of war with his last breath
a loosed arrow, not a chariot ascending...

But when they throw a dead man into his grave
behold: *he revived and stood up on his feet*
and we don't even know his name.

HEZEKIAH AND ISAIAH

HEZEKIAH, his back against the wall,
challenged by Sennacharib, the Assyrian king.

Isaiah speaks up for him: Isaiah the strong,

the prophet stronger than the king.

Israel has fallen: the shadow has come down,
Isaiah lifts up a mountain.

Hezekiah, pure of heart, lacks fire
Isaiah is the blast against suffering.

He shall not come into this city
the field mice shall gnaw at his bowstrings.

And as Hezekiah lies, sick unto death
Isaiah: *set thine house in order*

as he places the figs on his boil
and brings back the shadow ten degrees.

But still Hezekiah is naive
he shows the king of Babylon all he has

the gold, the spices, the ointment: hiding nothing.
Isaiah: what have you done?

It will all go to Babylon.
Your sons will be eunuchs in Babylon!
But Hezekiah is content with what he has
peace and truth in his own days

with no thought for the future
which is Babylon.

THE DESTROYER

MANNASEH, Amon, Josiah
the lineage made and broken
the son does not follow the father.

Josiah the child-reformer
walks the line of the Lord,
the curse of the old gods on the land.

Israel fallen, and still falling
Josiah will do what he can
saviour and destroyer.

He goes to gather the silver
to renovate the temple,
giving it to the builders in trust

and in the heart of the house
the high priest finds
the Book of the Law in the dust

waiting there, in the silence.
He reads it to the king.
Josiah is aghast.

How far have we come?
What have we done?
We have strayed from the path of fire.

Huldah the prophetess agrees. 'Tell Josiah.
And tell him because his heart was tender,

he will come to his grave in peace.

His eyes will not see the evil...'
Josiah gathers the elders, up to the temple
stands by a pillar, makes his covenant.

Then the purge begins.
The vessels of Baal, the idolatrous priests,
the incense burners, all into the river.

The houses of the sodomites
where the women were weaving,
and all the high places;
the left-hand gates of the city
and Topheth where they walked the fire,
and the chariots of the sun with fire
and the altars beaten down
with Solomon's adulteries...

before Nebuchadnezzar arrives
to bring them all into Babylon

leaving only the poorest of the poor behind
to be vinedressers and husbandmen.

Jerusalem, burning
and the temple he had saved

Josiah turning
sleeping peacefully in his grave.

NEHEMIAH

HE HAS THE COURAGE of his sadness,
to be sad in front of the king
at his feasting—

handing him his wine, his queen beside him.
Ataxerxes sees him:
This is nothing else but sorrow of heart

and seeing him, grants him.
Being seen is everything.

He's a man on a mission, too, and he's alone
the walls of Jerusalem lie broken, the gates burnt
the stamp of defeat like a curse.

Nehemiah travels by night
with a handful of men, and a mule.
He enters in unknown.
He sees it all: the waste.

Daylight will bring the high priest
and all the workers to the fore
healing the hurt, gate by gate
name by honoured name.

But the vision is in the night
while they're all asleep
and only one flame burns
in a heart that can only rest

when its dream is awake
in the light of a New Day.

THE PROPHETS

The Prophets: Moses, Elijah, Elisha—and now we have seven of the major prophets in this tradition, remarkable also because with them we also have the first political poets who represent truth beside ego, materialism, ambition, convenience—literally speaking truth to power. Here, like Rahab, and in the form of the dramatic monologue, they speak directly in their own voice: they tell us about themselves beside and within what they are saying, living in a timeless present.

AMOS

I AM A LION OF GOD...a herdsman of Tekoa,
I have heard the fire inside, and the bush burning;
I am the spectre at the feast in your dreams.

I'm the spectre from the South, come North
in among your riches and palaces...
I'm the poor boy with fire in his mouth.
Then the Lord opened my eyes...
I have seen fire on the house of Hazael

fire on the walls of Gaza, and Tyrus
for all your transgressions, and because
you pursued your brothers with the sword
and showed no mercy!

And you butchered the pregnant women
for the sake of a little more land,
and you lied in the name of the Lord,
and you sold out the poor *for a pair of shoes,*
and *the righteous for silver.*

So now it goes badly with you!
The peaceful are dismissed,
father and son take the same woman,
and you drink to oblivion in the house of your god.

But think about the Amorite:
tall as a cedar, strong as an oak
yet I brought him down
from the crown to the roots...

this is what He tells me to remind you!

And what do you say to the likes of us?
'Prophesy not.' You don't want to hear us.

But I tell you, your strength shall leave you
and you will run away naked before this day is out.
Who do you think knows His Secrets
His Way of moving and being?
Who do you think moves the people?
So you're sent an adversary.

And the horns shall be cut off from your altar,
yes, even here.

You, who oppress the poor
you who disregard the needy
—you now, and in the future—
the days shall come upon you
and you'll be taken away with hooks,
lifted like so many fish
from the ocean of your ignorance!

He says: I gave you everything
freedom from Egypt, manna from heaven
more than enough food in all your cities
and still you will not return.

And every bad thing that happened to wake you up
still left you refusing.

Now look: the innocence of your country is broken,
and there's no one to restore it,
to make it rise again. Israel!

So I tell you this place will come to nothing
until you see the watcher in the skies.

There will be grief, crying in the streets
highways, vineyards, houses
For I will pass through thee, saith the Lord.

And what is His Day? It is darkness
not the light you long for

or the meat you eat, or the music you love to hear.

Woe to all of you in your complacent ease!
Do you think you're better than the Philistines?
I am the spectre at your feast.

I am the lion, and the plumb line
hanging from this very ceiling!

You'd like to hang me with it
but I have to tell you what I've seen:

the summer come to an end,
the temple songs turned into howlings,
dead bodies in every place...
and nowhere to escape,
as the waters rise again...

No, you don't want to hear me
your eyes cast down whenever I speak

but don't say I didn't tell you
don't say you weren't warned
by a simple country shepherd!

Farewell, Beth-el. I'm gone.

HOSEA

THIS is what He said to me:
Go, take one of them and be with her

those fallen women, in a fallen kingdom
and so I found Gomer: my shadow, my other.
I didn't know His secret purpose was love.

I found her, and it was fertile between us;
my semen sang in her!
My gorgeous whore became a mother
the lovely woman she always was
(Love knows no separation *in that day*).

We conceived three children—You named them.
Jezreel, to bring down Israel
Lo-ruhamah, to scour Israel to its base
then Lo-ammi, to sever its people
before they can return to the Living God.

Israel, and all its children *as the sand of the sea*
which cannot be measured or numbered
returning into unity!

But first this journey.

She will be naked. She will be thirsty.
She will wander in a thorny wilderness.
She will lose her way. She will search
for all her lovers, but not find them...
then she will say

'*I will go and return to my first husband...*'
that is You.

So I will take away her clothes, her jewels

her feast days, her humour
her sabbaths, her vines, her fig trees...
before she can return to Me
(herself, as she is, within)

then I will bring her into the desert
and speak kindly to her
And I will give her vineyards from thence
and the valley of Achor for a door of hope
and she'll sing there, as when she was young,
when she was freed from bondage;
and she will call me 'Ishi.'

Then I will make a covenant for unity
with all the animals and the birds
the ants and the worms

And I will break the bow of the sword
and the battle out of the earth

and she will be with me for always
in kindness, discernment, compassion
she will be as she is: Woman.

And on that day
I will hear the heavens
and they shall hear the earth
and the earth shall hear the corn
and the wind and the oil;
and they shall hear Jezreel...

because I am not a God of Rage

My fire is the cleansing
the kingdom means to love,
falling like dew on the ground
on a New Day.

Hosea is my name.
I didn't understand any of this.
I thought I hated women
until You gave me Woman.

I owe it all to her.

MICAH

THIS IS MICAH, who is in God.
We have seen the Assyrians come
and the tribes scattered and divided
now the South (Judah) is threatened too.

Israel, for all its sins, is broken
melted down like the Lord's feet on the mountain
where the valleys are cleft *as wax before the fire*
and the stones roll down in a torrent.

One way, one movement to the root, the foundation
where the graven images are broken
the harlot-hirelings.

And so look at me:
I am wild, I shall wail
I will go naked in the fire

grieving with the cry of an owl

Owl-harbinger
of the wisdom that is dark

Owl medicine
                    from the root.

And so I pray you—you heads of state
see what you have done
hating the good and loving the evil
(as we say—)

you have devoured your own people
tortured and broken your own people
like animals for the cooking pot.

The Lord will not hear you.

And you, prophets, even you
who bite and say 'peace' in the same breath
who profess, and take money for your profession
your divination is worthless
as your dream of protection.

This is how the sun shall go down
this is how Zion is ploughed like a field,
and Jerusalem reduced to rubble.

But: it shall rise again
When? In the last days...I have seen it
and it is a blessed seeing

The Dangerous Book

The mountain of the house of the Lord
shall be built again on the mountain
and people shall flow into it

I can see them. Many nations, too
saying 'Let's go up there!'
to listen, and receive.

And the emanation of the mountain
will spread among the people
and they shall beat their swords into ploughshares
and their spears into pruning hooks
I tell you, there shall be no more fighting
no more war, or the study of it,
and every man shall sit under his vine
and his fig tree without fear.

And everyone will walk in the name of his god,
and we will walk in the Lord as One People.

So gather yourself, prepare for the worst
dark as the sun is at midnight
one shall come

one shall arise
a true man, a new man
whose goings forth have been from of old, from everlasting.

He shall come
in the fullness of time, and its birthing
and he shall stand and feed in the strength of the Lord

in the majesty of the name of the Lord his God
he will be royal in his knowing.

And this man shall be the peace,
and Assyria will fall.

War before peace
leaving this remnant
who will be among all peoples
a dew, a rain, that waits for no one
like a wind that blows...

And I have seen this:
You, asking your own people
'What have I done to you?'
'How have I exhausted you?'
'Testify against me.'

So how shall I come before You?
With burnt offerings, sacrifices,
rivers of oil? My own eldest son?
No.

I will come in all humility, as I am
naked as I am

to do justly, to love mercy
to walk humbly with my God

there is no other way.

ISAIAH

Who was I? Who am I? Many have come in my name
dreaming me, dreaming themselves within me—
the live coal in my mouth, in their own
and the Lord's terrible answer of desolation
for Israel's loss of its majesty
beside the dream of His House rebuilt on the mountain;
but in truth I saw something different, and kinder.

It was that dream for all time, and is
—and it is what separates us from it.
Everything He told me to say for Israel
as true for any nation. Everywhere,
all the Earth being His...

Who was I to see it? I was no one
in a world of transience and change
A voice commands 'Cry!'
And I answered 'What shall I cry?'
—All flesh is grass
and it's beauty like the wild flower's...
It was only His Breath that took me beyond
like a well of everlasting strength
seeing the world as He made it.

I was high born, a privileged boy.
I had a life before. Is anyone born to be a prophet?
No, he is chosen: he is made.
Light-blinded, heart-opened, struck—He comes,
and there's no turning away or turning back
there is only one turning: into Him.

142

You know about military training
and this is the work of the spirit.

But this was *joy*, and for joy
not desolation and damnation
for resurrection and return, not rage.
He told me: *the time of service is ended*
Jerusalem's suffering for its sins—
and this was my city I was proud to be in.

He told me: be a joyful messenger,
shout without fear: tell them I am here!
And He showed me Himself like a shepherd
tending his flock, not sending them fire,
earthquakes, plagues, privation...
He saw that we had suffered enough.

Then he showed me the nations. Eagle-eyed I soared
and saw as He had seen
down to where we seem like grasshoppers
under His shielding wing
where princes are reduced to nothing
made of nothing but seeming...
and the storm carried them off like straw.

I saw all this and heard Him say
'How can you say your destiny is hidden
or your rights ignored?'
Did you not know?
Had you not heard?
His strength is all we are:
His Breath. His Greater Being.

143

He only wants to show himself clearly
to help us all come home.

He showed me Cyrus, then. Ah, Cyrus
unknown, unexpected liberator
metaphor of all we cannot imagine
that could happen in the name of freedom
beyond our conceiving...but not His.

Cyrus: and so He says *I AM WITH YOU*
Fear not: if I can make this happen
I can make anything happen!
Cyrus: our saviour—His instrument
as I am His servant.

And the poor, everywhere and always
closest to pain...He showed me water,
water for them: rivers *on barren heights*
and fountains in the midst of valleys
and in the wilderness *cedar trees,*
acacias, myrtles, olives—fecundity
because He loves you more than princes,
more than you may ever know.

This was the New Exodus
the song of the earth without sleeping
that came to me in a dream—and in waking
as clear as counsel stating its case
for anyone who would argue against Him.

He said all I had seen myself, that
in the whole of Jerusalem there was no one

who could witness Him
even as He shone like the sun!
And so I came.

This was my solemn profession
to be that witness in poetry
as Cyrus was in action.
And so He upheld me.

He said: sing a new song!
He said *praise*—learn how to praise
then you will be as strong.
He likened Himself to a woman in labour
birthing all He does
lifting the veil of darkness from our eyes,
turning darkness into light.

And so I say to you: listen
this God you take for granted—do not.
You have seen many things but not observed them;
your ears are open but you do not hear
it was always His Will that you should see
the glory that is your own being in Him
—not Lucifer, son of the morning.

He says: you are already redeemed
saved, safe, if you could only see it
you are a man with your Father and your God
and a woman, and the child that will lead you
holding your soul in his hands.

This the new journey, the next

everlasting journey out of slavery
the slavery of sense and nonsense.
Ah, but Israel was not listening;
you know that: you know our story.
He still has to bear, to shoulder it for us—
like a father we give nothing but our foolish pride.

Idols! The work of our own hands
we worship without compromise...idols
that stand between us and Him,
between us and everything.
They are our separation from Him
in a world of make-believe ego dreams.
I called it worshipping a block of wood—
it's that ridiculous when you see it.
You use wood to burn and make your food
but you don't bow down before it!

Deluded hearts who believe they can,
bound into their own slavery of self
for a deliverance that never comes
and so all they live is a lie.
We were made to be with Him
in Him, of Him...I saw even the heathen rally
with more heart and soul than these so-called priests,
to say nothing of these self-elected seers.

This is a God who speaks clearly
not in darkness and declivity
drug-induced insanity
—and all he says is Turn to Me;
turn and return, and everything you dream of

you will find, even as you turn grey
I will still be the same.

Babylon fallen: world Babylon
typifying our complacency
a people who have never known suffering
glib, slick, self-centred, barely human
heir to *unforeseen ruin*
abandonment, powerful friends all gone
evaporating like the morning dew
like manna that never was.

The crown of pride shall be trodden under feet,
and the desert shall rejoice and blossom with the rose.

But first: obstinacy, resistance, refusal
your neck an iron bar
your forehead bronze. Iron man,
with your iron will that has to be broken.

I have seen all this, and it aged me
the world in a crucible like silver
to its uncertain awakening...
I thought sometimes I'd worked in vain,
and worn myself out for nothing.

Such is the servant
even as he dreams of the light of nations,
of all his master has shown him
in time and beyond it.

I have been a man of sorrows

147

even as I've been shown the greatest joy
a man can know in this life.
I've never stopped fighting for Jerusalem,
even to the edge of night.

And I have seen it in jewelled glory
seen it as Blake, who followed me
faithful servant of this Living God
who transcends what any tongue can tell.

Yes, many have followed and spoken in my name
but I knew a Lord of kindness and love
whose power was only for the sake of love
being one God for everyone.

We had no word for it as the battle raged.
One day it will be our saving grace,
and on that day my soul will rest.

HABBAKUK

I AM A QUIET MAN: I have seen too much
but my cry has echoed down the centuries;
you know it, although you don't know me
How long oh Lord, how long?
My heart is troubled.

While Nahum trumpeted the great Assyrian fall
with his vision of red and lightning
how could I be convinced?
An eye for an eye? Assyria falls,

Babylon is poised to rise.

It goes on: and it is still the same
where unholy war banishes love in your day.
Israel, Syria, Sudan...what difference?
Well may you ask, what has changed?
For myself, it was all this question.

When we know so clearly what is right and true
how can what is manifestly wrong prevail?
And yet it does. It goes on—
(it is enough to reduce any man to silence)
and so this great asking swelled in me,

deep within, keeping me sleepless
even as I was awake. I had to ask it,
ask Him, ask You—God of gods—
even as it seemed like lack of faith
perhaps even tempting fate...

It was a cry, then, and it was a question
so great, perhaps, there had to be an answer
but not, I prayed, an answer of my own making
(spare me that, whatever I must hear)
your prayer, my friend, should be the same.

You showed me the Chaldeans
fierce as they are dreadful
their horses swifter than the leopards
flying in the wind, ruthless as eagles
determined to eat—

insolent as kings, princes as nothing,
unmoved by every stronghold
for they shall heap dust, and take it.
But then, they will also take the credit
imputing this his power unto his god.

Can you see what I meant?
That was their turning away
and it has always been the same.
You give us Your Grace: we claim it,
and worship our own godlikeness.

It's savage. It's what savagery means
to acknowledge nothing beyond yourself.
Not even a man in a far away land
living among standing stones would do that.
How else might the harvest fail?

But still I asked Him—
I had a story, yes, but not an answer.
I prayed He would speak more directly
I will stand upon my watch...

You have my words to prove it.

Then He spoke (my hand still trembling)
'*Write the vision and make it plain upon tables*
That he may run that readeth it.
For the vision is yet for an appointed time
But at the end, it shall speak and not lie...'

And the vision is all in the waiting.

Consider a man who looks the part
but his soul which is lifted up is not upright in him
he drinks, he is vain
he doesn't really care about his home life,
his secret desires are hell
and is as death and cannot be satisfied.
Sounds familiar to you?

And yet *he gathereth unto him all nations,*
Heapeth unto him all people.
Name him, name them all for yourselves
these are the fallen illuminati of the world.

And always a moment comes when people see
through them as clearly as glass to the day.
Our leader has feet of more than clay
—and now there will be hell to pay.

Consider this same man, or someone like him
amassing secret wealth inside his house
that he may set his nest on high
...and be delivered from the power of evil!
What irony! And in truth

he's a narcissist, using people to feed himself
and has sinned against thy soul.
He hasn't much soul of his own to speak of
he's been so busy sucking at other people's
and the stones of his house shall cry out: fraud!

Likewise anyone *who buildeth a town with blood,*
it's not a City of God and never shall be.

For the earth shall be filled with the knowledge
                    of the glory of the Lord,
as the waters cover the sea.

I do believe it, as I did.
This knowledge is the great transparency.

And so thou art filled with shame for glory,
and shameful spewing shall be on thy glory
—there was no other way of saying it.

All we do returns to us
for better or worse, cloaking us
with shame or glory—there is no escape.
No graven image, or royal portrait
can make up for whatever we have done.

Meanwhile You stay in your Holy Temple
in the heart-height of the mountain
where silence reigns, until one day
we have the humility to listen.

And until that day it will always be the same.
Only your burden, like mine, may be lighter
because you know this

even though you find you're still waiting
for a day that never comes—until it does.

JEREMIAH

I AM A STONE. A stone in your hand
a stone in the rucksack on your back,
I bring you down to the ground.
I bring you further, as I was brought
to say what you have to though no one likes it
no one thanks you for it in this world—and worse
because there is no escape
no escape from what you know.

It was ever thus for me:
my family, a long line of priests.
It was ordained in the womb.
I was a stone there!
What choice did I have? It was chosen.
Bad news for Israel, and I was the messenger.
And they could not, would not see it coming.
The rod of an almond tree,
and a seething pisspot pointing north
(where else, but to Babylon?)
A desolation and an astonishment
a savage awakening—and why?
Because we had all forsaken You
forsaken the fountain of living waters
and hewed them with cisterns, broken cisterns
that can hold no water.

Israel, holding no water!
Israel living in illusion
worshipping convenient fantasies
just as you do now. And worse,

burning their own children in Tophet,
'the valley of slaughter'...I named it.

And so I saw a great darkness, and it
weighed in me like a stone.

Do I really have to speak of this, Lord?
Yes, you do.

I beheld the earth and lo it was without form and void
And the heavens, and they shed no light

And I had no light
Only His Word
—and His Fury, which is yours
when you face the world as it is.

You pour it out—you have to
when all you see
is lies and deceit all around you!
Otherwise, you'd explode—you'd be
a meaningless explosive...

But He never withdrew hope,
it was only that I could not feel it.

The ways were always there for us to walk
but we refused them: and now the hour has come.

Cities of the Night across the globe
flickering in their abomination...you know them
and they sink in you like a stone.

All the old paths, and all the old questions:
how can people be happy who behave like complete shits?
Pull them out like sheep for the slaughter
*And prepare them for the day of slaughter...*that was it.

He showed me a girdle. He told me to wear it.
He told me to go out and bury it.
Then He told me to go and fetch it
and it was rotten, *good for nothing*
of course it was. It was Israel.

I told the king and queen: I told them
sit yourselves down, as it will all come down
your lands, your wealth, *even the crown of your glory.*
They didn't like it, of course.
And can a leopard change his spots?
My question to you in all your majesty.

Show me Lord, something I can believe in!

It's dark out here; dark and drear;
it's not dark yet, but it's nearly there.

Ah, the heart is deceitful above all things...
I judge a man by what he actually does
and so I tell you: the rich man who sits
on his eggs like a silly partridge
but never hatches them—
will one day abandon them—
and end his days like a fool!

Jeremiah is telling you!

One morning He said 'Go down to the potter's.'
I did as I was told. And I watched him
throwing one pot that got spoilt
and then another...the clay wet, yielding
to the slightest impression or error
and He said: this is how it is
I can make a nation, or destroy it
—just like this simple artisan
I hold the whole world in My Hands.

The potter gave me a bottle to take to Tophet,
and smash over their desecrated innocence—
I did so with gusto.
And they didn't like that either.

Pashur really didn't like it.
He struck me in the face for it.
Then he put me in the stocks, for a laughing stock.

That was my darkest hour.
I cried out to You: 'You have deceived me!
You promised me protection—
and all they do is poke fun at me
deaf to my word, as to Yours?'

And I would have turned away,
but there was no turning
there was only the burning
of Your Fire within me:
then I knew You were with me
—this part of me knew—

even as I cursed the day I was born
and wished my mother could be my grave.

And after the disaster came
He showed me two baskets of figs
'Jeremiah, what do you think?'
I told him the good ones were good to eat
but the rotten were unspeakable.
And he told me what they meant.

A dark truth: those taken captive would return,
but those that stayed would be damned
(by their own stupidity, as I later saw)

I told them again: *metanoia*
there is no other way, or it's desolation
the wine cup of His Holy Rage among nations
disunited as they stand falling

and the temple like Shiloh...SHILOH!
Then they yelled at me, threatening me
to death with their own pain, those priests.
It was the princes who stuck up for me!
Then the elders, too; bless their grey hairs
remembering our brother Micah
as his name rang like a high sound in my ears.

Micah the Morasthite, you've met him.

I wrote to the captives in Babylon, I told them
seventy years...then He will come for you

And ye shall seek me, and will find me, when ye
Shall search for me with all your heart
And I will be found of you...

Shemaiah tried to defame me,
because he couldn't stomach what I was saying
any more than Zedekiah, who would not listen
until he was bound in chains and blinded.

And Jehoiakim, burning my words
that Baruch had faithfully transcribed on a scroll
—he inked it all out again, and more!

Maybe I *was* iron, stronger than I knew
but You alone know how I suffered
while all I could dream about was a New Land
You promised to us in my waking
out of Your everlasting love...
Virgin of Israel! Innocence restored,
innocence beyond experience, and a good shepherd
bringing us all home to the fold
and all of life become an innocent joy
turning and returning to its Source.

Meanwhile *every man that eateth the sour grape,*
his teeth shall be set on edge.
Bitterness is its own reward.
And Your Law in our inmost parts
written—where else? But in our hearts.

And forgiveness like rain and like dew.

Meanwhile they threw me in prison,
accusing me of plotting with the Chaldeans
and the floor of that dungeon was shit.
I sat in it.

Was I dreaming, after all?
One of the eunuchs spoke up for me
so they brought old rags and ropes,
told me to put them under my armpits;
then they hauled me up. It was agony.

But ah the air, even in the prison courtyard
in no man's land where the likes of us live.
I was still here when they arrived
to burn the city...and Babylon's king
took more than pity on me
because everything I'd said he could see
to the letter, with his own eyes.

They gave me a free man's choice then;
food and water. I went down to Mizpah
to live with those who were left
the poorest of the poor, and as honest.

I told them, stay: don't go to Egypt
there is no way back. But they left anyway
taking me with them, an old man in tow. Disaster
—but I've already said enough. I am stone.

They always threw stones, and in the end real ones
—like my Babylon, bound, and flung into the river.

One day, when my work is finally done,
you will hear every one of them singing.

EZEKIEL

IT WAS MY THIRTIETH YEAR to heaven. I was a child of the Captivity. You have to imagine: we were not treated badly. There was freedom of a kind. We could live almost normal lives: and we did, but we could not return.

Jerusalem, our Holy City, was behind us. Jerusalem, and all the disaster of our homeland.

And yet we were told we would return. But when? In seventy years? That was a lifetime. And until then? We were waiting. Waiting for something to happen...waiting like old men sitting in the sun.

It was limbo, a sentence of uncertain duration with no right of appeal.

And that made it worse. It was a limbo, and a life, but it was a living death.

A valley of dry bones.

What vision? What possibility?

What on earth was there to say?

*

It is hot here. Mesopotamia. It is always hot, and when it isn't hot, it is humid. This is a place of thunder...of storms sudden as the air's grey curdling.

The first distant rumbling like a huge metal ball rolling over a bare floor.

Then lightning, flickering white when it's dark, zig-zagging or blinding across the sky.

Torrential rain then, sometimes loud as a waterfall, striking into the sand and dust and liquefying it to mud.

God is in the thunder...and the rising seething wind.

And then something is happening.

*

I was by the canal at Chebar (now Kabour), as I often was, to the north of the city where there is a sandy plain. The waterway is the borderline between Man and Desert—or so it was for me.

I came here to pray. My birthday was coming. I was a priest. The Temple awaited me.

Cleansing, fasting, ablution.

I wanted something to happen.

*

It knocked me to the ground. It electrified my brain. It blinded
my eyes

—but the sky within the sky was opened

And I saw...as I can still see it now

A great whirling wind came out of the North
like a cloud, a tornado, and a fire
folding back in on itself as it moved
and it was bright, not grey
its heart was sunset-amber...

And out of its centre
four living creatures, like men
but with four faces each, and four wings
their feet like calves' feet, animal, rooted
shining like burnished brass
the closest we can shine to gold.

Human hands under their wings,
joined, as if stitched, to each other's
and not turning, but facing straight forward
decisive. I peered closer

and their four faces were evangelists
each a man, and a lion on the right
and an ox and an eagle on the left,
supreme strength—

Fearless lion
stubborn ox

high-flying eagle!

Wings stretched upwards,
their inner wings covering their bodies
also folded in...

And wherever the spirit was to go, they went
no turning, no hesitation...

They burned like coals, they shone like lamps
the movement of light and fire coursing up and down
as if inside them and around them

while out of the fire flashed lightning!
Storm lightning—
and they ran and returned like lightning
as the spirit moves.

Like lightning inside lightning.

And beside each of them, a wheel
shining green, the colour of beryl
in the High Priest's breastplate!

And their work, their very being
each a wheel inside that wheel—
(wheels within wheels, but no spin doctors, these)
and when they moved, the whole of them was moving.

Their rings, rims, high like eyes
all around them, all seeing—
lifted up with their wheels as they rose

a fantastic sight, like chariots
of earth and fire, stillness and light.

They were *Life*. They were alive
and so much more intensely alive
than you can easily imagine...

They were Spirit Life: above them, crystal
a sky, terrible and transparent
a wholly spiritual sky at another level of being
their wings stretched straight out under it,
angelic, standing

And their wings whirred like waters as they moved
like the voice of God, His Speech, utterance
like great birds, and when they stood still again
their wings drifted down by their sides.

And a Voice was above them
a voice and a throne
that streamed upwards from them

bright as a rainbow after the rain,
a bow of burning gold
throne and storm and glory...and

I fell, I fainted onto my face.

Then the voice spoke: 'Stand up! And I will speak to you'
I had to stand.
And the spirit streamed into me and through me
lifting me up into my quivering feet.

164

It said: 'I send you to Israel
this rebellious people who have ignored Me
even unto this very day
(that is now, killing their own near-neighbours)
they are children, and their hearts are closed.
You will say thus, I say
and whether they hear you, or are deaf to you,
they will know a prophet has been among them.

Don't be afraid of them or what they say
scratching like brambles, or stinging like scorpions
—don't be dismayed. Say it to them
but don't be like them. Here, take, eat'

...and a scroll was handed to me
covered in writing:
it was full of grief but it tasted sweet.

It entered my throat, my heart, my belly
and my bowels...to excrete.

He comforted me, told me
my forehead had been forged harder than flint,
adamant.

No turning away, but going: straight.

Then I was taken up, as if into the air
with a rushing like a waterfall in my ears
that was the blessing of the glory of the Lord.
I heard their wings again, too
and their wheels

And it was as bitter to leave them as
the scroll had tasted sweet.

But what I am I saying? I was stunned, speechless.
I could barely move for seven days.

*

Then He said: 'here, take a tile
and make a sketch of Jerusalem on it
then *lay a siege against it.*
Just as you would with an army, the works.
And put an iron pan between you and it,
a wall of iron. This is your sign to them.

Then lie on your left side to bear their iniquity
one day for each year of it, that's 390
a year and a month: then on your right side
40 days for Judah, for her wilderness
setting your face against Jerusalem:
I shall bind you here so you do not move

but you will have food, meat, water, measured
according to your need for the siege
baked as barley cakes with human excrement
to signify your protest.

Ezekiel, go to it.
You are a living installation
a credible madman…

to shock them awake.'

I protested: I had lived a pure life
for the priesthood, as I told you...
my only consolation was cow dung instead!

I had to do it. It was insane.

And he told me to cut off my hair and beard,
burn some of it in the city; thresh some of it with a knife
scattering some of it to the wind—
keeping the residue to weave into my clothing,
then feeding the fire with it

as a sign for the Days of Fire to come.

This is Jerusalem, damned
when father and son shall eat of each other
this is the City, and it is Hell.

And He said He will show no mercy there
—sickness, famine, and the sword—
meted out like my shaven hair...

to the end of his Rage like a storm.

But there was more.

Jerusalem the whore: here she is,
a female child thrown out into a field
her father an Amorite, mother a Hittite
in no land but Canaan: unwashed, unswaddled
still bloodied with afterbirth

...and I found her, and said *Live*
I brought her into womanhood
I loved her as a father should
covered her with fine linen and silk
ornaments, bracelets, a chain for her neck
a jewel on her forehead, and a crown:
I crowned her, and she ate like a queen
but she believed in her own beauty and not in Me.
She believed in men, gave herself to them
she even gave her children to them!
building thy high place at every head of the way
a brothel for one and all.

Egyptians, Philistines, Assyrians...
Here she is, in a headdress of black feathers
thigh boots and crimson panties
striding out to the front of the stage,
with her pretty blond face: her lovers
in skintight leotards all around her
gyrating to the beat, haunches bent bared,
faces as cold as the air, as they fawn (or seem to)
swarm, or mean to, after her every step...

But she will be naked before them
stripped of her roving microphone, her song
until she leaves them: until she changes
into a half-bridal dress, *remembering who she is*
singing her heart-song alone...

Only then will His Raging cease
as she shines newborn in all she is...

   *

Think of it like this: two great eagles;
the first, landing in the top of a cedar
plucks off the top branch with his beak,
carries it to the marketplace of Money City.
Then he carries off a very young vine;
plants it in fertile ground by a wide stream
like a border. It grows there—
its branches reaching up towards the eagle-sky.

Then a second bird, like the first
finds the vine inclining towards him
twisting its roots, extending its branches—
away from the ground where it has been planted.

Can a vine like this thrive, even survive?
Israel is that vine: turning away
from the truth of the covenant it made
with Babylon, even in the darkest day
trying to raise Egypt on its side!
How can such stupidity survive?

It was God's will we should be in Babylon
and we rebelled against even *that*.
So the eagle has us in its talons
and it's not a pretty sight.

However (parable concluding): He says
I myself will take a topmost cedar branch
and plant it on a very high mountain
(the mountain of the Temple of our returning)
and it will become a Great Tree
sheltering *every* kind of bird.

Then every tree will know where it comes from
how it is levelled, and how it rises
in life, and from death to life again.
Now, do you see it?

*

It means: we have to let the concept of sour grapes go. That the
sins of the fathers are ours, and we are doomed to repeat them.
He told me: abandon this, because it is not true. *All souls are
mine.* If the soul of a father is His, then so is his son's. Each,
individually.

And *the soul that sinneth, it shall die.*

What does it mean? It means we are each responsible. As you
will say 'each man is the captain of his fate.' And each woman,
too.

It has always been true: and it is the Law Made New.

It means we have to do what is right. And to do the right thing
is to live—it is Life.

(Life, like those wheels, full of light...)

It means we have to *turn* from Death to Life. That is the
turning.

I saw it so simply, even in the midst of my grief. I saw it simply
as light, in my mind's eye.

All the rest were examples in writing at the time. You can read them for yourself.

But remember this above all: *He derives no pleasure from the death of the wicked.*

We may do: he does not.

What is my grief, or the loss of my wife, beside His?

Ezekiel, you are so small. And those too who bang the drum in your name full of righteous hate.

The essence remains: *make you a new heart and a new spirit.*

How can we not, in the name of Life, obey?

*

My grief was my rage, and my rage was my grief. And so I saw Aholah and Aholibah, and the Cup of Bitterness passed from one to the other: one whore to the other; all her sex turned bitter as my own. It was the Assyrians and their persecution, their merciless machinery against us, and for so long: then it was the Chaldeans, and even the Egyptians—all we had been freed from! And where was Israel? Nowhere, and betrayed. And so I raged and I was not alone. We were a tamed, a castrated people. We often spoke of it.

And so I saw Tyre, too, as I saw Israel: once of perfect beauty, connected on all sides, with the best of men and mariners, wholly refined. It was all we could have been, should have been...and it

171

was all ruined, lost, broken in mid-sea...

this was the voice of my grief,
the ocean of my grief.

*

But a new sun shall rise, out of the pit
where all the Egyptians are lying in it.

What use is Ra and Pharaoh to them now?

*

And the shepherds of Israel...where are they now?

He said to me: *Woe be to the shepherds of Israel that do feed themselves! Should not the shepherds feed the flocks?*

These shepherds, our officials and leaders, feed themselves but they do not feed us. Hear them filing their papers and braying like donkeys in their Parliament of Fools! They don't look after the sick or the poor (they punish them), or the black sheep from abroad...so what kind of shepherds are they?

But with fire and with cruelty have ye ruled them.
And so the flock is scattered *upon all the face of the earth.*

And so His Judgement upon you! You pseudo-elected shepherds...

He says: I will take the flock back into Myself. He will seek us out and bring us home to good pasture and a safe fold.

I will seek that which was lost, and bring again that which was driven away, and will bind up that which was broken, and will strengthen that which was sick, but I will destroy the fat and the strong; I will feed them with judgement.

The Lord is my shepherd.

And He says to us that he will distinguish among us: cattle from cattle, rams and he-goats. He will see us as we each are, and He will ask us 'Do you really think it's a good thing to have eaten up all the good pasture and then trodden down its residue into mud?' And to have drunk deep of the water, and the reserves of water, and yet polluted it? The poor eat and drink what is left, do they not?

I tell you, the whole flock is responsible: and this is what He is telling us.

And there will be a new shepherd, as David was, but no longer a king of this world. And He will make a new covenant with us, a Covenant of Peace, so that the evil beasts will cease their ravening and we can be safe in the wilderness and the woods.

And He will make this place a place of blessing; there will be showers of blessing. The earth will be fertile—tree and field— *and we will know it is the Lord.* The Lord who has freed us from those who served themselves through us.

Read what I have written carefully, and you will see it is there.

And we'll no longer be a prey to anyone: with a new crop for the ground.

Hunger and shame shall pass.

A new sun shall rise.

And ye my flock, the flock of my pasture, are men; and I am your God.

*

And the dead shall rise...

Dry bones fill the valley. It is humanity! So many dead, from so many wars, all of us

dead as we are, the dead and the living dead. We are bones in the valley and the long unbroken silence.

We waited and watched and nothing changed: only the dying. Moment after moment, monument after monument.

Our death like a trance.

Bereft.
And He said to me: *Son of Man, can these bones live?*
And I said: God knows (I don't).
And He said: *Prophesy upon these bones...*

And He said: breath will enter them, the spirit will enter them, into every cell of them

they will be gathered and joined, bone locking to bone
muscles will be re-formed on them
skin will begin to cover them
breath and heartbeat will follow then

and they will stir, they will wake
they will stand, they will open their eyes

they will gaze around, they will see one another...

There was a noise then, and a shaking like an earthquake. And
it came to pass.

But there was no breath until He said
Prophesy to the wind, to the four winds
for breath, for Life to come again

And so it did. And so they stood: we stood, like a great army.

Then he said: these bones are the whole house of your country:
they are dry, without hope, they are disconnected.

And He said: I will open your graves now, and My Spirit will be
in you and you will live, and you will know I am the Way and
the Life.

These bones shall live—in You.

And I wept for the hope and my heart opening, like rain falling
and splashing. It was rain, the humid day at last breaking.

*

That was long ago, and I was alone.

Gog lay before me, and Eternity like the sky and the sky within the sky, beyond me.

Know the spirit that walks within you
in your every movement, every step of the way.

Call it by its True Name.

They say I am not a great writer, that my style is poor and full of repetition; but no matter. I have seen what I have seen.

RUTH

A GLOSS

*Ruth, we felt, is a standalone chapter not just as a celebration of
another remarkable female figure but as an evocation of feminine
love—the love we will later see among the women of the Gospels.
At the same time, Boaz (Ruth's husband) is a gentle man. I have
summarised the prose story here as a poem. Hence 'a gloss.'*

ALL THE MEN have died:
the women return
husbandless now: a mother
and her two daughters-in-law.

They're already displaced, between borders
bound with love by their loss.
Where do they belong?

Mother-in-law tells them to go
she's old: but Ruth will not leave her.

Her love drifts down the centuries,
become a song

Wherever you go, I shall go
and I shall be buried beside you;
we will live together forever—
and our love will be the gift of our lives.

What love is this?
It's not the love
of heroes or kings—
it is a woman's love, unseen.

It crosses all divides.

But one man can see it, that's Boaz
welcoming her to his harvest fields
and protecting her —
(he commands the young men).

This is a *gentle man* who knows his own mind.

We haven't seen the likes of him either
among so many priests, patriarchs, prophets even.

She will go to him on the threshing floor tonight,
she will *uncover his feet,* says mother-in-law.

What is it in a woman that can surrender
like a river to the sea—her destiny?
But he surrenders, too:
to buying her land twice over

for the mother, and Ruth who becomes his wife.

This is his sacrifice.
(Another kinsman could have had her
but when it comes to it, his heart
is not as great, he's not willing
to pay the price).

And this is the foundation.

A tale, a song from long ago
when something good that's done
creates an unknown future...

and a woman who can love beyond the day
becomes the great grandmother of King David.

THE PSALMS

based on originals by William Tyndale, c. 1530

These had to be translations, and of course accurate, so I went back to Tyndale's originals because of his extraordinary ear for rhythm as well as his modernity of speech—which I have carefully updated. This is a selection we of the psalms we felt most significant for us now, for their emotional range as well as faith.

'The Lord tests the righteous, but in his soul he hates the wicked, and all those who love violence.' A different kind of God is emerging next to the tired Old Testament God we've come to know too well.

8

L ORD, HOW EXCELLENT is your name in all the earth
who have set your glory above the skies!
Out of the mouths of babes and sucklings
you have ordained strength
to stop the enemy and the avenger in their tracks.
When I think about your heavens, the work of your fingers,

the moon and all the stars you have created
who are we that you are mindful of us?
And the children of Eve that you watch over us?
For you have made us only a little lower than the angels
crowning us with glory and honour!
You have given us control of the work of your hands
you have put everything under our feet.
Sheep, oxen, yes, and all the wild country animals
the birds of the air, fish of the sea
and whatever passes through the paths of the deep.
Oh Lord, how essential is your name in all the earth!

11

to the chief musician: a psalm of David

I PUT MY TRUST in the Lord
so how come you say to my soul
flee like a bird to your mountain?
For look, the wicked bend their bow
they tauten their arrow on the string
so they can sneakily shoot the upright in heart.
If the foundations are destroyed, what can the righteous do?
The Lord is in his holy temple, his throne in heaven:
his eyes see, his eyelids flicker at the children of men.
The Lord tests the righteous, but in his soul he hates
the wicked, and all those who love violence.
And he shall rain fire, and horrible storms on them
—this will be the portion of their cup.
Our just Lord loves justice: he looks for those who stand tall.

22

to the chief musician on Aijeleth Shahar: a psalm of David

MY GOD, MY GOD why have you forsaken me?
Why are you so far from helping me
and the tongue of my fiery cry?
God, I cry in the daytime but you don't hear me
and in the night—I'm not silent!
But you are holy still, in the praises of Israel
our fathers trusted you, they trusted and you set them free
they cried to you and were freed, they trusted shamelessly.
But I am a worm, and no man: an embarrassment
and people despise me...
those that see me laugh me to scorn
they pout, they shake their heads saying
'He trusted in God, so let God deliver him
—since he delighted in him so much!'
But you, you took me out of the womb
you gave me hope when I was on my mother's breast
you are my God from my mother's belly.
Don't be far from me, trouble is near, there's no one around!
A gang of bulls has surrounded me: strong Bashan bulls
gape at me like ravening, roaring lions...
I'm poured out like water, all my bones out of joint,
my heart's like wax, my bowels have melted; my strength
has dried up, my tongue sticks to the roof of my mouth;
—you have brought me into the valley of dry death.
Dogs are barking at me: an evil council has enclosed me
they're piercing my hands and feet...
I tell my bones: all they do is stare back at me.
They divide my clothes among themselves,

then they cast lots for my linen...
Don't be far from me, oh Lord my strength, help me
deliver my soul from the sword: my darling from the dog
save me from the lion's jaws...
you have heard me cry from among the unicorns!
I will state your name to my brothers: I will praise you.
You that fear the Lord, praise him: all you blood of Jacob
glorify him, fear him, all you seed of Israel
for he has not ignored the sufferings of the suffering
nor has he hidden his face from them
but when they cried out to him, he heard.
I will praise you in the great congregation
I will honour my vows with those who fear you.
The meek shall eat and be nourished: they shall
praise the Lord and their hearts shall live forever!
All the ends of the earth will return to the Lord
the kindred spirits of nations will worship him
for the earth is the Lord's, he is the governor of the nations.
And the well-fed will also worship,
all of us who go down into the dust
will bow before him, because no one alone
can keep his own soul alive.
Descendants also will serve him
and this will be told to a new generation.
They will come and affirm his righteousness
to a people as yet unborn, that he has accomplished all of this.

23

THE LORD IS MY SHEPHERD, I shall not want
he makes me lie down in green fields

he guides me by still waters.
He restores my soul: he leads me in the paths
of rightness for his own name's sake.
And yes, though I walk in the valley of the shadow of death
I will fear no evil: you are with me
your crook and your staff will comfort me.
You lay a table for me in the presence of my enemies
you bless my head with oil, my cup runneth over.
Surely goodness and mercy will follow me
all the days of my life—
and I will live in the house of the Lord, forever.

24

a psalm of David

THE EARTH IS THE LORD'S, and the fullness of it
the world, and everything that lives in it.
He has built it on the seas, the rivers, the floods.
Who shall climb the hill of the Lord?
Who can stand in his holy place?
He who has clean hands and a pure heart
who hasn't raised his soul into vanity, or sworn lyingly.
He will receive the Lord's blessing
and rightness from the God of his salvation.
This is the generation who seeks him, and your face, Jacob.
Lift up your heads, ye gates and everlasting doors
and the King of Glory shall come in.
Who is this king? The Lord strong and mighty
the Lord mighty in struggle.
Lift up your heads ye gates, and again, you everlasting doors

and the King of Glory shall come in!
Who is this king? The Lord of hosts: he is the King of Glory.

40

to the chief musician: a psalm of David

I WAITED PATIENTLY for the Lord: he leaned to me,
   and heard my cry.
He brought me up out of the horrible pit,
   out of the cloying clay,
set my feet on a rock, and made me steady.
He's put a new song in my mouth that's praise to our God
many shall see it, and shall fear and trust in him.
Blessed is the man, the woman, who trusts in the Lord
unswayed by the proud, or those who turn to untruth.
Many, Lord, are your amazing works:
   like your thoughts towards us
they can't be accounted: if I would speak of them
they could not be numbered!
You didn't want sacrifice or burnt offering
you have opened my ears: you didn't want these things.
Then I said, 'Look, I'm coming':
   it's written in the weight of the book.
I delight in doing Your Will, your law is inside my heart.
I have preached righteousness in the great congregation,
I have not held back my mouth: you know it.
I've not hidden your righteousness in my heart,
I've declared your faithfulness and salvation.
I've not hidden your loving kindness
or your truth from the great congregation.

Don't hold back your tender mercies from me
may your kindness and truth continually preserve me.
Innumerable evils have hedged me about
my sins have taken hold of me, so I can't look up
they are more than the hairs on my head—
my heart fails me!
Be content to free me; Lord, make haste to help me
let those who stalk my soul to destroy it
be ashamed and confounded!
Let them be driven back and shamed in their own evil,
let them be desolate as a reward
for their shame that laughs, Aha, at me!
Let everyone who sees you rejoice and be glad in you,
let those who love your salvation say 'The Lord be magnified!'
I am poor and needy, but you think about me
you are my help and deliverer: oh God, don't tarry.

62

IN TRUTH MY SOUL is waiting on God:
    my salvation comes from him;
he alone is my rock: my defence: I shall not be moved!
How long will you hold a grievance against someone?
You will be slain, all of you; like a collapsing wall,
    a tottering fence.
They only consult to cast him down from his excellence
delighting in lies, they bless with their mouths,
    but inwardly curse.
My soul, wait only on God: expectation is from him alone.
In God is my salvation and glory,
    the rock of my strength and refuge.

Trust in him at all times:
    people, pour out your heart before him...
God is our refuge! Selah.
Surely people of low degree are vanity, yet people
of high degree are a lie to lay in the balance—
they are even lighter than vanity!
Trust not in oppression, and the vanity of theft,
if your wealth increases, don't set your heart on it.
God has said—twice I've heard this
    —that power belongs to him alone.
Also mercy is his: because he gives to everyone
according to their merits.

86

a prayer of David

BOW DOWN YOUR EAR, Lord: I am poor and needy,
keep my soul in its divinity: oh God,
save your servant who trusts in you!
Be merciful to me: I cry unto you daily
rejoice in my soul: I lift it up to you!
For you, Lord, are good and always ready to forgive
generous in mercy for all who call upon you.
Lord, hear my prayer: listen to my supplications,
in my day of trouble I'll call on you, because you will answer.
There's no one like you, Lord, among all the gods
nor are there any works like your own.
All the nations you've made
will come and worship before you
and glorify your name.

For you are great, and you do wondrous things
you alone are God.
Teach me your way, I'll walk in your truth
cohere my heart to fear your name
I will praise you, God with all my heart
I will glorify your name forever
because your mercy is great and you've freed my soul
from the lowest of hells.
God, the proud are risen against me
and the council of violent men have stalked my soul
not seeing you in their own minds at all.
But you are a God full of compassion
gracious, longsuffering, plenteous in mercy;
oh turn to me—have mercy upon me
give thy servant your strength
save this son of your daughter!
Show me a sign that those who hate me
might see it and be ashamed
because *you* have helped and comforted me!

100

a psalm of praise

MAKE A JOYFUL NOISE unto the Lord, all ye lands!
Serve the Lord with gladness:
    come into his presence with a song!
Know that the Lord is God: it's he who made us,
and not we ourselves: we are his people
and the sheep of his pasture.
Enter his gates with thanksgiving!

And his courts with praise
be grateful to him, and bless his name.
For the Lord is good, his mercy everlasting
and his truth endures from generation to generation.

104

BLESS THE LORD, my soul.
God, you are great, you are decked with honour and majesty
covering yourself with light as if with clothing
stretching out the heavens like a curtain—
laying the beams of your rooms in the waters
making the clouds your chariot
walking on the wings of the wind!
Making your angels spirits—
your ministers a flaming fire
you laid the earth's foundations
so they could never be removed.
You covered the deep as if with a cloak;
the waters stood above the mountains.
At your command, they withdrew
at your voice of thunder, they began to drain away!
They go by the mountains and into the valleys
into the places you've found for them;
you've set a boundary they may not cross
so they will never again cover the planet.
You send springs into the valleys, among the hills
they are drink to every wild animal
the donkeys quench their thirst.
By them, the birds of the air have their dwelling
chirruping among the branches.

You water the hills from your rooms,
the earth is more than happy with your labours.
You make the grass grown for the cattle
and all kinds of green plants in man's service
that he may bring forth food,
and wine, that makes his heart glad
oil that makes his face shine,
bread that strengthens his being also.
God's trees are full of sap like the cedars
of Lebanon he has planted
where the birds make their nests;
for the stork, the fir trees are her house.
The high hills are a refuge for the wild goats
and the rocks for the rabbits.
You appointed the moon to mark seasons,
the sun knows why it sets.
You make darkness and it is night
when all the forest animals rustle.
The young lions roar after their prey
seeking their meat from God.
The sun rises, they gather themselves together
and lie down in their dens.
Man goes to work, his labour till the evening.
Oh Lord how manifest are your creations!
You've made them all in wisdom
the earth is full of your treasures.
So is this wide ocean with its innumerable
creeping things, small and huge creatures.
There go the ships, and there is that blue whale
who you've made to play in it!
They all wait on you, that you give them
their food in due time.

They gather what you give them
you open your hand: they're filled with goodness.
You hide your face, then they are anxious
you take away their breath, and they return to dust.
You send their spirit forth—they are reborn
and you renew the face of the earth.
The glory of the Lord will last forever,
the Lord will glory in his creations.
He looks at the earth, and it shakes
he touches the hills, and they smoke.
I will sing to the Lord for as long as I live
I will praise my God while I have my being.
My meditation will be sweet
I will be glad in him!
Let sinners be consumed,
and the wicked disintegrate.
Bless the Lord my soul, only that. Praise him.

108

a song of David

GOD, MY HEART IS FIXED: I will sing and praise
you with my gift from you, my glory.
Wake up, psaltery and harp! I will wake early.
I will praise you among the people
I will sing praises to you among the nations.
Your mercy is great above the heavens
your truth reaches into the clouds!
Be exalted, God, above the heavens
in your glory above all the earth

that your beloved may be delivered.
Save me with your right hand: answer me.
God has spoken in his holiness: I will rejoice,
I will divide Schechem
and apportion the valley of Succoth
Gilead is mine, Mannaseh too
Ephraim the strength of my crown
Judah my sceptre
Moab my washpot—over Edom
I'll throw my shoe; I'll shout over Philistia!
Who will bring me into the strong city?
Who will lead me into Edom?
Won't you, God, who cast us down?
And won't you now go forth with our army?
Give us help in this trouble: there's no help from man,
through you we shall do valiantly—
because it's you who will vanquish our enemies.

121

a song of degrees

I WILL LIFT UP my eyes to the hills
where my help comes from—
my help comes from the Lord
who made heaven and earth.
He won't let your foot be moved
he who keeps you will not sleep.
Look, he who keeps Israel
will neither doze or sleep!
The Lord is your keeper

he's the shadow on your right hand.
The sun will not burn you by day
or the moon stun you by night.
The Lord will protect you from all evil
he will guard your soul.
The Lord will protect your going out
and your coming home
from this time forth, and for ever more.

127

a song of degrees, for Solomon

UNLESS THE LORD builds the house
the builders work in vain.
Unless the Lord keeps the city
the watchman watches in vain.
It's vain for you to rise up early
or sit around up late
eating your bread of sorrow
while he gives his beloved sleep.
Children are his inheritance,
the womb's fruit is his reward.
The children of youth
are like arrows in a strong man's hands.
Happy is the man
whose quiver is full of them—
they won't be ashamed,
but will speak directly
with the enemy at the gate.

130

a song of degrees

OUT OF THE DEPTHS I've cried to you, Lord
hear my voice, let your ears hear me.
If you count all my sins then who will stand?
But you forgive, awesomely.
I will wait for you: my hope is in your Word.
My soul waits for the Lord longer
than they who watch for the morning.
I say, more than they who wait for the dawn!
Let Israel hope in the Lord
for with him there is mercy
and enormous redemption.
He will redeem Israel of all its sins.

148

PRAISE THE LORD, praise the Lord from the heavens
praise him in the heights!
Praise him and all his angels: praise his hosts.
Praise him, sun and moon: praise his stars of light.
Praise him, heaven of heavens
—and you waters above the heavens—
let them all praise the name of the Lord;
for he uttered it, and thy were created.
He has made them for ever and ever
he's made a decree that shall not pass.
Praise him from the earth, you dragons and deeps,
fire and hail, snow and vapour

storm-wind fulfilling his uttered word
mountains and hills, fruiting trees and cedars,
animals, and cattle, creeping things, flying birds.
Kings of the earth and all peoples
princes and all the judges of the earth
young men and women, old men and children
let them praise the name of the Lord—
for his name alone is essential
his quintessence is above the earth and heaven.
He exalts the horn of his people,
the praise of all his saints
even the children of Israel, near him.
Praise him!

150

PRAISE THE LORD, praise him in his sanctuary
praise him in the high dome of his power
praise him for his great acts, for his excellent greatness!
Praise him with the sound of the trumpet
with the psaltery and harp—
praise him with the timbrel and dance,
with stringed instruments and keys.
Praise him with loud cymbals, high clashing cymbals!
Let everything that breathes praise the Lord.

JOB

a one act drama

Job is the first ever recorded attempt at verse drama. But because of the length of the speeches (so long you can get lost in them) I've taken the liberty of rewriting it as a one-act play. Job is such an important figure because he brings up the whole question of faith in the midst of suffering and loss, and beyond the 'easy answers' that Job's companions unwittingly torture him with. Meanwhile God's famous 'answer' is represented in full...but even with the storyteller's happy ending, it may still leave you wondering.

The characters are (in order of appearance) Storyteller, Job, Eliphaz, Bildad, Zophar, the young man Elihu—and GOD.

The stage is set simply. The Storyeller is in contemporary modern dress.

He enters with the curtain still up to address the audience.

JOB

STORYTELLER

THERE WAS A MAN CALLED JOB (like, globe—), who lived in a wise part of the land in a place called Uz (not Oz), south of Edom—not Eden!

He was straightforward, sound, honest—known to be—and God-fearing too...in other words, *mindful of God*. In fact, he was a model of virtue.

He had a lot—seven sons, three daughters, seven thousand sheep, three thousand camels, five thousand oxen, five thousand she-donkeys—and many servants. That's a lot to lose.

His sons had a great time in their respective houses wining and dining and inviting their sisters.

Job made sure they were purified afterwards of their various hangovers. He was a kind daddy. More kind than cool, but very kind none the less.

One day God's angels turn up to meet with God...Satan among them.

'So where have you been?' asks God.

'From going to and fro in the earth
And from walking up and down in it,' Satan cryptically replies.

'So did you see my servant Job?' asks God. 'There's no one like him: God-fearing, shuns evil...you know how unusual this is.'

'Yes,' says Satan—who sharpens God's pencil. 'But not for nothing, eh. Look at the wall round his house and all his land. You've blessed all he does, and his flocks thrive. But stretch out a finger to all his possessions and I bet you he'll curse you to your face!'

'O-K,' says God (after a long pause, and slowly), 'all he has is in your power now. But keep your hands off his person.'

Satan leaves with what he wanted.

Then when Job's kids are all having a party, drinking wine etc.

at the eldest brother's house, a messenger runs up to him, bows,
and says

'Look, bad news. While your oxen were all ploughing
with the donkeys grazing at their side
a bunch of predatory nomads swept in
and stole the lot. I'm so sorry.'

He'd hardly finished speaking when another messenger turns up
(like, out of breath—)

'Look, all your sheep have just been struck by lightning
your shepherds too—
only I was able to escape to tell you'

But then another messenger trumps him:

'Those Chaldeans, ohmygod—three gangs of them—
have raided all your camels, and made off with them.
They've killed your servants, too...I ran as fast as I could.'

And then another:

All your children at their eldest brother's, just now
were eating and drinking and suddenly a gale sprang up
battering the house...then all the walls fell in
and crushed them. But here I am—'

An unfathomable silence.

Job gets up and tears his robe.
Then he shaves his head.

Then he falls to the ground and says to God
(immortal words—)
'Naked I came from my mother's womb
Naked I shall return.
God gives, God has taken away
Blessed be His Name.'

No cursing God, then.

Once again, God's angels come to meet with God...and Satan
rocks up too.
Again, God asks 'Where have you been?'
Satan: 'Oh, you know, wandering about.'
God: 'So did you notice my servant Job? There's no one like him
in all the earth etc. The point is, *he continues just as he was* despite
your trying to persuade me to ruin him.'

'Ah, skin for skin,' Satan replies. 'A man can give all he has to save
his life, but lay a finger on him—and he will curse you. Believe
me.'

'Very well,' says God. 'But spare his life!'
Satan slips away.

Job breaks out in ulcers from tip to toe.
He takes a piece of pot to scrape himself with,
and sits in the ashpit.

His wife is furious:

'Not still worshipping that Fat Arse are you? Curse him, Job, he
deserves it.'

'That's how a silly woman talks,' he replies. 'If we take happiness from God, then we have to take sadness too!' (i.e. the rough with the smooth)

So, no cursing God.

The news of these disasters reaches the ears of three of Job's friends—Eliphaz, Bildad, and Zophar. They message each other like people did in those days, then set off from their homes.

'Let's go and see what we can do for him, poor sod!'

Seeing Job from a distance, imagine...they can barely recognise him. They shout aloud, they tear their clothes, they put dust on their heads in solidarity.

Then (the story goes) they sit down with him seven days and nights, absolutely speechless.

Finally, Job himself breaks the silence.

SCENE 1

The curtain parts. The storyteller steps to one side and leaves the stage. Job is sitting, his head in his hands, with his friends sitting around him looking somewhat apprehensive. Job speaks looking downwards at the floor.

JOB
Curse the day I was born—and the night I was conceived! May it be darkness, lightless, Godless! Deep in shadow as I am.

Dismal, joyless. Call up Leviathan! No stars at dawn. Why didn't I die newborn? What were there two knees for, two breasts to suck? I'd be in peace now with the kings of this earth, with all their riches; or swaddled like a stillborn. Down there, you know, evil men no longer do their thing; down there *the high and the low are one...and the slave is free of his master.*

Why make a man conscious when he's born for grief? Why give light to those who long for a death that never comes? Or to anyone who God just blocks on every side? Tell me.

My only food is sighs. My worst fears come true. I am in agony!

ELIPHAZ *(leaning forward)*
Can you hear, can you bear anything in return?

We can't say nothing. Job: think of those you taught, the strength you gave them, the way you set them right. But now your turn has come, you've lost all patience! Friend, you're overwhelmed—of course you are. But doesn't your faith give you hope? You've lived an exemplary life!

Have you ever seen a good man brought to nothing? Have you? You know that those who seed iniquity reap the same harvest. All it takes is a breath from God.

Now: a whisper came into my ears like a secret revelation. In the early hours, when our dreams master us, *a shiver of horror ran through me.* I felt breath on my face, my hairs stood on end. Someone was there...though I couldn't see him. There was silence, then I heard a voice:

'Was any man ever found blameless in the presence of God? He doesn't even fully trust his own servants or angels! So how much can he trust us, fallible as we are?'

So, ask then. Where will you find an answer? It's we who make trouble for ourselves *as surely as eagles fly to the heights.*

If I were you, I'd ask God direct: I'd lay my case in front of him.

He is the Great cause. So, then, don't refuse this Shadow Lesson. He who wounds is also he who heals. You'll be safe then, you'll see.

JOB *(still looking down)*

If only misery could be weighed, and all my suffering put on the scales! But they're greater than the sands of the seas. So no wonder my words are wild! Those shadowy arrows stick in me, they poison me. God stands against me like an army. It's like eating everything I hate the most. God give me hope! Or maybe he could just crush me—that at least would give me some comfort. Can I go on waiting? What use is it when doom is already so close. I'm not made of stone. What strength?

(Begins to look up).

My brothers have been fickle as a torrent...like ice, and like vanishing. Are you going to be like that? Will you run? Have I asked you for anything unreasonable?

Put me right and I will say no more;
show me where I've been at fault.

'Fair comment can be borne without resentment'—yes: but what is the basis for your critique? Mere words—desperate speech? Come on, please look at me as one human being to another! I won't lie. Or relent. My case isn't yet tried!

(They stare).

Tell me: is a man's life here nothing more than forced labour? I've been living in fantasy. This is depression, friends, this is what it's like. The day crawls by. And the night. And I'm loathsome, like it. And my life is like a breath—you'll look twice, and I'm gone. That place...Sheol...no one comes back up again!

So no wonder I can't shut up about it? Could you? Do you think I'm like some wild animal to look at me like this? Eh? For pity's sake! And what have I done to YOU, watcher in the skies? Why did You choose me as your target?

BILDAD

Job, Job, is there no end to this? Can God stop whatever is right—can justice be falsified? If your sons have sinned, they've paid for it—so you too must seek and petition Him! Then he'll restore everything to you—the good man's house will be rebuilt! How you are now will seem to you like nothing, I promise you. Think about our fathers. What do we know? *Our life passes like a shadow.* But they will tell you 'Does papyrus flourish, except in marshes? Pluck them fresh, they wither fastest.' Such is our fate when we forget God...but believe me, God never denies a sinless man, or helps an evil one. Your cheeks will fill with laughter again—and your mouth will be a cry of joy! And your enemies will be shamed to a man.

JOB

I know what you're saying: 'how can a man be in the right against God?' Who can defy him, mountain-mover, earth-shaker? Star maker? He never goes back on his anger. So how do I plead my case with him? Even if I *am* in the right, what use is my defence? He's the judge, after all. How can I be sure he'd listen to my voice? He who—for no reason I can see—crushes and wounds me? And what strength do I have? Who calls him to account? He can say what he likes about me: I have no defence. Am I innocent? I don't know: but my life is hateful. I'll say this: it's all one—*innocent and guilty, he destroys all alike.* He even laughs about it!

If I try and stifle my feelings and put on a mask, I'm overwhelmed with fear at everything I've suffered. And if I'm guilty, what's the use anyway? The bottom line is I'm a man, and he's not. No argument, then. No dialogue possible.

No mediation either.

(Looks up)

However, I shall speak! Since I've lost the taste for life, I'll give myself free rein. I'll say to him: TELL ME YOUR REASON. Is it ok for him to hurt me and turn a blind eye on the wicked? Have you even got human eyes—can you see as we see? You know damn well I'm innocent and that no one can challenge you. Your own hands made me! So now you want to destroy me?

(Lifts his fist)

Maybe you were just pretending all along...biding your time... looking for anywhere I'd gone wrong. So, bad news if I'm guilty: if not I hardly dare raise my head. *(Gets to his feet)* And if I make a stand, you'll hunt me down like a lion.

So why was I born? I should have died then. Can you not leave me a little joy?

ZOPHAR

Job, you're babbling. Does your wordiness make you right? Do you really think you can silence everyone so you can rant with no one to answer you? This is what you said:

'My way of life is faultless

and in your eyes I am free from blame'

But if God wanted *to show you the secret of wisdom that put all cleverness to shame*...my God, you would not think he's calling you to account! Sinless—are you really? Come on! Can you claim to know God's mystery? *(Gestures.)* It's higher than the heavens, deeper than Sheol.

What can you know? Only this: *he sees iniquity and marks it well.* Come, you've got to get things straight, and reach out to him. Renounce whatever sin you have! Then you can be fearless, innocent. Then you will forget your sufferings! People will seek you out. You'll be protected, as well.

JOB *(sarcastic)*

Everyone would agree with you—and when you die, wisdom will
too! Listen, I can think as deeply as you: do you think I'm
inferior to you? So who hasn't thought as much? After all a man
becomes a joke if he cries out to God and expects an answer. The
blameless innocent? That's even funnier. Meanwhile those who
are doing absolutely fine patronise us. You know what they say,
Zophar. And yet listen: *the tents of thieves are left in peace*—and
those who defy God live in safety! Every creature knows this is
how it is. God holds everything in his power—everything.

No one can rebuild what he destroys: no one can free whoever
he imprisons! Drought or flood, it's all his. He robs a nation's
counsellors of their wits, turns judges into idiots. *His hands untie
the belt of kings*...he makes priests walk shoe-less. Meanwhile the
cleverest speakers can be struck dumb as old men without
discretion. *(Gestures)* He builds a nation up: he strikes it down.
He leaves a people wandering *in a trackless waste*...you know it.

I've seen all of this with my own eyes. Whatever you think
you know, I know too. I'm no way less than you! But my words
are for Shaddai—I mean to argue with him about all of this!

(Emphatic)

As for you, you're charlatans! Physicians according to
yourselves! I wish someone would teach you SI-LENCE—the
only wisdom that suits you! Listen to my accusation, try
empathising with what's in my mouth. Will you plead God's case
for him? Will *you* be his advocate? *(His eyes narrow)* Would it
be good for you to meet his scrutiny? What do you think?
Would he be duped?

He'd tell you where to get off, I'm telling you. Your old
chestnuts are just that—*proverbs of ash*—your responses
mechanical and breakable. Shut up!

(They look at him).

Now I'll do some talking. Whatever comes of it, I don't care. I'll take my life in my own hands. He can kill me if he likes— what other hope? Only to justify myself to him. Courage alone feels like freedom to me.

Now listen carefully: *I'm going to proceed by law.* Innocent until proved guilty. So who's going to accuse me? *(Raises his voice)* LET HIM COME—I'm ready to be silenced or to die. But just grant me this: TAKE YOUR HEAVY HAND AWAY FROM ME. Then by all means accuse me, and I'll reply. I'll speak—and you can answer me.

(Shouts)

How many faults and crimes have I committed?

What law have I broken or offended? Why do you turn away and look at me like an enemy? You accuse me while my life is crumbling away and broken. This is what you're looking at!

(Quietly)

Who can bring the clean out of the unclean? No man alive!

Leave him alone to finish his day. There's always hope for a tree—but for him? He dies, he's gone. He rises again? I don't think so.

God, if you'd only hide me in Sheol till your anger is past! *(Makes a face)* You might even be glad to see me again. But no, I don't think so.

(Lights dim...then slowly come back up again)

SCENE 2

ELIPHAZ *(his voice rising)*
Does a wise man deal with airy fluff? Defend himself with vacuous talk? And mere wordiness? You do worse, Job, *you flout piety itself*...you even dismiss meditation in God's presence!

Actually, you have a guilty conscience—evidence: your devious language! *Your own mouth condemns you*—not us.

Are you Adam? Have you listened at God's council? Do you have a monopoly on wisdom? *(Ironically)* 'I don't think so!'

You scorn our moderation. But look how your passion takes you, how bad you look, ranting away like this.

How can any man be innocent? God knows. How much less so the likes of us.

Listen, I'll tell you what I've experienced. The life of an evil man is always painful! A tyrant's years are always numbered. The danger is always in his ears: he can never relax completely. He's no hope of running from the darkness he's created...he's marked down like meat, and he knows it.

He raised his hand against God...he tried to defy Shaddai with his fat face and massive shield, living among the ruins of all those he's dispossessed. But all his own buildings will be ruined like this: he'll no longer cast a shadow over the land. Name him— you know the likes of him down the corridors of time.

Conceive mischief, and you breed disaster.

JOB *(impatient)*

I've heard all this before! What lousy comforters you are! Give me a break—all you want to have is the last word. All you're trying to do is make yourselves feel better. I could talk like you. I could overwhelm you with sermons till I was exhausted, too. But my suffering is real, and it remains.

Rage drives me crazy: everyone is against me—you all are, too—rushing at me, rushing after me ! I've been handed over to the godless!

I lived in peace until he shattered me. I'm like a target for his arrows. He butchers me. I've rubbed my forehead in the dust, but still it continues. *(Pauses)* However, I have not retaliated.

Witness me, grief is my advocate: let this plead my case.

My days are numbered: the gravediggers aren't far away. I'm the butt of mockers: I brood on their spite. So you've abandoned me—ONLY YOU CAN CHAMPION ME. IMAGINE! Come on, then, do it all again. *I shall not find a single sage among you.*

Look, I'm heartbroken: can you not see that? All I look forward to is Sheol...making my bed in the dark. Grave, you are my father: worm you are my sister, my mother. Hope? Where is it then?

BILDAD

Will you never learn to control yourself? Your very expression is the problem! And how can you think we're so stupid? *Tear yourself to pieces if you will*—but the world isn't going to burn because of you.

A sinful man's light is bound to be put out: his own cunning brings him down. You know it: he's trapped, he's snared...hunger finds him, disaster stalks him. Then disease claims him.

Lilith makes her home under his roof.

His roots wither, his branches are blasted. His memory fades: his name's forgotten. He's an exile, a nobody then—and this is the fate of anyone who separates from God.

JOB *(still upset)*

Will you never stop torturing me with stuff like this? Ten times at least—you're shameless! Suppose I have made a mistake: it's still true that God is my oppressor—it's *his* net closing around me. And if I protest: No Reply.

He's built a wall across my path—I can't get over it. My honour, the crown of my work, is gone. He breaks through me on every side: I succumb.

Meanwhile my brothers—where are they? My family shuns

me. Even my servant...I'm reduced to begging him. My wife can't stand my breath...*I am a thing corrupt.* Even the children laugh at me in the street. I'm friendless—I'm stuffed. Please have some sympathy at least, and stop hounding me like he has!
(His tone shifts...half to himself)

Would this were all written down...
inscribed on some monument...
cut into the rock forever.

I need a writer!
But I know this: my advocate lives even as I die...I shall be vindicated. And even as you're muttering about your next pretext against me
(Menacing)
You will learn that there is indeed judgement.

ZOPHAR

Job, you're making me impatient; I don't like these arguments. But my spirit is whispering to me! Don't you realise that since time began the victory of evil has always been brief? It may have towered sky-high—but then it vanishes like a phantom. Meanwhile his descendants have to clean up the mess. God makes him vomit up all his wealth! The poison he's sucked poisons him...what he's done to the poor rebounds on him. *Misery descends on him with all its force.* God pours fire on him, all his rage. No use running away now! He's stuck with arrows...

JOB *(interrupting)*

Stop! Just listen to me, that's all I ask. It's all you can give me! *Let me have my say*—you can cavil when I've finished.
Do you think I bear a grudge or something? Have I no reason

to be impatient? Don't you realise what's happened to me? But listen: there's a question that will silence you...I tell you, it makes me shudder.

(Pauses)

Why do evil people survive—*and thrive?* Fearless of God? Nothing goes wrong for them—that's where you're wrong. Their children dance, they live their lives to the full, and they die happy. Now how is that?

And these are the ones who tell God to go to hell!

Isn't it true: *they hold their fortune in their own two hands...* and there's no room for God!

Do we really often see an evil man's light put out—do we? God, you say, punishes his children: I say, let him suffer. But once he's gone, where is his suffering?

(Quotes)

But who can give lessons in wisdom to God?

A good man and a rogue lie in death both the same...that is what you're not seeing.

Meanwhile, I know what's in your mind, and your miserable thoughts about me. Who is there to accuse *anyone* once they've gone...their funeral procession, perhaps?

What nonsense are your answers!

(They all, including Job, freeze...lights down)

SCENE 3

ELIPHAZ

Can we be of any use to God when a wise man's wisdom is only for *himself?* Does Shaddai gain a jot from your integrity? Would God punish you for your piety? No! But for all your failings, Job! You've pressurised us all on your behalf. Think of the cruel things you've also done—can I imagine them for you?

God can see everything—but because he's above us all you ask what does he know?!

You mistake his generosity, too: what he gives to *everyone* (and not just you). So then *make peace with him, be reconciled...* and your happiness will return. Welcome his teachings—keep his words close to your heart. If you come back humbled you'll find Shaddai abundant as gold and silver! Then you'll lift your face up: you'll pray, he will hear you and *light will shine on your path!*

He'll bring you freedom.

JOB

Ah, then I'm rebellious. His heavy hand is still on me. If only I knew how to reach him and reach his place! I'd set out my case— my argument would be lucid, I can tell you. I'd note his defence, every word of it! He'd have to give me a hearing! He'd realise I'm a honest man, too.

But any direction I go in, he's not there. Yet he knows every step I take.

(Affirms)

Let him test me in the crucible; I shall come out pure gold.

I've walked with him: I know I have. But once he's decided, who can change his mind? No doubt over my sentence, then. And that's why I'm scared: and the more I think about it the more terrifying it is. He's made my heart absolutely sink...

And the gloom veils his presence from me.

Why can't his faithful ones see him? Look at how honest ordinary people suffer. I've no conscience about it, either. May my enemy be damned—my opponent likewise! What hope has

211

a godless man anyway? Is God going to hear his cries? I'm trying to show you how he *actually* works, and if you'd understood me you wouldn't be wasting your breath in empty words.

Here's the fate God has in store for the wicked: the sword. Plague. His clothes on the back of a good man. His money redistributed among the innocent. The rich man wakes up—he's lost everything. He's panicked in broad daylight—later, night terrors get him. No pity for him! His downfall's only cause for applause...hear the hissing that meets him on every side. Then he's on the run—an outlaw from the moon.

So, he's lightning-struck—him and all his kind.

But tell me, where does wisdom come from?
Where is understanding to be found?

It can't be bought with gold or paid with silver, or priced by any crystal standard. Nothing can match it in value! Pearls are not even worth diving for.

Now listen.

It's outside the knowledge of every living thing, hidden even from birds in the sky. Even damnation and death can only say 'We've heard rumours of it.'

God alone has traced its path. And so he said to us

'Wisdom? Is fear of the Lord
Understanding? Not to do evil?'

(Pauses—looks out over the audience)

But who will bring me back to the time that's gone when he was my guardian, his light over my head?

212

Will I ever see my ripe days again with my children round me?

When I went to the city gate, the young men stood aside; the older men got to their feet. People stopped talking—they waited on my words. I paused, and they were still listening. *They waited for me as men wait for rain.* They watched me for the least sign of a smile.

My praises echoed...they smiled at me. I freed the poor man, and the orphan too. Dying men had my blessing as I had theirs. *(Gestures with his hand, remembering)* I was dressed in my cloak and turban. I was eyes for the blind and feet for the lame, they said. And every stranger had his case heard—I made sure of that.

So I thought I'd die in honour!

But now I'm the laughing stock of young men whose fathers I didn't see fit to put with the dogs that looked after my sheep! They had no strength, they chewed roots: they had nothing. They were outcasts living on the edge, in caves, clefts. And these are the ones who gossip about me!

I'm loathsome, a tramp, even to them. They'd throw stones if they could. It's terrifying.

(He moves as if to dive forward)

Grief has me in its maw—thrown into the mud.

So I appeal to You but you give me no answer. Only cruelty. You're taking me to death, I know it...*but have I ever hurt anybody?*

Haven't I wept for people's hardship? I only hoped for happiness—and this darkness came.

(Paces)

My stomach is never still.

I promised not to stare at young women. Now we know what God deals out from on high—but hasn't he seen how I've been? Have I been untrue? I don't think so.

(Quotes)

213

If ever I lost my heart to any woman
or lurked at my neighbour's door;
let my wife grind corn that isn't mine
let her sleep between another's sheets—

I've not been lustful—and if I had what would I do when he calls me up? Let my own land accuse me and grow wild with brambles!

Have I been insensitive to others' needs? I don't think so. Have I ever denied anyone in my reach?

(Looks at his hand)

Have I ever put my trust in my money? Or gloated over what I've got? Has my heart been seduced and kissed my mouth?

Have I taken pleasure in others' pain? Have I ever cursed them to death?

My door has always been open to the traveller.

Have I ever lied about my blunders?

Stood in fear of gossip?

(Emphatic)

Who can get me a hearing from God?

I've had my say: let Shaddai answer me.

I'll wear it royally!

SCENE 4

Enter a young man, Elihu. Light comes up and illuminates him at the back of the stage as he approaches the gathering. He is momentarily uncertain, then quickens his step. He bows respectfully to his elders who are present. Each of them could be his father.

Job turns from the front of the stage, and sees him. Then Elihu addresses him as the others turn to listen.

214

ELIHU

I'm still young—sir, you're old: so I was afraid to tell you what I know. I thought 'Old age should speak—advancing years will utter wisdom.' But it's not necessarily so. Wisdom is a breath, and an inspiration. Old age doesn't mean wisdom, or longevity either.

So I'm asking you all for a hearing.

There was a time when I hoped for a lot from you: I gave you my whole attention...and I can honestly say that not one of you has disproved anything that Job has said!

So don't think *you've* found wisdom, or that your teaching is from God and not yourselves. I'm not going to argue like you— I'm taking a different tack.

There's a lot to say and it fills me like new wine in a skin! I've got to speak; I'm not going to flatter anyone either.

Job, be kind enough to listen, and listen well. I will be honest, I promise you. Refute me if you can. It was God's breath that made me—but I'm not a demi-god, I'm human.

How could you say 'I am perfect—yet God is inventing grievances against me?'

I tell you, you are wrong.

God does not fit man's measure.

So why do you rail at him like a judge? God speaks first one way, then another...but we don't notice. He speaks in dreams, and visions...he whispers in our ears. He may frighten us too, sometimes, to turn us away from doing bad. So he levels our pride. He saves us from Sheol.

When we suffer, too, he's working on us. And there's an angel beside him—a mediator—chosen to remind us where our duty lies, and to have pity on us. He intercedes. Then we recover. And we give thanks...and we're closer to God than we were before.

215

So we share our good news far and wide, and say something like this:

'I missed the mark and left the path
but God hasn't punished me as he could have—
he's rescued me from death
and is letting me live in the light'

God does this again and again.

Job, listen. Do you have anything to criticise? I'm not against you. And there is wisdom.

You elders, too. Let's discover together where justice truly lies!

Now, Job has said 'I'm in the right—and God is refusing me. My wounds are beyond healing.'

Are there many people like him? Who keep company with bad people? Did he not say himself that it's useless for anyone to merely try and please God?

God is so far removed from evil that he treats everyone as their particular way of life suggests. He never gets it wrong— have no doubt! The course of right is always there. God is its breath...if he drew back the whole universe would collapse!

So could an *enemy* of justice ever prevail over us? It makes no sense. And would any of you dare to condemn a God *who tells kings they are good for nothing...and makes no distinction between the rich and the poor?*

He can take out a tyrant just like that. He keeps sight of everyone...not even the deepest shadow prevents that. He doesn't summon anyone to court either: he just decides.

You may say: 'they've so ignored him that the poor cry out— but he's unmoved. Nothing can touch him—he hides his face.' But it's not true...he takes pity on nations as well as people, freeing them from the ganglia of distress.

If a man like this says to God: 'I was led astray, I'll sin no more. *If I did wrong then tell me about it...*' then do you think he should be punished?

So this is what I have to say: there's no wisdom in what Job has said...his words lack actual sense. He calls justice itself into question—so as a result, whether he likes it or not,

he's abusing God!

(Job flinches)

Job, are you going to go on saying you're in the right and insist on your innocence? Even to asking God how *you* affect *him?*

(Job turns away)

Look up at the sky: look at it clearly. See how high those clouds are? If you do wrong what on earth do you achieve against him? Nothing. How then do you think you benefit him?

Your fellow men and women are the ones who *suffer—humanity* gains if you're good. He only doesn't answer because of our pride. But to maintain he doesn't see or hear is ridiculous. He sees it all.

You even claim: 'he doesn't see me' or even 'he doesn't seem aware of our wrongdoing.' This is nonsense. Your talk here is idle words. You're simply being emotional...

(Job raises his hand—he's heard enough...)

But wait while I explain just a little more—I want to prove my Maker just! God *never* rejects a blameless man, or lets a wrongdoer live on in all his power. He just doesn't. He *always* supports a good man's rights. When kings grow proud *he fetters them with chains!* Then they have to see all they've done. He whispers in their ears: the writing's on the wall. And if they listen, all *can* be well.

Or it's a thunderbolt.

(The sound of distant thunder, briefly...everyone looks up)

Stubborn people come off worst of all! But he can save people *because* of their suffering. He uses it to open their eyes.

For you, Job, it's the same.

Please consider: you lived in luxury. You had everything anyone could want. But you didn't give justice to those well-off people—and I've heard you cheated orphan children out of their rights?

(Job glares back)

So you were led astray by your wealth: you were complacent. *Prosecute the rich, not merely the penniless!*

This is why you've been tried.

God is supreme. No one can tell him he's done wrong. Turn your mind to *praise*, Job, to what goes beyond your mind. He holds the balance in everything, in rain and sun. And so there's food for us. He's the master of lightning and where it strikes... thunder is his warning.

(Thunder rumbles again...closer).

Doesn't it move your heart? It does mine. Listen to His Voice!

See how he brings us to a standstill as the snow flakes down, too...then he's the God of Ice.

Listen to all this, Job: no backsliding now!

Meditate on God's wonders.

Light vanishes in darkness—but then it returns again. This is His Splendour. There's no other word for it but *awe*.

(Brief pause)

SCENE 5

Storm wind starting to gather as the thunder rolls again. Slowly the company all stand. Dim flickering lightning silhouettes them as they look around.

218

Then a loud clap of thunder as if directly in the theatre, as they jump.

WHO IS OBSCURING MY WORK
WITH HIS EMPTY WORDS?

Brace yourself: now it's my turn to ask the questions.

Where were you when I laid the earth's foundations?

Tell me, since you seem to know so much!

Who designed it, who decided it, do you know?

Who laid its cornerstone?
Who held back the sea? I did.

Have you ever in your life given orders to the morning?

Have you seen it *stealing the light from wicked men?*

Have you been to the Source? To the deepest?
To the Gate of Death and the Borderlands?

Have you an inkling of the extent of the earth?

Tell me about it!

If you know all this, you must be ancient.

Did you know I also keep snow for times of great stress, battle and war?

That I rain on desert places?

Who is the father of the rain?

Do you understand celestial law?

Have you ever found prey for the lioness so she can feed her cubs?

Who feeds the raven?

Who gave the wild donkey his freedom?

And would any of these animals serve you?
Consider the ostrich and how she survives being precisely ostrich-like!

Or the horse that can leap like a grasshopper!
And is afraid of nothing.

Does the falcon obey you? Or the female eagle feeding her young on blood?

Job, who are you? Are you opposing all of this?

JOB *(ashen-faced)*
My words have only been my own: what can I say?
   I'd better be silent.
   I've said all I can—I can't add anything.

GOD

So, brace yourself again.

Do you really want to put me in the wrong to put yourself in the right?

Has your arm this strength?

If so, be royal: be furious! *Humiliate the haughty at a glance!*

Cast one look at the proud...then I will acknowledge you.

Think of Behemoth—he's the masterpiece of all my work. But I had to discipline him, to forbid him the mountains to protect my other animals. And so you find him under the lotus and among the reeds in the swamp. It's perfect for him. Who is going to catch him there?

Leviathan, too. *Can you catch him with a fish-hook?* Will he plead with you, cajole and coax you to be his slave for life. I don't think so!

Think about him. He is also as I am—WILD. Made without fear. Do you see it now? Job? Do you see what life is? This is my answer.

(The sound of rain beginning)

> JOB *(steps forward to kneel)*
> I know you can do anything, Lord.
>   All you conceive you can perform.
>   I am the man who questioned you. I see I've been holding

forth beyond my understanding.

> I knew you then only in my mind
> but now I've seen you face to face
> I take back all I said.
> I repent.

Job slowly lifts and smooths ashes onto his head as the light brightens around him. His tears begin to fall.
   The company stand back speechless in the shadows.
   Single spotlight on Job, slowly fading.

CURTAIN

The Storyteller re-enters after a pause as the houselights come back up.

STORYTELLER

So you see when God had said all this to Job he turned to Eliphaz and said 'I am burning with anger with you and your two friends for not speaking honestly as Job has done. So now, find seven bulls and seven rams and take them to him. Consider yourselves dismissed—Job can pray for you. I forgive you as he will too!'

   Satan was nowhere to be seen.

   Then God, you know, restored all Job's fortunes because *he'd prayed for his friends.* In fact, he gave him everything he'd lost twice over—so the story says.

   All his brothers and sisters and old friends came to see him and sat down with him. They showed him every sympathy for his ordeal. Each of them gave him a silver coin—and a gold ring.

And Job, well, Job came to own fourteen thousand sheep, six thousand camels, one thousand oxen and she-donkeys. He had seven sons and three daughters, too—Turtledove, Cassia, and Mascara. What about that?

There weren't any more beautiful girls in all the land than his. And he gave them his inheritance with their brothers.

Job lived till he was well over 100—140, it is said! And so he saw his grandchildren for several generations.

When he finally died he was 'full of days'—and full of Life. Here's to Life!
Goodnight.

The Storyteller takes a bow

THE SONG OF SONGS

a one-act verse drama

Again The Song of Songs had to be translation as the first and finest love poem of its kind. And, despite being described as a 'wedding idyll' there is more to it than meets the eye when you realise the story inside the poem isn't a wedding—it's an affair, and how the Shulamite suffers and eventually resolves that as one of Solomon's many women. The poem is no less passionate for that!

Please see extended note on this at the back of the book.

SCENE I

Shulamite

LET HIM KISS ME inside my mouth.
Your love is lovelier than wine
the smell of you more subtle and fragrant
your name is like oil silken pouring
and that's why the girls all love you.

Daughters of Jerusalem

Just look at us, and we'll run after you!

Shulamite

This king of a man has taken me into his bedroom.

Daughters of Jerusalem

We'll be happy for you—we'll celebrate,
we'll talk about your love that's greater than wine.
It's right that he loves you.

Shulamite

I am black and gorgeous,
you daughters of Jerusalem,
like the tents at Kedar
like Solomon's own curtains.
Don't see me as swarthy,
imagine the sun has scorched me!

My brothers were angry with me
they made me look after the vineyards,
but I haven't taken care of my own.

Tell me, oh you that my soul loves
where you feed your flock, and rest in the noonday heat

why should I be like an outcast
among your friends?

King Solomon

Loveliest woman; if you don't know why
follow the flock's footsteps
and feed your young ones by the shepherd's tent on Zion.
Lover, I've compared you
to a horse among Pharaoh's chariots,
your cheeks gorgeous with their plats
your neck with its string of jewels.
I will order you plats of gold
studded with silver.

Shulamite

While my king sat at his table
my spikenard wafted towards him.
My beloved is like sprigs of myrrh
bound between my breasts.
My beloved is like a cluster of henna flowers
among the vines of Engedi.

King Solomon

God, you are beautiful, you are truly lovely
your eyes are like doves.

Shulamite

And you are beautiful too, and kind
and our bed is green.
The beams of our house are cedar
our rafters, evergreen.

I am a rose of Sharon,
a red lily of the valleys.

King Solomon

A lily among thorns,
that's my love among all the others.

Shulamite

An apple tree among all the others in the wood,
that's my beloved beside other men.

I sat down under his longed-for shade
and his fruit was sweet in my mouth.

He brought me to his banqueting house,
the banner he raises over me is love!
Feed me with raisin cakes, comfort me with apples,
I'm lovesick.
His left arm is under my head
his right hand is touching me.

I ask you, daughters of Jerusalem,
by the gazelles and the hinds in the fields,
don't titivate my love, don't stir it up
until its ready to awaken.

SCENE II

Shulamite

MY LOVER'S VOICE! Look, he's coming
jumping on the mountains
racing over the hills.
He's like a roe, or a young stag,
look, he's standing beside our wall.
He's looking in at the windows
he's visible through the lattice.
Then he spoke, and said to me
'Get up, my lovely one, come out
look, winter is over
the rain has gone
the flowers are with us;
birdsong has returned
you can hear the turtle dove,
the fig tree is ripening
the vines are blossoming;
you can smell them.
Get up, my love, and come out
oh my love, hidden in the depths of the rock
and the steep places
let me see your face
your voice is sweet, and you are beautiful.'

The Brothers

Go catch the foxes, the little foxes
that make havoc in the vineyards
because they're blossoming now!

Shulamite

My beloved is mine, and I am his:
he's feeding his flock among the lilies.
Until the day's cool, and the shadows fly
Return, my love, and be like that roe, that young stag
on the Bether mountains.
Lying on my bed at night, I search for him
but find him not.
I said: 'I will get up, and go out into the city
into the streets and the squares
I will search for the man I love.'
I looked for him, but couldn't find him.
The watchmen on their rounds found me
and I asked them 'Have you seen him?'
It was only a little way on from them
that I found him—
and clasping him, wouldn't let him go;
until I'd taken him into my mother's house
and the room she conceived me in.

I ask you again, daughters of Jerusalem
by the gazelles and the hinds in the field,
don't titivate my love, don't stir it up
until it's ready to awaken.

SCENE III

Daughters of Jerusalem

WHAT IS THIS rising up out of the desert
like a column, a plume of smoke
scented with myrrh and frankincense
with every perfume a merchant knows?

It's Solomon's sedan chair!
Sixty strong men around it,
champions of Israel.
They're all expert with the sword,
every one wears one on his thigh
against the dangers of the night.

Solomon has made himself a throne
out of Lebanese wood.
He's made the posts out of silver
the bottom is gold, his seat purple
the middle paved with ebony the colour of love
from Jerusalem's daughters!

So go, daughters of Zion, and look at Solomon
wearing his crown his mother gave him
on his wedding day, and in his heart's joy.

King Solomon

God, you are beautiful, my love, you're truly beautiful
your eyes behind your veil are doves.

Your hair wild as a flock of goats
that stray along the side of Mt. Gilead.

Your teeth white as newly shorn ewes
come up from the washing:
each one has its twin
no one is lonely among them.

Your lips are a gash of scarlet
and your mouth is gorgeous:
your temples, behind your veil,
are halves of a pomegranate.
Your neck is like David's tower
built for defence
hung round with a thousand bucklers;
shields of all the strong men.

Your breasts are like twin fawns, gazelle twins
which feed among the lilies.

Until the day's cool, and the shadows fly away
I'm going to the mount of myrrh
the hill of frankincense!
You are beautiful, my love
there's no blemish in you.

Come with me from Lebanon, be my wife,
look out from the summit of Amana
from Senir and Hermon,
from the lion's den and the high place of the leopards.

You have ravished my heart, sister, wife.

You ravish my heart with just one of your eyes,
with one glimpse of your neck.
Your love is so exquisite
so much more delicious than wine!
And the smell of you, than all the other spices!
Your lips exude wild honey
honey and milk lie under your tongue
and the scent of your clothing
is like Lebanon.

She's an enclosed garden, my sister-wife
a paradise garden, a sealed fountain.
Her shoots are a pomegranate orchard
laden with precious fruit;
henna with spikenard
spikenard and saffron,
calamus and cinnamon,
with all the incense-bearing trees;
myrrh and aloes, all the vital spices.
You are a fountain in the gardens,
a well of living waters,
and flowing streams from Lebanon.

Shulamite

Wake up, north wind, and blow south.
Breathe on my garden, propagate its perfume.
Let my beloved walk in this garden
and eat its precious fruit!

King Solomon

I've come into your garden, my sister-wife
I've gathered myrrh and spice
I've eaten your honeycomb, your honey
drunk milk and wine.
Eat, friends; eat and drink like this;
drink deep as you like, beloved.

SCENE IV

Shulamite

I WAS ASLEEP, but my heart was awake
it's the voice of my beloved knocking—he says
'Open to me, sister, my dove, my perfect love
my head is filled with dew
and my hair with night rain.

I've taken off my coat: do you want me to put it on?
I've washed my feet: should I dirty them again?'
He slid his hand through the hole in my door
and my heart jumped.
I got up to open it to him
my hands ran with myrrh
liquid off my fingers
on the handle of the bolt.

I opened my door to him...
but then, where was he? He'd gone.
My soul blanched: he was there, speaking to me.

233

I went out immediately, but he was nowhere around.
I called out his name—no answer.
The watchmen on patrol found me
they hit me, they hurt me;
they ripped my cloak off me.

I only ask you, daughters of Jerusalem
that if you find him, please tell him
that I'm sick with love.

Daughters of Jerusalem

Why is your lover-man better than any other,
lovely woman?
What makes your lover so special
that you put this on us?

Shulamite

My beloved is white—he's ruddy,
he's the best among ten thousand.
His head is like gold, pure gold
his long hair black as a raven.
His eyes are dove's eyes beside the water
washed as if with milk, and well set.
His cheeks are a bed of spices,
a bank where sweet herbs grow.

His lips are like lilies secreting myrrh.
His hands like gold rings set with beryl.

His body, ivory inlaid with sapphires.
His thighs, marble set into gold...
his face is Lebanon, and its amazing cedars.

His mouth is the sweetest: he's altogether lovely.
This is my beloved, and my friend
you daughters of Jerusalem.

Daughters of Jerusalem

So where has he gone
loveliest woman?
Where has he turned
that we may find him again with you?

Shulamite

He's gone down to the garden, to the spice beds
to feed himself there, to gather lilies.
I am my beloved's, and he is mine
he's feeding his flock among the lilies.

SCENE V

King Solomon

MY LOVE, you are beautiful as Tirzah
lovely as Jerusalem
scary as an army with banners.

235

Turn your eyes away from me,
they've captured me!
Your hair still wild as that flock of goats,
lying along the side of Gilead
your teeth white as ewes
come up from the washing
where every one has a twin
and no one is lonely;
your temples two halves of a pomegranate
behind your veil...

There are sixty queens, eighty concubines
and countless women
but you, my love, are unique
the only daughter your mother had
and her darling—
the daughters saw you, and pronounced you blessed;
yes, and all the queens and concubines too.

Daughters of Jerusalem

Who is she that gazes out like the dawn
white as the moon, clear as the sun
awesome as an army with banners?

Shulamite

I went down to the nut orchard
to see the new growth in the valley
if the vine was budding

and the pomegranate in flower.
Before I knew it, my soul had thrown me
among the chariots of my princely people!

Daughters of Jerusalem

Come back, come back to us;
return so we can gaze at you!

Shulamite

Why do you want to look at me
as if on a dance between opposites?

King Solomon

How beautiful your feet are in sandals, princely woman
the curve of your thighs is jewelled
by the hands of a master craftsman.
Your navel is like a golden cup
that's never short of wine—
your belly a heap of harvest wheat
surrounded by lilies.

Your breasts two fawns,
twins of a gazelle
your neck an ivory tower
your eyes, the pools in Heshbon
by the gate of Bath-rabbim;

your nose the tower of Lebanon
facing towards Damascus.

Your head is Carmel
your hair dark mauve
this king's a prisoner there.
How beautiful and sensitive you are
for making love with!
You stand like a palm,
your breasts are grapes in abundance.

I said 'I'll climb into that palm tree
—I'll take hold of its branches.'
Let your breasts be like the vine's clusters,
and the smell of your breath like apples
your mouth like the rarest wine
that slips as smoothly down your throat,
and on the parted lips of the sleepers.

Shulamite

I am my beloved's
and he wants me.
Come, my man, let's go into the fields
let's stay a night in the villages
then get up early to the vineyards.
Let's see whether the vine has matured
and the pomegranates are flowering.

I'll give myself to you there.
The mandrakes exude their scent

And all around us are the fruits,
new and old, that I've kept for you!

Let's do it all again.
Oh how I wish you were my brother
suckled at my mother's breasts!
Then if I saw you outside, I'd kiss you
without people thinking I'm a whore.

I would lead you into my mother's house
and you would guide me there—
I'd make you drink spiced wine,
the juice of my pomegranate.
Your left hand would be under my head,
and your right hand would be caressing me.

And I'd ask you, daughters of Jerusalem
not to titivate or stir up my love
until it's ready to awaken!

SCENE VI

Daughters of Jerusalem

WHO'S THIS now coming out of the desert
leaning on her beloved?

King Solomon

I made love to you under the apple tree

where your mother was in labour with you,
and then she was giving birth to you.

Shulamite

Keep me like a seal in your heart, and on your arm:
love is stronger than death.
Jealousy's as cruel as the grave,
its flashes burn
like the flame of God.
A flood of water can't put out love—
nor can a torrent drown it.
If a man could give all he had for love
he would be utterly contented.

The Brothers

We have a little sister,
but she's too young for breasts:
what more can we do for her
on the day she'll be betrothed?
If she's a wall
we'll build a silver turret on her
if she's a door
we'll protect her with planks of cedar.

Shulamite

So I am a wall: and my breasts are towers

then, in his eyes, I'd found peace.

Solomon had a vineyard at Baal-hamon,
then he let it out to overseers.
Everyone was supposed to bring a thousand pieces
of silver for its fruit.

But my vineyard is in front of me.
You, Solomon, can have your thousand
and those who manage it, two hundred.

King Solomon

You that live in the gardens:
friends listen to your voice,
now let me hear it.

Shulamite

Hurry, my beloved, remember:
Be like a gazelle, a young stag
on the mountain of spices...

WISDOM

With Wisdom we have the first direct expression of Sophia, the Feminine Divine—she (as we are explicitly told) that was with God from the beginning. A different dimension opens here as a result... we might say God is no longer alone. This was the broader-minded thought in the first century Alexandria of its time where Jew, Egyptian, Muslim and Christian lived side by side. It's also a lengthy exploration of virtue beside our basic attitude to life, and how that can change; and in that it strongly links to the secularism (and negativity) of our own time.

Meanwhile the light of Wisdom reveals a God of Love, named so for the first time on the edge of a new testament and a new and vulnerable world where only our hearts can show us the way.

I AM THE GREAT I AM. I am everything in Creation. I was with Him from the beginning—I was by His side; they called me 'a master workman.'

Sapientia Dei: I am Ruach, I am Woman. My essence is rejoicing.

The Lord possessed me in the beginning of his way
I was daily his delight
I came out of the mouth of the Most High
I dwelt in high places

and walked in the bottom of the deep.

I had power over the waves of the sea
over all the earth
over every people and nation...

I rejoiced in Creation.

I was a tree: a cedar   a cypress   a palm
a rose plant   an olive   a plane   a turpentine
I am a scent   cinnamon   asplanthus   the best myrrh

I am the mother of fair, beautiful love

I am given to all my children

Receive Me.

*

Wisdom is my spirit, and is your friend
she hates foul language, though—
because He sees into your innermost soul
and, knowing your heart,
listens to everything your tongue tells.

His spirit fills the whole world.

A lying mouth deals death to the soul.
Don't flirt with death with your mistakes,
always learn from the errors you make.
Death was not his intention!
You've heard it said: *He takes no pleasure*
in the extinction of the living.

He created everything from Being
there's nothing toxic in what He intended.
The hell we've made of things holds no power
on *His* earth—

because virtue—

                alignment—

                              is eternal

before and beyond the grave.

    *

But the godless deal in death every day,
he's their ally and their pact.
You know what they say:

'Life is short, and transient
and there's no relief at the end of it.
We're born merely by chance
and after all this, there's nothing.
Our breath might as well be smoke...
Reason's a mere spark from our heartbeat
put it out, and our body is ashes
—the spirit vanishes.

Nearly all of us will be forgotten,
no one will remember what we've done
we dissolve like cloud, wisps, the mist
the sun's heat burns through...
I tell you: our days are like this, too
and then there's no turning back.

No one comes back from the grave.

So: let's party while we can
and have some fun with the whole damn show.
Carpe diem—and her rump
let's leave our litter everywhere
as proof.

As for the virtuous man, damn him
the grieving widow and that old geezer.
Let's put our vitality in their place
what use is weakness anyway?
Let's annoy him for making us feel bad!
Let's throw him one—po-face
with all his pious pretensions.
The very sight of him is a burden:
We're phoney to him, and look, he
disdains us with his nose in the air!

Let's see if what he claims is true
and what will happen to him.
Let's be cruel and rack him
poke and prod his gentleness
test his endurance—

245

Actually, we might as well kill him
since he's already so well provided for.'

What a stain on the Page of Life these people are,
blinded by their egos—
ignorant of the hiddenness of God:
hopeless in their nihilism.
But He made all of us immortal:
Death was the child of envy.

Envy, born of emptiness: an empty self.

But those souls who do right
are in the Hand of God
and there, no pain will get near them.

In the eyes of the unwise
they seem simply to die
their demise looks like disaster, annihilation—
but they are at peace.

Although it looks like they've been punished
their secret heart is full of eternal life
and having suffered, they'll be more blessed
than we can easily conceive.

God has proved who they are
he's tested them like gold in the fire
and taken them home to the light
—no more sacrifice.

When they're full of the spirit, they will shine

and race like sparks through the stubble...

They will judge the nations
and all the world's people.
He will always be their king.

Those who trust in Him will know the truth
and those who are faithful to Love
will be with him.

Grace and mercy is there for us, then;
he cares infinitely for those he's blessed.

And for the rest?
People who scorn Me are miserable
their hope is void
their work unending
their achievements worthless;
their wives a nightmare
their children all over the place
their descendants weighed down
with their memory!

Hear me.

The harvest of honest work is a glory,
the root of wisdom never decays.

Harsh is the fate of a race of evil-doers.

Better to have no children
                            but have virtue

eternal life holds its memory
it's transparent: everyone sees what it is.
Present, we strive for it
absent, we long for it—
crowned, it resonates forever
having given all we have for it

                and its victory.

Without virtue, no firm foundations
shallow-rooted, branches swaying in the wind
torn up by the storm.
                Fruitless,
immature, no good for anything—
and these are the children who inherit, then.

Although a virtuous man dies before his time
he will find rest.

So it is said.

Old age isn't about how long you live
wisdom alone is in a man's grey hairs:
glorious life is its harvest.

God has loved him so much for what he's done
he's raised him up

above all the Tribe of the Unwise around him.

He's gone—where?—to a pure place
where evil can't distort his mind
or betrayal seduce his soul.

248

Evil, like a kaleidoscope, twists light into the shadow
and the raging of desire eclipses
a simple, true heart.

He came to the truth early
his name will long outlive him,
the Lord has taken him home.

And people gawp, not getting it
it doesn't seem to occur to them
how grace and mercy await us.

His soul, by its very existence
judges those who survive
beside hideous old men.

They see him, but they don't understand
and because they don't, they jeer...
but He alone will have the last laugh—
soon enough, they'll be in faceless crematoriums.

Hear me, and the scribe who is My Voice.

A man who does right will stand as if on fire
before his persecutors and oppressors
who counted his work as nothing
                    and they're
gripped, as if drugged, with an unfamiliar fear
amazed at the strangeness of his salvation
so far beyond anything they've known.

They'll know remorse then

and they'll say to each other:

'This was the guy we laughed at
as a proverb of stupidity—
how stupid we were!
We thought he was a nutcase
only fit to be sectioned.
But here he is: a Son of God
given a place among the saints!
That's how far we've gone off track
the light hasn't shined for us
the sun didn't kiss our day.
All we've done is break and twist the law
crossing pathless wastes.
God's way hasn't been on our map
and what have we gained?
What use is all our pride now?
It's all gone like a shadow
a dream that has dissolved away
like a boat's keel through the waves
leaving no trace...
Or when a bird has flown
leaving nothing of its passing
but the light beaten by its wings—
or when an arrow is loosed
parting the air closing behind it
so swiftly you can't see where it went
that's how it is with us—
we're absolutely transient
and we've nothing to show for it instead.'

Yes, the hope of a man who has no faith

is like dust, sand carried on the wind
a thin froth driven away with the storm
smoke blown here and there...
gone like a guest who visits just for a day.

But those who live right live forever
their place is with Him and his care
theirs is the Kingdom, and its crown
covered with his right hand and his arm.

*

So listen, kings, queens, and understand
you world-leaders of far-flung lands: a warning
to you who have millions under your sway,
inflated by their sheer number—
Power is the Lord's, not yours
it is a gift and a commission.
He will see right through you, all the way.

And if you haven't played your part
or behaved as He would have you do
he'll come down on you like an eagle
—and rip your imago apart.
Judgement is sharpest for the likes of you,
the poor will sooner be pardoned
than your sins forgotten.

He isn't awed by greatness,
why should he be? He's made everything
great and small: but you, in your power
will be scrutinised to the end.

Remember.

These words are for you,
written here in Alexandria
that you may learn what wisdom is and not transgress.

Those who see things as sacred
will be held sacred
and find all their resource and guidance there.

Listen, then: align yourselves
be saved by His breath.

> *

Now, Wisdom taught me all of this
She who infuses everything
with total understanding
she's manifest, subtle, lively, clear
she's undefiled, direct, beyond hurt
loving everything that's good
she's quick and always ready
she's kind and she isn't flakey
she's carefree too: she has the power
she oversees everything, she reaches
through all we can conceive
in the most sophisticated way.

She's more moving than any kind of motion
she penetrates everything because she's pure
she's the breath of the power of the Divine—
a river from His Glory they both share

so nothing can occlude her.

She's the brightness of the everlasting light
an unclouded mirror of all that's fine
and she can do anything—
she makes everything New.

Down the corridors of time, she enters
into souls who are sacred, holy
making them friends and prophets.

God only deeply loves those who live with her:
she's lovelier than the sun
she's high above the stars
she's older and younger than the light.

For after this cometh night:
but vice shall not prevail against wisdom.

I have spoken. Meanwhile
she's organising everything to the detail.

*

In the greatest number of the wise lies the world's salvation.

*   *   *

You can show your strength any time you want to
but who can resist the power of your arm?
The whole world, to You
is as a little grain of the balance

253

a drop of dew glistening on the ground.

But You have mercy on everything
because You can do anything...
you illuminate our errors so they can be amended.

You love everything that is,
which is in Creation—
you would never have made anything you hated!

And how could anything have survived
if it wasn't Your Will?

Or been preserved if it wasn't by Your Calling?

You forgive us all
because we are Yours
thou lover of souls.

You are the God of Love.

*

*

THE NEW TESTAMENT

*

INTRODUCTION TO
THE NEW TESTAMENT

J AY'S JOURNEY through the books of the Bible is also a journey through God's own journey as revealed in the Books from a tribal god to the God of universal love. The question Jay confronts us with is: is God learning too or is it that God simply lets us understand little by little the true nature of God?

One of the most telling stories in the New Testament is the one told in Matthew and Mark of the Syro-Phoenician woman who out argues Jesus! The version in Mark 7: 24 to 30 captures this moment particularly well. As Mark says, Syro-Phoenicians were 'pagans.' Even worse, it is a woman who challenges Jesus begging him to heal her little daughter who 'had an unclean spirit.' Jesus's reply is frankly sexist, racist and tribal. 'The children should be fed first, because it is not fair to take the children's food and throw it to the house-dogs.' Remember that in the ancient Middle East dogs were effectively vermin so this was incredibly rude.

The woman however argues back 'Ah yes sir, but the house-dogs under the table can eat the children's scraps'.

Jesus is being challenged by a pagan woman to think bigger

about who he is, why he is here and what sort of God he follows. And Jesus learns. He has to change his mind and approach and says, 'For saying this, you may go home happy; the devil has gone out of your daughter.'

Interestingly, in the standard Catholic and Anglican prayer of Humble Access just before the communion bread is shared, the prayer uses this image of 'not even being worthy to eat the crumbs under your table.' In other words, as 'pagans'—that is gentiles, not Jews—we know we can come to the communion because Jesus' invitation is to all regardless of race. Something he had to learn.

So if Jesus as the Son of God learns, perhaps Jay is right in exploring that God also learns throughout the Bible.

As Jay worked into the New Testament I think he was surprised to see the extent that the struggle between a tribal god and the Universal God of love was still a major issue. For example, St. Paul's Letter to the Romans. This letter was the single most important book of the Bible for Martin Luther (sixteenth century) whose actions launched the Protestant Reformation. He found within it a call to abandon any idea that we can help ourselves through acts of kindness or goodness, to draw closer to God. Only God's grace could reach us, damned as we were by the very nature of Adam's sin and through the sexual act which brings each person into birth. This is known as Original Sin, a particularly pernicious teaching which only appears in Christianity in the fifth century AD.

I recall my friend Diarmuid McCulloch telling me he had been invited to Reformation Day in Germany – the annual celebration of the Reformation and its creation especially of Lutheranism. He was rather astonished to be asked what was the current thinking in England about the Letter to the Romans and was somewhat stuck for an answer, as it has never been that important in England. I had never understood why the German and Scandinavian princes had found Luther's fascination with the Letter to the Romans so important. Then Jay worked on it and rather casually said that he found it very interesting. When I asked why he said, 'Throughout the Old Testament, I have struggled with the fact that much of it is tribal, my god not Our God—and then occasionally you get a flash of Our God and that God is the origin of all and is love for all. I didn't expect to find Paul was struggling with both. Paul can't work out whether to believe in a tribal God or a Universal God—between God as Judge and God as Love. In Romans he veers between tribal god and the God of Love, never quite sure which he wants to proclaim.'

I then realised that this tribal/universal is what lies at the heart of Lutheranism. The princes who backed the Reformation wanted to be in charge of faith in their own lands – tribal – yet also wanted to feel they were part of a universal religion as well. Paul's grappling with his tribal Jewish background, and the challenge to this that a universal God presented, had found an echo 1600 years later when politics and faith came dramatically together. Romans was perfect for the Reformation princes because they too couldn't quite work out which god or God to believe in and Romans gave them bits of both!

I have always argued that the Book of Revelation should never have made it into the Bible. It is a tribal, disturbing book and one which I have found very hard to understand, let alone want to read as the final book of the Bible. In some ancient Christian traditions it is left out. But Jay's version takes me on a journey into the dark side, the shadow side of faith and fear and has shown me how this book is perhaps the most shocking and yet at the same time the most revealing of books.

However. We do not finish with Revelation. Instead we go round to the Creation, to Genesis, again because to understand where the journey has taken us we need to echo T.S. Eliot in his poem 'Little Gidding:'

> We shall not cease from exploration
> And the end of all our exploring
> Will be to arrive where we started
> And know the place for the first time.

That is the brilliance of Jay's work and his relationship with this most dangerous of books, the Holy Bible.

Martin Palmer
Bath, September 2018

*

*

PAUL

How Saul becomes Paul is an enduring story of fascination. So we begin on the road to Damascus and that archetypal moment of change for the unbeliever that gives us that phrase as a metaphor. I have told Paul's story with as much relevant detail as I can because it helps us to see his character as well as the challenge of his circumstances: I have drawn the material from Luke (Acts) to illuminate this complex Man of Light, divided as he was between the tribal past and an emerging future where only Love has meaning.

His Letter to the Romans is one of the most challenging texts in the Bible—I've tried to make new sense of it here in a voice that speaks to us now. Two shorter letters follow, both uplifting, giving us real insight into the community of the early church and its will to survive.

THAT LIGHT, where it all began...and always begins. The dusty road. The afternoon heat. I remember we were walking, not saying much. Damascus ahead, still some distance away. I remember my sandals as I glanced down...then it came, dazzling, instantaneous, like a sun that had come out of the sun, piercing my eyes, my mind...and a ringing in my ears—a high sound, and then a voice, a voice I'd always dreaded hearing: 'I am Jesus, and you are persecuting me.' I stopped still...the men speechless around me.

Then the darkness, the blindness. The darkness full of light, but as I moved my eyes I was blind. I called out, I cried out. They had to lead me by the hand...as if in a dream. My sandaled feet I could no longer see. Five minutes ago...but that was over.

I'd crossed the line.

Finally we came among streets, people. My head was down. They led me to a room down a sidestreet...the sounds ebbed away. Then there was only darkness.

What was I to do? I tried to pray. The hours passed. No food, no water. But then a knocking came at the door—and there was a man, they said, who claimed he'd come to help me. Had I dreamt him? Ananias. Of course I wanted help; someone, anyone. But who was he? Was he one of them?

He was one of the brothers. He'd heard inside, been told where to go, and who he was to see: his obedience was pure. I felt him close to me. Then the touch of his hands...the touch of a man who was my enemy...and the lie of that in his trust, his humanity.

He laid his hands on me, telling me slowly and clearly why he'd been sent, and as he spelt out the words 'sight' and 'Holy Spirit' the darkness, my darkness, loosened and fell like scales from my eyes onto the floor...and, oh mercy, I could see again.

My life, but another life, my sight for another life given back. Alleluija.

So then I was preaching in those very same synagogues. Of course everyone was amazed. But my power increased steadily as the light came through me, with me, as all I had...the old life

266

gone, already fast retreating like a coastline from the sea.

The Jews were devastated. They'd lost their main man. So their complacency turned to hatred...so much so that the brothers lowered me down from the city wall one night in a basket. I had to get away!

But when I tried to join the brothers in Jerusalem, they were afraid—who could blame them? Barnabas helped me no end, then. He was the closest. And the light among us that was for all of us between our eyes and minds, as we prayed, talked, decided what to do next...this still growing light that has never left me, even in my darkest hours...this is what has sustained me, and somehow kept me safe.

His face, as I often imagine it, unseen, in my mind.

I was still Saul then, and while we were in Antioch (where we were first called Christians) a great famine came just as Agabus had predicted, wide-eyed. We organised a collection and sent out all we could to the brothers down in Judaea.

Then we were sent to Seleucia, and sailed to Cyprus. And there was a man there called Elymas—a self-styled magician— who was, you know, just as I had been. He tried to stop me talking to the proconsul, Sergius Paulus, who wanted to hear about the Lord. I confronted him face to face...and he was blinded too! I saw *myself* as he groped around. I can still see him in my mind's eye.

Then I was Paul: Saul really died.

Paphos to Perge to Antioch in Pisidia. And there I spoke to them, the orthodox Jews there, I gave them the whole history that led up to you, Lord: with Moses, Samuel, David and John... John of the Desert blinded by light not by darkness...my other, wilder, better half.

Then your story: how many times have I told it now in the

name of salvation? And my own? How often have I argued it in the style I learnt from the Stoics and the Cynics with their rhetorical questions designed to draw in the listener so it becomes obvious what they're saying Yes to?

And always we'd say 'stay faithful to the grace God has given you'...and this was all we could do.

But those legalistic Jews didn't want to know—the pagans were much more open-hearted when it came to it (which is why I became their apostle)...and that was our strange joy as we walked on to Iconium.

And there, the people were divided: they loved us and they hated us almost regardless of their own faith. It is what happens to an individual man when he hears. You couldn't even guess who he might be in a crowd. He could surprise you—he, or she, frequently does.

Something happens in the heart and mind in a moment of silence when people hear about you. Or it doesn't, and their fear turns to mockery, to anger. And this is when we had to move on.

Lyaconia was extraordinary. Jesus had said we could do 'all this and more,' but of course the brothers didn't really believe him. But here was a man who could hardly move who was looking at me repeatedly until something came over me like a command and I told him, like Lazarus, to stand up—and my God he did! I was as surprised as he was.

There was an uproar. The crowd there shouted we must be gods: they called Barnabas Zeus. I was Hermes! Then they wanted to offer sacrifices with their garlanded oxen. No, no. We rushed towards the gates to tell them 'We are only human beings like you,' and to turn them to You. My God we had to work hard!

But then those Jews arrived and made them want to stone us. One flung struck me on the side of my head, and I went down.

They dragged me towards the city gate...and the brothers (bless them all) came gathering around as I came to, and I thought of that cripple. Be strong. I stood up again. How many times?

Then there was all that dissension about circumcision, the established custom in Israel for men at that time. I know it wasn't right to impose it on a people who had just changed their hearts and minds—it would have seemed like a punishment. But still they insisted on the old Law. Peter spoke brilliantly, seeing we are all one faith and saying so.

We almost competed in oratory, building on the example of each other. And Barnabas was my brother. We were sent. The matter was decided. Triumph in Antioch!

That is, until Barnabas and I fell out.

I wanted to go back over the old ground we'd covered—and he wanted to take John Mark along with us. But how could I trust him after what he'd done in Pamphylia? Barnabas was giving him the benefit of the doubt (because he was his cousin), but he wasn't listening. The mission, and our alignment to it, was so crucial we couldn't afford this.

That's what we fought over—we just could not see eye to eye. (After all, who was right? How often have I talked about forgiveness?). So they went to Cyprus—and I asked Silas to travel with me.

We went to Syria and Cilicia then, and I found Timothy there. I only recommended he was circumcised so he could be accepted there—everyone knew his father was a Greek, after all.

We were all out to give enough to the churches that were like little potted seedlings.

And all the time we listened to our intuition and sometimes it was like He was with us, when we thought to cross into Bithynia and He said 'don't go there.'

One night I had a vision that was like a waking dream: a Macedonian is standing in front of me in his tunic and greaves and he is saying 'Come and help us.'

So we went by boat to Phillippi.

And it was there I preached to the women sitting on the ground...one of them, Lydia, her heart opening, her eyes looking at me but at the same time around me; seeing you, Lord. She asked to be baptised, with her husband, then invited us to stay with her. She wouldn't take no for an answer.

Then we encountered the slave girl too who kept following us and exposing us by announcing loudly that we were saviours. It was embarrassing, but most of all it was dangerous. But then I realised what was speaking through her and I asked it in no uncertain terms to be gone!

'I order you in the name of Christ to leave that woman!'

But when her owner saw he couldn't make any more money out of her soothsaying, he and his cronies turned on us and had us accused of making a disturbance. Then it rapidly escalated. We were stripped and ordered to be flogged—there and then, and manhandled into prison.

But still we prayed and sang to God.

Then suddenly with a rumbling like feet running downstairs the ground started to shake and vibrate... the prison doors snapped open around us...and our chains fell off the wall. The janitor woke up, grabbed his sword, and was about to fall on it (in the Roman way) when I shouted at him *stop, man, stop.*

Then he threw himself at our feet and asked me what he needed to do to be saved.

It was simple enough to tell him (I'd said it so many times before), and he drank the words in, his eyes still wide.

Later he took us back to his family and was washing our wounds with a care he'd only shown his own kind. He kept staring at us with what was dawning in his mind.

The magistrates sent orders for our release, but I insisted in no uncertain terms they escort us out of the town themselves. When they realised we were Roman citizens, they were mortified.

And all this time the strength and clarity to speak were growing in me. Every time I witnessed Him it was as if his presence, his body was within mine like a light. 'I am always with you,' as you said, Lord!

The knowing reached as far in as my words to people reached out. This is where I am now. It has made me a writer with my voice, a dictator of letters handwritten on scrolls.

Lord, you gave me speech and you gave me peace...especially when those negative-minded Jews were stirring things up against us. You gave me eyes to understand with, too. I saw it was inevitable. Their position, their inheritance, was being challenged to the core. But they also twisted the truth by claiming Jesus as a rival emperor to Caesar—and that was a lie. 'My kingdom is not of this world'—he said that to us, but they couldn't understand it. If they had, they wouldn't have so routinely attacked us.

It helped me not to take it so personally. And it only increased my resolve. I had one life, and it was in His Light.

They were fighting for their beliefs: in my own way, I was fighting for mine. But not with swords or lies. That is the difference.

Anyway, Silas and I left for Beroea in the night. When we arrived, we went straight to the synagogue. And here they had ears! The Greek women, too. Then the Thessalonikan Jews arrived to stir up trouble...so I left for Athens.

Athens! The whole city rank with idolatry: statues, prostitutes, self-styled sophists. I spoke in the Agora (the market place) to anyone who would listen, because I could speak their language well enough, even though it wasn't my own. Some of them argued with me and tried to put me down—they called me *spermalogos*—a propagandist for more of their own outlandish gods.

Resurrection—the goddess Anastasis! I don't think so!

I addressed the Council of the Areopagus: I told them that their altar to the Unknown God was exactly what I was talking about. I told them the Lord doesn't make his home in shrines made by human hands. I told them that he is never in need of anything since he has given us all we have—breath, bone and body. I told them about the origin of the human race and the destiny of nations. I told them—as some of their poets had also said—that we are all his children.

And I told them about the judgement to come in the Last Days, and that he, the Lord of Love, is our judge...risen from the dead.

Always it was that, the *kerygma*, the central miraculous fact. I wanted to dazzle their minds with it as I had been dazzled.

They laughed at that, throwing their heads back...but there were two at least who really listened and saw: Dionysius the Areopagite—not the god!—and a woman who introduced herself as Damaris.

Two out of twenty five, was it?—where two or three can be greater than all.

I left Athens then and went to Corinth where I met Aquila and his lovely wife Priscilla. They were tentmakers just as I'd been, and exiles too—banished by Claudius from Rome. We worked together in the synagogues.

272

Then Silas and Timothy arrived from Macedonia and we started work in earnest. When the Jews there railed against me I took off my cloak and shook it in front of them...'on your heads be it!,' I told them. It grew harder to be patient with them.

However, Corinth listened and many came to the faith, and we baptised them. We took them to the Water of Life, down into your death, Lord, then up again into the light as they shook their wet hair and put their palms to their eyes. And in the night you came to me, Lord, and reassured me telling me to Fear Not, and how 'there are many here that are your friends.'

And so I stayed, for nigh on eighteen months.

But still the orthodox Jews would not let up. But then Gallio, the proconsul, turned the tables on them when I was brought before the tribunal. And how strangely like Pilate he sounded, unable to find any crime in me...as if history was repeating itself. Meanwhile Sosthenes, their president, got the brunt of their anger—what an ugly scene it was to see them beat him like that outside the court house.

Anyway, we left soon afterwards—Aquila, Priscilla and myself—by boat for Syria...and then on to Ephesus where we parted. There again, they listened to me, and even asked me to stay longer...but I was called on. There was so much to attend to among all our communities.

'I will come back another time, God willing.'

I stayed where I could. Ephesus became a kind of home for me, and it was there I first started writing all the best of my thoughts down that could last beyond the moment of speaking. And as I did—with Tertius as scribe, attentive to my every word—they took on a life of their own. But as I said, they were not in my first language—the language that was breath to me—so I was translating myself as I thought out loud. I'd go over the same sentence several times trying to get it right, and it was difficult. Tertius was very patient, and sometimes he'd suggest a word or phrase as well. It was always a task that has left what I was saying open to interpretation, but also misunderstanding.

But I wanted our groups to have something, most of all, that would unite them when there was so much trying to break us apart. Yes, and I wanted them to have something of me as well that would outlast me, and that was why I always signed my name at the end. I wrote to our friends in Corinth, in Galatia too (as you know), and Phillippi.

There was always a sense of living on borrowed time. I was never completely well either, the wretched illness was always with me. A little wine was sometimes my only solace.

Meanwhile virtually everything I'd touched—a cloth, or an apron—was taken to the sick...and it was their belief in them that healed them, and in You.

Who was I after all? Only your witness.

And the fire that was also light stayed strong within me. I didn't always know when to stop! Sometimes I preached into the night—and once (I'll never forget this, in Troas)—a young man perched on a window sill fell asleep and dropped like a stone three floors down. We rushed to him, but even as I held him I knew he would revive. They said I'd raised him from the dead!

Meanwhile Macedonia beckoned again; and then Rome.

Danger was never far away, whether in front of us like those silversmiths yelling 'Great is Diana of the Ephesians!' or, as ever, the adversary behind our backs—those unbelievers that sharpen our own edge for all time.

I was dictating this to be sent ahead of me...

LETTER TO THE CHURCH AT ROME

DEAR FRIENDS,

First of all, thank God for all of you and the way your faith is talked about everywhere. The God I love by talking about his Son knows that I always say your names aloud in my prayers. I'm longing to see you to share the strength of the spirit with you. I've often planned to come, but I've always been waylaid until now. The way I see it, I owe this trip to everyone— pagans, Greeks, educated, uneducated—I want to bring this message to everyone.

I'm not ashamed of the Good News! It's the power of God saving everyone who has faith because this is what reveals God's ways to us. *Faith leads to faith,* or as it's traditionally said 'The upright man finds life through faith.'

God's rage is transparent with those who keep truth imprisoned in their evil ways. What we can know about God is plain as daylight because God himself has made it plain! Ever since Creation, his everlasting power—however invisible—has been here for us to see in all the things he's made. That's why people like this have no excuse: they know God, but refuse to honour or thank him. They have no gratitude. Instead, they have nonsense logic and endarkened minds. The more they think of themselves as philosophers, the more stupid they become...exchanging His Glory for a worthless imitation, in other words the *image* of mortal humanity, and likewise animals. That's why he left them to their depravity, because they've given up divine truth for a lie, *and worshipped creatures instead of their Creator*...who is blessed forever, Amen!

That's why God has left them to their own devices, and why their women have been part of this distortion as well. Perversion and lust on both sides.

In other words, God has left them to their own ideas, and their own Saturnalian behaviour. They're steeped in negativity as a result: depravity, greed, malice, envy, murder, fighting, disloyalty, spite. Liars, become enemies of the divine: crude, grandiose, arrogant—as it is said 'only enterprising in sin.' They dishonour their parents, without love or compassion. They know what God thinks of all this (it's plain as day—) but still they do it, and what's worse, encourage others to do the same.

So whoever you are (or think you are) if you judge without seeing this, you only judge yourself because you behave no differently! We know that God judges impartially—but when you judge, while doing exactly the same things, do you think you will somehow escape his attention? Or are you simply abusing his abundant goodness and tolerance without realising *his goodness means your repentance?* Your stubborn refusal to say sorry only fuels the fire he has for you on the day His Judgements will all be made known. You see, he rewards each of us as our works deserve. For those of us who keep our eyes on eternity will have eternal life—while those of us *who refused to take truth for their guide,* there will be fire. Pain and suffering come to every one of us who work for the wrong side. Good reputation, honour and peace are for those who do right. God has no favourites, either...no jobs for the boys.

Keeping to the Law, not just having it in mind, is what makes us clean in God's eyes. Pagans who never heard of the Law but who are still guided to do what it says may not know of it—it doesn't matter, they *are* it. They can point to it in their own hearts—they can call a witness which is their own conscience. They have prosecution and defence as well, as in any court, which is part of their own mental process.

If you call yourself a Jew and trust in the Law, and know God's will as well as what is right—if you're convinced you can guide the blind and be a light to those in darkness teaching those who don't know, *then why not teach yourself as well?* You preach against theft, but you steal: you decry unfaithfulness, but you're doing it anyway, you denigrate idolatry, but you lust after it in your dreams. Seeming to uphold the Law, and then breaking it, is a betrayal of God with contempt. It's your fault that his name is taken in vain among unbelievers. It's plain hypocrisy to them.

To be a Jew is not just to look like one—as for male circumcision, it's much more than an operation. A real man *is inwardly a man:* and the real operation I'm talking about is in the heart. It's not of the letter, see—it's of the spirit. A man like that may not be recognised by others, but he's seen by God. Of that you may be sure.

So is a practising Jew better off? Well, they are the people God's message was given to. So what if some of them have been unfaithful? Does that lessen God's fidelity? Of course not: *God will always be true even though everyone proves to be false.* But if our lack of awareness makes God demonstrate his, how can we say he's unfair? Of if he gets angry with us in return? That would be absurd—it would be like saying he could never judge the world. It would be like saying that since my untruthfulness makes God demonstrate *his* truth, I shouldn't be judged as a sinner at all! That would be like saying 'do evil as a means to good.' Some people have even accused us of teaching this!

So are *we* any better off? Not at all—we're all equally capable of getting it wrong. And so, as it's said:

There's not a good man left, not one
not one who gets it—
not even one who's looking for God.
They've all turned away...
their throats are like yawning graves
their tongues full of lies
snake's spittle on their lips
curses fill their mouths...
their feet race when there's blood to spill
wherever they go, there's ruin.
They know nothing in the world about peace
there's no spark of God in their eyes.

Now the Law says all this for those who live under it, but actually it's meant to *silence all of us* and open the whole world to the awareness of judgement. No one is vindicated in the sight of God simply by keeping the Law. All the Law does is tell us what isn't right.

God's way, revealed originally through the Law and the Prophets, has never been revealed outside the Law—because now it's the *same justice* that comes through faith to everyone who recognises Jesus Christ. Everyone has sinned and betrayed God's glory and *anyone* can be freed through the gift of his grace...redeemed in Jesus, the Christ who was called by God to sacrifice his life so as to open the way for all of us through faith. This is how God makes his way known; first, in the past, when sins went unpunished—and then, for us now, where he justifies everyone who believes in Jesus.

So what of our pretensions? There's no room for them. What sort of law excludes them? The sort of law that tells us 'what to do'? Actually no, it's the law of faith because a man is validated by faith *and not by doing something the Law tells him to do.* This God is the God of everyone. So, then, do we understand that faith makes the Law pointless? Not at all: we're giving the Law its true existence and value.

Think about this with Abraham. If he'd been validated as a reward for his actions, he'd have something to boast about— though not in God's eyes because (as scripture says) *Abraham put his faith in God, and his faith was what justified him.* When a man is working, his pay isn't seen as a favour but as his due. But when a man has nothing to show but faith, then it's his only his faith that validates him. David says the same: a man is happy if God thinks him virtuous, *irrespective of his good deeds.* Happy are those whose failings are forgiven whose shame is deleted— happy the man the Lord sees as he essentially is.

The promise of inheriting the world wasn't made to Abraham

and his descendants because of any law *but because of his faith.*
If the world is only inherited by those who stick to the Law,
then faith is pointless. Law by definition includes the potential
for punishment—only when there's no law can that not
happen. That's why what fulfils the promise depends on faith,
so that faith can be what it is—a free gift for all of Abraham's
children, not only those who belong to the Law *but those who
belong to faith.* As it's said: 'I've made you the father of many
nations.' In God's eyes, Abraham is our father: Abraham put
his whole trust in a God who can also bring the dead back to
life and call into being what has never been seen.

Though it looked like Abraham's hope couldn't be met, he
hoped and he believed and through that he became the father
he is and was promised to be: 'Your descendants will be as far-
flung as the stars.' Even the thought that he was well past
fatherhood (as Sarah was past motherhood) didn't shake his
belief. Because God promised it, Abraham refused to deny it
or doubt it, but got his strength from faith convinced that
God had the power to do what he'd promised. This faith is
ours too if we believe in a power that raised Jesus from the
dead—the Jesus who gave his life for our sins and rose again in
a body of light to save us.

So far, then, we've seen that through faith in our Lord we're
judged to be in the right and at peace with God because it's by
faith we've entered that state of grace where we can talk about
'looking forward to God's glory.' But that's not all we can talk
about—we can talk about our sufferings. They bring patience,
as we know all too well, and patience creates perseverance
which brings hope—a hope that isn't illusory because it's God's
love that has been poured into our hearts by the Holy Spirit.

280

We were still pretty much helpless when Christ died for us. It's not easy for a good man to die—though you might be prepared to for someone really worthy—but the proof of God's love is that Jesus died for us *even when we were still sinners to a man.* And having died for us, isn't it likely that he would also save us from his father's anger?

When we were brought back to God by the death of his Son, we were still like enemies...but now we've been reunited with the Source, surely we can count on being saved by Jesus' life? Not just because we've been re-united, but because we've been filled like vessels with the wine of a joyful trust in God through Jesus who brought us home.

Sin, you know, came into the world through one man—and through sin came death. Death exists because we've all sinned. Sin came into being long before the Law was given. Death came to everyone from Adam to Moses, although then there was no law as such to break.

Long ago, Adam prefigured the One to come—and that gift to us outweighed his fall. If we know that 'through one man's fall, so many died,' it's even clearer that divine grace through Jesus came to as many of us as an abundant free gift. The repercussions of that gift far outweighs one man's sin! After Adam's fall, judgement came into being—however now, after numerous falls, comes grace and forgiveness. If death took hold as a result of one man's fall then it's just as certain that one man—Jesus—will make everyone royal in life who receives a gift he doesn't even deserve. *Made right, clear, clean; reborn again.* One man's fall brings judgement on everyone—and the great act of one man brings everyone life and a reason for living. One man's disobedience created sin—'one man's obedience makes as many righteous'...think of that. When law came into being it only multiplied the opportunities of falling—however, grace remained even greater, so now grace can reign bringing eternal life because of what came through the power of Christ.

So, do we stay in sin so that grace has a greater reach? Of course not. We're already dead in this place so how can we go on living in it? You've been told that when we were baptised in Christ Jesus *we were immersed in his death*—we go into the tomb with him, then we rise out of the water with a new life.

So, with him, we imitate his death then we join him in resurrection. We realise that our old selves have been 'crucified'—the old sinful body has been dissolved and freed from its slavery. When a man physically dies he's anyway finished with sin.

But we believe that having died with Jesus we return to life with him—and having done so, *we will never die again.* Death has lost its dominion. When we die like this, we die once and for all. Our life is with the Divine now. So, friends, think of yourselves as 'dead to sin,' but alive for God in Christ.

That's why you mustn't let sin control any part of your body or your desires—but instead surrender to God and think of yourself like a dead man brought back to life, with every part of your body fighting for the light. Then, and then only, sin will no longer control you *because you're living by grace and not by law.*

Does this mean we're free to go on sinning now? Absolutely

not. You know if you agree to obey a master you become his slave. You can't be a slave to sin, and at the same time a slave of divine obedience! You can't serve two masters! You may have been freed from sin, but only so you can come into right being. Think about what you are putting your body in service to.

When you were slaves to sin you felt no loyalty to virtue—and what did you get for this? Nothing but memories that now make you blush. But now you've been set free you've been made slaves of God—and your reward is eternity. *'For the wages of sin is death'*—but God's gift is eternal life in the being of Christ.

Friends, those of you who've studied law know that laws only affect people in their lifetime. For example, a married woman has legal obligations to a husband while he's alive, but not when he dies. So if she goes with another man while her husband is still alive, legally she's an adulteress. However, when he dies all that changes. And that's why you are now dead to the Law and you can get yourself a new man! We're freed from the Law, free to serve in a completely new way.

So: is the Law sin? No. But, personally, I wouldn't have known what sin is without it. I wouldn't have known what it is to lust if the Law hadn't said 'Thou shalt not covet.' But it was this same commandment that sin (so to speak) also took advantage of to evoke all kinds of wanting in me.
Once upon a time when there was no Law, *I was alive*—but when this commandment came into being, sin came to life... and I died. The Law is sacred. Does that mean something sacred killed me? No. But what it does mean is that sin *used something good against me* and through that commandment

(for example) it exercised its insidious power.

The Law, of course, is spiritual—but as a slave to sin, I am not. I can't understand my own behaviour. I don't do the things I want to—and I find myself doing the things I hate. When I act against my own will that means a part of me acknowledges the Law is right—and for the rest, sin is living in me. I know of nothing good in me per se—that is, in my unspiritual self—for although the will to do good is in me, what I actually do isn't that good at all. Do you see? That is how sin lives in me.

In fact, every time I want to do something good, something like this happens. In my innermost self I love God's law, but then my body rebels against it and what my reason is telling me. This is what makes me a prisoner.

What a fallen man I am! Who can rescue me from death? Thanks be to God and Jesus Christ our Lord!

So I serve the Law of God; and in my unspiritual self, I serve the law of sin.

———————————————————

So the reason why those of us in Christ are not condemned is that the law of the spirit, of true life in Him, frees us from sin and death. God has done with the Law what we couldn't do because of our nature. God resolved sin by sending his own Son in a body as physical as any sinful one—*and in that body God transformed sin.* He did this so that spiritual law could be achieved in us, when we behave not as our unspiritual nature *but as the spirit dictates.*

Unspiritual people are drawn only by what is unspiritual—for us, it is the opposite by definition. It's death to limit yourself to the unspiritual—true life and peace can only come with spiritual immersion. That's because to limit yourself to the unspiritual is actually to be *against God*—such a mindset can never be open to Divine Law. People who are only into unspiritual things can never be 'pleasing to God' as we would understand it. But you care about spiritual things because the Spirit of God has made its home in you. Actually, unless the Spirit of Christ was already in you, you couldn't belong to him in this way. Your body may be 'dead' because of sin, but if Christ is in you then your spirit *is life itself*—and if the spirit of him who resurrected Jesus is living in you then he will animate and energise your body...through the Spirit that is living in you.

So then, friends, there's no need for us to pander to our unspiritual selves or live merely secular lives! If you live like that you're dancing with death, but if (through the Spirit) you draw a line under your body's unhealthy distortions and imbalances, you will, in every sense, live.

Everyone who's moved by the Spirit is a Son or Daughter of God. The Spirit you've received isn't a slave bringing fear into your life again—it's the spirit of being a son or daughter, and it makes you want to cry out 'Father!' And if we're children, we're inheritors as well—inheritors of God, co-inheritors with Christ, sharing in his suffering to share in his glory.
You know, I think whatever we suffer here can in no way compare with the glory that's waiting for us. I say: the whole Creation is waiting for the revelation of the sons and daughters of God! It wasn't Creation's fault that it was unable to attain its own conscious purpose—it was designed like that—but it still

dreams of being freed from its bondage to revel in the same freedom we have. From the beginning of time, Creation has (as you've said) *been groaning in one great act of giving birth,* and not only creation *but all of us who possess the first fruits of the spirit;* we too labour inwardly as we wait for our bodies to be set free. We must be content with the hope that we'll be saved. Our salvation isn't even in sight (we couldn't be hoping for it if it were!) but we *must* hope for it, and wait for it with patience.

The Spirit, too, comes to help us in our hour of need. When we can't find words to pray with, the Spirit speaks for us in a way that could never have been put into words in the first place—and God, who knows our hearts, knows perfectly well what our prayer means...just as he knows the saints' prayers are attuned with his own psyche, resonant, returning like butterflies to him.

We know that God works with everyone who loves him—*he turns everything to our good.* He works with everyone he's called to his purpose. These are the people he chose long ago to become like images of his Son—so that Jesus is like the eldest of many who follow on from him. He's called all those he's intended for this, and those he calls, he justifies; and with those he justifies, he shares his glory.

What can we add to this? With God on our side, who can really be against us? Since God gave up his Son for all of us we can be sure, after such an unbelievable gift, he won't refuse anything in his power that he *can* give. Can anyone condemn those God has chosen? When God releases a man, can anyone pass judgement on him? Would Christ? No! He's there at God's right hand, intervening for us.

Friends, nothing can come between us and the love of Christ. Even if we're troubled, fearful, lacking food or shelter, being threatened or even attacked. As scripture says 'For your sake, daily, we're being seen like sheep for slaughter—.'
These are the trials we triumph through, because of the power of his love for us.

I'm certain of this: neither death or life, angel or prince, nothing that exists, nothing yet to come, or any power or entity in height and depth can come between us and the love of God made visible in Christ Jesus, our brother and our Lord.

What I want to say now isn't pretence—I say it with Christ, and it's the truth. My sadness is so great, the ache in my mind so endless, I'd willingly be judged and severed from Christ if it could help you dear ones in Israel, my ancestry, my own flesh and blood. We were adopted by God, we were given the glory and the covenants, and promises were made to us. We're descended from the patriarchs, and from us the flesh and blood of Jesus came, who's above all.

Does this mean God hasn't kept his promise? Not at all. But not all those descendants of Israel *are* Israel—not all Abraham's children are his true children. Remember 'It's through Isaac your name will be continued'—in other words, it's not physical descent that is the real thing here, it's only the children of the promise who are the true descendants. The actual words of the promise are: 'I shall visit you...and Sarah will have a son.' Even more to the point is what was said to Rebecca, Isaac's wife, before her twin children were born or had done anything good or bad. To emphasise that God's choice is free (depending on the one who calls, and not on *deserving* as we would understand it), Rebecca was told 'the elder will serve the younger.' Or as scripture says elsewhere 'I showed my love for Jacob and my hatred of Esau.'

Does it therefore follow that God is unjust? Of course it doesn't. Take what God said to Moses: 'I have mercy on those I want to, and I show compassion to those I want to as well.' In other words the only thing that counts is not what we want or try to do, *but God's mercy.* He also says to Pharaoh: 'The only reason you're Pharaoh is to show my power and make my name known throughout the world.' In other words, if God wants to show mercy, he does, and when he wants to harden someone's heart (for reasons we don't know), he does so.

You'll ask me 'In which case how can God ever blame anyone, since no one can oppose his will?' But what right have we to cross-examine God? The pot can't say to the potter 'Why did you make me this shape?' Surely a potter can do what he likes with the clay?

Or else imagine that though God is ready to express his anger, he still patiently puts up with the people who make him so, whatever they deserve. He also puts up with them for the sake of those other people he wants to show his mercy to, people he'd prepared for glory long ago. And well, we are those people—Jews or pagans, we are the ones he's called.

That's exactly what God says through Hosea:

I'll say to a people that wasn't mine
'You are my people'—

and to a nation I never loved
'I love you'
Instead of being told
'You are no people of mine'
they will now be called
the sons and daughters of the living God.'

And, referring to Israel, Isaiah had this to say:

'Though Israel shall have as many descendants
as there are sandgrains on the seashore
only a remnant will be saved—
for without hesitation or delay
the Lord will pass his sentence on the earth.'

And as he added:

'If the Lord hadn't left us descendants
we'd now be like Sodom and Gomorrah...'

So it follows from this that pagans who weren't looking for
virtue found it all the same—a rightness that comes of faith—
while Israel looking for it from Law actually failed to do what
the Law required! Why? Because they relied on good deeds
rather than trusting in faith. In other words, they stumbled
over the stumbling stone:
See how I lay in Zion
like a stone to stumble over,
a rock to trip men up!
Only those who have faith in Him
will have no reason for shame.

Brothers, I've the warmest love for the Jews and I pray for their salvation. I can swear to their passion for God...but their zeal is misguided! They don't recognise the rightness that comes from God—*instead, they try to promote their own idea of it.* But now the Law has come to an end with Christ, and *everyone* who has faith can be justified. That is how it is now.

When Moses talks about being justified by the Law, he says 'those who abide by the Law will draw life from it.' But the rightness that comes from faith says this:

'Don't tell yourself you have to bring down Christ'—as in the text 'Who will go up to heaven?' or that you have to bring him back from the dead ('Who will go down to the underworld?'). It also says 'The Word (the faith we affirm) is very near you, it's on your lips and in your heart.' If your lips affirm that Jesus is Lord and you believe in your heart that he was raised from the dead, you will be saved. The very affirmation is salvation. When scripture says 'Those who believe in him have no reason for shame' it makes no racial distinction between anyone. We all belong to the same Lord who embraces us all. 'For everyone who calls on the name of the Lord will be saved.'
But: they won't ask him until they believe in him, and they won't believe in him till they've heard of him, and they won't hear of him unless they get a preacher...until one is sent! Ah, 'the footsteps of those who bring good news is a welcome sound.' However, not everyone listens. Isaiah: 'How many believe what we affirmed?'

Is it possible they just don't hear? But they have heard. Again, is it possible that Israel just didn't understand? Moses answered this long ago—Isaiah said it even more clearly.

'I've been found by those
who didn't come looking for me—
I've revealed myself to those
who didn't even consult me—

And each day I stretched out my hand
to an ungrateful and resistant people.'

So has God rejected our people? Absolutely not. I am an
Israelite, descended through Abraham and the Benjamites, and
I could never agree God rejected us! He chose us particularly
to carry something: a story and an unfolding, and long ago.
Do you remember how Elijah complains to God about Israel's
behaviour? 'Lord, they've killed your prophets and broken
down your altars. I'm the only one left—and they want to kill
me as well!' And God says 'I've kept 7,000 men who haven't
gone over to Baal.' Today it's the same thing—and perhaps
always will be—there's a remnant, chosen by grace. By grace,
you notice, not by good deeds!

So it wasn't Israel as a whole that found what it was looking
for, but only a chosen few. The rest weren't allowed to see the
truth—'God has given them a sluggish spirit, unseeing eyes,
inattentive ears...and they're still like that today.'
David curses them for their rigidity!
So has Israel fallen forever, or just stumbled on the way?

Obviously, not fallen forever—however their shortcomings are
reflected in those pagans they could easily be jealous of. Think
of how the pagans would have benefited! Let me tell you this:
I've been sent to you as your pagan apostle, and I'm proud of
it! And the purpose here is *also* to make Israel jealous...imagine

if they could admit to that!

A whole batch of bread is made sacred if the first handful of dough is holy. All the branches are holy if the root is. And even if some of the branches have been cut off and grafted like wild olive among the others, remember it's not you that supports the root but the root that supports you. You'll see that as intentional—they were cut off because of their unbelief—but if you hold firm it's only because of your faith. Rather than making you proud, it should make you aware. God didn't spare those branches—will he necessarily spare you? Don't forget that God can be as severe as he can be kind—and he's also kind for as long as he chooses to be!

Friends, there's a hidden reason for all of this which I don't want you to miss, thinking you know more than you do. One part of Israel has stayed blind, but this will only be the case until the pagan world comes in—then, I predict, the rest of Israel will awaken. The Jews are enemies of God only as regards the Good News, and only for the sake of you—but as a chosen people, they are still beloved of God. God never takes back what he gives or reneges on his choice.

Just as you changed, so will they: and they'll only be shown mercy because you have been. God has incarcerated everyone in their disobedience only to demonstrate the capacity of mercy to human kind.

How rich are God's depths
how deep his wisdom, his knowledge
how impossible to penetrate his motives
or understand his methods!

Who could ever know the mind of the Lord?
Who could ever be his counsellor?
Who could ever give or lend him anything?

Everything comes from him
it's all by him, and for him:
Glory to Him forever.
Ameyn—we promise.

Think of God's mercy and worship him in a way that is worthy
of your intelligence. Offer your bodies to the Spirit. Don't be
like the world around you—be yourself, and in the new mind
you have now. It's the only way to find God's will, knowing
what he wants for you. It will clarify in your mind as 'the
perfect thing to do.'

Don't exaggerate your own importance. You've each got to
judge yourself by the standard of faith you've been given. Just
as our body has different parts, so all of us (together with
Christ) *make up one body*—and as parts of *that* we belong to
each other. Our gifts vary according to what grace has given
us—whatever it is, accounting, administration, teaching—use
it. Let us do what we do best.
Never let your love be a pretence, and always choose the good
over the bad. Love one another, and respect each other as
deeply too. Work for the Spirit with unstinting effort. And if
you have hope, you'll be happy about the work. Don't give up
if trials come: keep on with your prayers. Hospitality should
always come naturally to you too.

Bless those who persecute you—don't curse them in return. Celebrate with those who celebrate—be sad with those in sadness. Treat everyone with kindness and don't be patronising—make friends with those who have a lot less than you.

Never repay evil with evil, but let everyone see you're only interested in the highest standards. Do all you can to live in peace with everyone. Never try and get revenge, either—leave that to God's anger! 'Vengeance is mine.' But there's more: 'If our enemy is hungry, give him food: if he's thirsty, get him a drink. And so you heap red coals on his head!'

Go with the governing authorities. All government also comes from God, so resisting it can only lead to pain. Anyway, a good man has nothing to fear from a magistrate—only criminals have anything to be worried about. If you want to live without being afraid of authority, *you must live honestly*—it's as simple as that. You may even be honoured for it! *The state is essentially there to serve God whether it realises it or not*...remember that, and live with your conscience. This is why we pay taxes, too. Society doesn't work unless we also submit to it.

Avoid all debt—except mutual love! Your greatest obligation is to this. All the commandments come down to this: *you must love your neighbour as yourself.*
Love is the answer to all the commandments. Real love harms no one.

The time has come: we must wake up. The night is almost over, the dawn begins to brighten over the hill. Let's surrender the things we do under cover of darkness—let's get dressed in the light. And let's live well and no longer be merely slaves to our addictions and desires. Forget about them!

If someone's faith is not very strong, welcome them all the same without starting an argument. People's faith varies as much as their diets—they're not to be condemned. Whether a man stands or falls is his master's business...remember the Lord always has the power to make him stand. Likewise holy days—each to their own. There are so many ways of thanking the Lord.

Each one of our lives influences each other's. We live and die for the Lord just as Christ is lord of the dead and the living. Wherever we go, he's there. That's why you should never judge your brother. We'll all have to stand before God's judgement— and it's God we'll have to explain ourselves to. Rather than judging him, decide never to be the cause of his tripping over, or falling. In other words, don't compromise your freedom, but remember it means *rightness, peace and joy brought by the Holy Spirit.* If you serve Christ like this, you can't go wrong.

Hold on to your own belief as something between you and God—and think of anyone as fortunate who can make a decision without going against his or her conscience. *Every act done in bad faith is a sin.*

Those of us who are strong have a duty to bear with the difficulties of those who are not. We should all think of our neighbours and help them in their faith. Christ didn't think of himself...'the insults of those who insult you fall on me,' as the psalmist said. And everything there is in scripture is meant to remind us how people who didn't give up were helped by God. So may he who helps us help you to bear with one another, as Jesus did, so that united in mind and voice you have the strength to praise.

It can only be for the glory of God that you treat each other in this way. So may the God of hope bring you such joy and peace in your faith that the Holy Spirit will dissolve everything that separates you from what you long for, in the name of hope.

Friends, I ask you in the name of Jesus and the love of the Holy Spirit to help me through my dangers by praying for me...

Greet each other with a holy kiss. And be on your guard against anyone who tries to interfere with what you've been taught. Your fidelity to Christ is the only thing that matters, and the thought of that makes me glad; as I will be to be with you.

Timothy, who is with me, also sends his greetings, so do Jason and Sosipater—and I, Tertius who wrote out this letter, am also saying hello! Also from Gaius, where we all meet in his house. Erastus and Quartus too.

Glory to him who gives you strength to live in the knowledge of Christ, the revelation of a mystery kept secret over the ages, but now as clear as the light—an Open Secret that belongs everywhere, and for everyone, as God wants it to be.
Amen.

LETTER TO THE CHURCH AT EPHESUS

proem

BLESSED BE GOD, the Father of our Lord
who's blessed us all with the heaven in Christ.
Before the world was made, he chose us
to be divine, and to live love with him
determining we'd be his sons and daughters
through Christ, and his Great Design
praising his freely given grace—
his gift to us in his beloved son
who gives us our freedom and forgiveness.

So rich is the grace
which God has showered on us like rain
in wisdom and insight!
He's let us know the mystery of his purpose
the hidden plan he made in Christ
from the beginning, to the end of time
when he would synthesise everything
in him, above and below.
And it's in him we've been claimed as God's own
in his original guidance, willed to be
chosen to be for his greater glory
as the people who would put their hope in Christ
before he came.

Now you as well, in him
have heard the message which is true
and the Good News of your salvation
and you've believed it—
and you've been stamped with the seal
of the Holy Spirit in its promise,
the promise of our inheritance
which brings freedom for all those
God has taken for his own
paid for with the life of his son
as absolute proof of His Love.

Friends, this will show you why I've always remembered you in my prayers, knowing your faith in Jesus and the love you show to all the saints...I thank God for you. May he grant you the spirit of wisdom and perception of all that's revealed to bring you to a fuller knowing of him. *May he enlighten the eyes of your mind* so you can see what hope he has for you and in you, what rich glories he's promised...and how infinitely great the power he has for us is, as believers.

You can see this from the strength of his power in Christ—and when he was resurrected to sit by him far above any sovereignty, throne or angelic dominion, or any other state that can be named, in this or any age to come. *He's put all things under his feet,* and made him the head of our church *which is his body*—and the fullness of him filling Creation.

You were dead, you know, with the crimes and sins you lived with following the way of the world...under the ruler of the air, the Lucifer of the psyche where our demons enter in. We were all among them, too; living compulsive lives, ruled by our own desires—and our own ideas.

We were as much under God's anger as the rest of the world!
But God loved us so much he was generous, he was forgiving...
and dead as we were, he brought us to life with Christ, through
grace—*he raised us up* and gave us a place with him in heaven.

This was to show us how infinitely rich he is in grace! Because
it's by grace you've been saved, through faith, not by anything
of your own or anything you've done...*but by a gift from God.*
No one can claim the credit! We're God's artwork, created in
Christ *to live the life he'd always meant us to live.*

Don't forget there was a time you were unbelievers—never
forget you had no Christ and were excluded from Israel;
outsiders, aliens with no promise, merely immersed in the
matter of this world, and alone. But now, in Jesus, you've been
brought very close—literally, *in his blood.* He is the peace
between us where he's made the two into one (as he does a
man and a woman) dissolving the polarity and destroying the
separation evoked by the rules and decrees of the Law.
This was to create the New Man he was and is, uniting us—
and uniting us with God. Do you see? *In his own person, he
killed the hostility.* He came to bring the Good News of peace.
Through him now, we can all come to the Father.

So you're no longer foreign! You are citizens here, you're part of
God's household. You're part of a building that has the apostles
and prophets as its foundations, and Christ as its cornerstone.
Every part of it is aligned with him, and we are all grown into
one temple together—and you are also being built into a house
where God lives in the spirit as he does in the walls.

So here I am: Paul, a prisoner in him for you...you've no doubt heard how I've been made into a messenger with the grace he has for you. It came to me as a revelation which I've just described—if you care to read my words you'll see something of the depths there are in Christ. This mystery is also what the apostles carry, and really it was unknown to people in previous generations...and it means we now share the same inheritance and promise, Christian and pagan alike, through the gospel and its living story. That's what I've been made a servant of— and I'm less than the least of all the saints, I can assure you!

Through all the ages, this has been kept hidden, kept secret in God the creator of everything. Why? So that the Sovereignties and Powers can realise what they're up against, and how all-encompassing God's wisdom really is—exactly as he planned it in the idea and then reality of his Son. This is why we can be bold enough now to approach him in complete confidence as well as faith—so, I ask you, never lose faith in the trials I go through on your behalf: *they are our glory.*

This is what I pray, then: kneeling to Jesus' father that every family takes its name from, where *pater* is also (as you know in Greek) *patria:*

Out of his infinite glory
may he give you
his power through the spirit
for your hidden self to grow strong;

May Christ live in your heart
through faith—
and seeded, built in love
you'll grasp the breadth and the length
height and depth

of knowing the love of Christ
beyond all knowing—
being filled with the fullness of God.

Glory be to him
with his light working in us
capable of more than we can see or imagine;

Glory to him
from generation to generation
in our church, and in Jesus forever. Amen.

So as a prisoner of the Lord, I'm pleading with you to lead a
life worthy of your vocation. Be patient with one another, in
kindness, selflessness, and gentleness! Do everything you can
to hold the unity of the Spirit as a sacred space, a *temenos* that
brings you together. There is (in truth) One Body and One
Spirit just as you were called into the same hope. There is one
Lord, one faith, one baptism and one God, the Father-Mother
of everything *over all, through all, and within all.* This is what I
want you above all to see.

But each of us individually have been given our share of
grace—given as Christ defines it. You know it was said:

'When we climbed to the height
he took prisoners—
and he gave us the downflowing gift of the Spirit'

When it says 'he climbed' (or ascended) what can it mean if it

301

doesn't also signify his descent into the earth's deepest depths? The one who rose higher than all the heavens *is the same as the one who descended.* That's the point. And to some his gift was being an apostle, to others, prophets; to some, evangelists, to others, priests or educators—so that all the saints together (as a white brotherhood and sisterhood) form a unity in the work of service, building up the body of Christ. In this way, we will all come into unification in our faith and knowledge of Jesus until *we become transformed people,* fully mature with Christ's own fullness.

Then we're no longer children! Or tossed emotionally one way or another, influenced by every breeze of doctrine, at the mercy of all those snake oil tricks people play in their cleverness and deceit. If we live by the truth and in love we'll grow in every way into Christ who makes the whole body, all its parts and connecting threads adding their own strength for each part to function as it does, so this body grows *as it builds itself up in love.* And particularly I want to urge you in the name of the Lord not to go on living the kind of aimless fantasy life that pagans can live. They're in the dark in their minds, and they're estranged from Divine Life—without really knowing anything because they've closed their hearts. Once their sense of right and wrong is blurred, they abandon themselves to demonic sexuality of every kind. That isn't what you've learnt in Christ, unless you weren't listening, when Jesus was here to show you what is loving and real. So you've got to let go of your old way of life, and your old self, which is blurred by illusory ambitions and desires. Your mind needs a spiritual revolution, a *metanoia,* so you can *be* the new self that's been created in God's way rather than your own—in all the goodness and health of what's true.

So from now on, *no more lies*—you must speak the truth to each other, since we're all parts of one another. Even if you're angry, don't miss the mark—*don't let the sun set on your anger* or else you've given a demon a neat foothold.

Anyone who's been a thief has got to let that go and find some real work helping those who are in need. Be on your guard against *foul talk*—let what you say be uplifting to others, as occasion offers, and good for your listeners or you'll only be wounding the Holy Spirit who has earmarked you with a seal of freedom when Judgement Day comes. Don't bear grudges, lose your rag or yell at anyone, or put each other down with disgusting names, or sideways anger and spite. Be friends with each other, and kind, forgiving each other as readily as God forgave you in Christ.

Try, then, to be like God towards his children he infinitely loves—and follow the example of Jesus by loving as he loved you, giving himself in our place as the ultimate sacrifice. Don't talk about sex for it's own sake—don't be coarse or salacious, it only poisons you like the wrong kind of humour...*raise your voices in thanksgiving instead,* in gratitude for the purity of life. No one who idolises impurity can come into the Kingdom.

Don't let anyone deceive you with empty rhetoric either— God's anger always comes down on those who deny him. Don't be like those people. *You were darkness once, but now you are light in the Lord: be like children of light...*the light speaks for itself in the goodness that it is, in the way we live. Try to find out what God wants of you, disowning darkness that's exposed by contrast.

Secrecy hides people's shame, but anything exposed to the light will be illuminated, and anything that is exposed to light *turns into light.* That's why it is said:

'Wake up from your sleep
rise from the dead—
and Christ will shine in you'

So be conscious about the lives you lead, being mindful and not senseless people. This may be an evil time, but your lives can redeem it! Don't be unconscious, but really see what the Lord is wanting of you. Don't dull yourself with wine, either— be filled instead with the Spirit, the true intoxication. Sing when you're together and go on singing and chanting in your heart: so that always and everywhere you're giving thanks to God our Father in the name of Jesus, Lord of our being.

Surrender to one another in Christ's love. A woman needs to see her man like this—just as Christ (our head) saves our bodies so a man can be to his wife. As the church surrenders to Christ so a woman should be able to, in anything. At the same time a man should love his wife just as Christ loved us and gave his life for us *to make her holy.* He purified her in water with his words (his love) *so that when he took her to himself, she would be glorious...*flawlessly herself. Again, men should love women the way they do their own bodies—*for a man to love his wife is for him to love himself.* A man should never hate his own body, but feed and nurture it; and that's exactly the way Christ treats his church, because it is his body and we are its arms, legs, chest, heart. And for this reason too, a man needs to leave his father and mother *and be joined to his wife, and the two will become one body.*

This mysterium has many echoes—but I'm saying it's an exact analogy for Christ and his church and what it's meant to be like. In sum: each one of you needs to love your woman as you love yourself—*and let every wife respect her husband.*

That is the unity of love.

Sons and daughters, listen to your parents in their awareness of the Lord. That's your only duty. The first commandment is *Honour your father and your mother*—and it's promise: *and you will thrive and live a long life in the land.* Parents, don't make your children resent you, but guide and support them as the Lord would.

Workers, be in tune with the men who are called your bosses. Show them loyalty and respect as you do to Jesus; not only when you're under their eye (as if you were only accountable to them) but because you're loyal to Christ in wanting to do the Will of God, and not just what you want. Work hard, work well: and do it for God, no less. You can be sure everyone will be rewarded as well as thanked for the work they've done—the Lord will make sure of that. And you employers, treat your workforce in the same spirit; without pressurising or bullying, remembering you both have the same Master, and he's not impressed by status.

Finally, friends, be strong in the Lord and his power. 'Put upon you the armour of light' so you can resist the demonic with light. Because you know it's not human enemies we need to fight—it's the forces of darkness in this world, the discarnate entities of evil that enter in. It's a spiritual war we're fighting. That's why you can only rely on Divine Light, or you won't be able to handle it when the worst happens—you won't have enough resources to hold your ground.

So stand: with *truth buckled round your waist and integrity for a breastplate;* your shoes winged messengers of the good news of peace. Always carry your shield of faith so you can ward off the dark arrows of the Demiurge. Salvation is your helmet and your crown—the word of God your shining sword.

It's a war. Pray, always, asking for what you need: *praying in the Spirit on every occasion.* Never get tired of staying awake to pray—and pray for me to be able to speak the mystery of this gospel without fear—and as a man in chains: pray I always speak with the fire and light of courage.

I'd like you to know what's happening to me, and what I'm doing—my dear brother Tychicus will tell you all. I'm sending him to you precisely to give you our news and reassure you.

May God our Father and the Lord Jesus Christ give peace faith and love to all of you.

May grace and true life be with everyone who loves our Lord, now and forever.

LETTER TO THE CHURCH AT COLOSSAE

FROM PAUL, asked by God to be an apostle of Christ, and from brother Timothy—to the community at Colossae, our family in Christ. Grace and peace to you.

We've never stopped remembering you in our prayers, and we give thanks for you to God ever since we heard about your faith and the love you demonstrate; because of the hope there is, held in heaven.

And it's only recently you've heard about all this!

The Good News that's reached you is now spreading everywhere, with the same results it had with you: understanding God's grace and what it really means. Epaphras, who was teaching you, is one of our closest associates and a real emissary—he told us about your love in the Spirit because he'd seen it for himself.

We've been with you in mind since then, and we pray you can reach the fullest knowledge of him through your best wisdom and spiritual understanding. You'll have the strength to never give up on this, and to bear anything with a measure of joy, thanking God you're part of the family of light.

That is what he's done—he's taken us out of the darkness and its powers, and made a place for us with Christ who gives us our freedom from the past.

He's the image of the Unknown God
firstborn essential *anthropos*—
everything was made in him
as it is in heaven and earth,
everything visible and invisible
Thrones, Dominions, Sovereignties, Powers
everything was created through him.

Before anything was, he was—
he holds everything in unity.
Now the Church is his body,
he its crown.

Because he is the Source
he was the first to be resurrected
so that he's the first in everything.
God wanted the pleroma,
the cosmos, to be found in him
and everything to be brought back
in heaven and earth:

when he stopped the world
with his death on Golgotha.

*

No time ago, you were foreigners and enemies of God in the
way you used to think and the things you did. Consider that.
But now he's *brought you back,* through his death and his
human, mortal body. Now you're able to be with him:

cleansed, purified, whole...and for as long as you stand firm in your foundation of faith. Don't drift away!

I gladly suffer for you, as I do in my own body, to make up something of what Christ still has to go through for the sake of his church. I became who I am for you when God made me responsible for this message—a message that was a mystery hidden for generations and now revealed to all of us who have been touched.

It was God's purpose to reveal it, and show its rich glory to unbelievers. This mystery is *Christ in you* and between you, and ain all you hope for. This is the Christ we proclaim. And this is the wisdom we train everyone in to make them resonant with Him. It's only for this that I struggle on, inspired by him with a force, a wind as if from the stars...I'm compelled.

I want you to know I labour for you, and those in Laodicea, and for so many others who have never seen my face. It's to help *bind you all together in love* and to fire your minds so that your understanding can come full term and you really know God's secret where all the jewels of wisdom and gnosis are hidden.

I say that to make sure no one misleads you with specious arguments. I may be absent in body, but I'm with you in spirit, and delighted to find you in a good place with each other seeing how firm your faith is.

So, some things to say to you now regarding this:
You must live your whole life in the Christ you've received.
You need to be rooted in him, grounded in him and held by the faith you've achieved. And in gratitude!

Make sure no one waylays you and takes away your freedom with some vacuous second-hand philosophy based on this world, and not on Christ.

Divine Life *is in his body,* and in him you'll find your wholeness. He's a Cosmic Christ: he's above all other power.

You've been operated on by him: and it's something much more radical than circumcision. You've been in the tomb with him, in your baptism, and you've ascended with him through your faith in God's power to raise him miraculously from the dead.

You were dead yourself in your old lives: he's brought you alive, and he's forgiven all your mistakes.

He's overridden the Law: this is the thing, and cancelled every third world debt we've had to pay—he's done away with all of it *by nailing it to the cross.* And he overcame all the other powers of air and earth that came behind him in his own triumphal procession in spirit.

From now on, let no one else decide what you should eat or drink, or whether you recognise annual festivals, New Moons or sabbaths. These were only pale reflections: *the reality is Christ.* Don't be taken in by angel-worshippers: people like that are always going on about their psychic experiences, inflating their own importance. Someone like this *hasn't united to the head*—and it's only the head, the crown that holds the whole thing together; the whole body with its joints and sinews—and this is the only way you can reach your full strength in God.

If you've really died to this world's principles, why do you still let its rules dictate to you? It's forbidden to pick up this, taste that, touch something else—all these prohibitions are about transient things anyway—fine examples of what rules and regulations are based on! You can argue that there's wisdom in these obsessions, abasements and austerities, but once the body starts to seriously complain they're absolutely of no use at all.

Since you've been brought back to true life in Christ, you need to look *for how it is in heaven*...where Christ is sitting at God's right hand. Think about things like this, not earthly things, *because you've died*—and now the life you have is hidden with Christ. And when he's revealed—glad day—he is your life, and you will also be revealed in all *your* glory with and through him.

This is why you need to kill everything in you that brings you down: bad habits, mean desires and wishes, and especially greed which is always an idolatry. God never likes any of this kind of thing. It's how you lived when you were surrounded by people doing the same kind of thing before: but now you really need to let these behaviours go: getting angry, being generally negative, miserable, spiteful, abusive, talking obscenely—and lying to save face. You've shed the skin of your old self and you've put new clothing on which will travel with you into true knowledge the more its renewed *in the image of the creator*...and in that picture, there's no room for racial differentiation (Christians, Jews, Greeks, Scythians etc.). There's only Christ: *he is everything, and he is in everything.*

You are God's chosen people: he loves you, and your real clothing is compassion, kindness, humility, gentleness,

311

patience. Bear with one another—forgive each other as soon as you can when an argument begins. The Lord forgave *you*, now you need to do the same. And over all of these, put on love, wear love, be love. And may the peace of Christ be in your hearts because it's for this you were called to be together and be one body. Always be thankful for that.

Let Christ's message find it's home in you. Teach and support each other in wisdom's higher sensing. With joy in your hearts, sing chant and pray—and never say or do anything other than in Christ's name, giving thanks to God through him.

Then you will be safe, as well as saved.

For my thoughts about the home and the household, marriage, relationships and work, please see my previous letter as I repeat its contents here.

Again, keep going with your prayers and be positive as you stay awake to pray. Pray for us especially, asking God to show us every opportunity to share the message and proclaim the mystery of Christ—in chains as I am!—with a clear and direct voice.

Be thoughtful and receptive with those who aren't Christians, and make sure you make the best use of your time with them. Talk to them warmly and with humour, and try to tailor your answers (to whatever questions they have) to the needs of each individual person as you see them.

Tychicus will tell you all about me. He's a brother I love very much: a loyal friend and helper in everything. I'm sending him to you exactly for this purpose.

Also Onesimus, that dear man who is one of your citizens. They'll tell you what's been going on.

Aristarchus, who's in prison here with me, sends his best—as does Mark, Barnabas' cousin—you were sent some guidelines about him, do welcome him!—also Jesus Justus says hello. Of all those that have come over from the previous situation these are the only ones actually working with me for the Kingdom. They've been a great comfort to me, I must say. Epiphas, your brother citizen, sends greetings: this servant of the Lord never stops working for you, praying that you'll hold fast to centre that is God's will. I can testify for him! Also greetings from my dear friend Luke, the doctor—also from Damas.

Please send my best to the community at Laodicea—and to Nympha and the gathering that meets at her house. After you've read this letter, please do pass it on to be read in the church at Laodicea, then get my letter to them (which I sent to Ephesus) back to read yourselves.

Tell Archippus this 'Remember what the Lord wants you to do, and do your best to do it.'

Here's a final greeting in my own hand—

PAUL

Remember the chains I'm wearing as you think of me.

Grace be with you.

*

THE ONE STORY

*

EVERYONE HAS THEIR OWN JESUS, including Judas: a vital part of our hope is projected onto him. The One Story is his, and I studied the four accounts of the Synoptic Gospels side by side and in detail for comparison and variation; at the same time this irreducible figure lives in the individual relationships and encounters we see him in.

Kahlil Gibran's fifty eye witness accounts in Jesus the Son of Man offers the same emphasis: who we are is also a reflection of each other, no man is an island. Jesus says that who we are in essence is the Kingdom, which is also what unites rather than divides us: this is a story that means all of us.

*

AND SO TO BEGIN WITH, THE WORD.
It was in God, it *was* God.
Christ—the word made flesh—
was with God from the beginning;
through him everything came into being,
not one thing was exempt.

It all came to life in him,
and that life was *light*
and the light of men and women,
a light that shines in the dark
that it can't overpower or comprehend.

The Word—the true light, enlightening
coming into the world
where Christ is already *in* the world
that has it being through him—
and yet the world does not acknowledge him.

He came into his kingdom,
and people did not accept him.

But to all who did, and do
the power to become Children of God is given.

The Word was made flesh here

(from The Gospel of John, ch. 1)

PRELUDE

NARRATOR:
An angel (Gabriel) comes to Mary. A brightening in the
room...a presence...then a voice
—*Mary, the Lord is with you.*

MARY:
What is this? Who are you?

ANGEL:
Don't be afraid...all is well. You have grace. Just know that
you're going to conceive a child, that his name is Jesus, and he's
going to change the world.
Of his kingdom there shall be no end.

MARY:
But how? I haven't slept with anybody!

ANGEL *(smiling)*:
The Spirit will come for you like a swan. Did you know that
Elizabeth is pregnant too, old as she is? Nothing is impossible
for God.

MARY:
(kneeling, reaching out her arms in front of her—)

She wakes up. Joseph is wanting to make love to her.

A plain stage. The Four Evangelists sit in a line on individual chairs in period dress, facing forwards. As each speaks a spotlight lights up above them.

MATTHEW:
When The Master was born in Bethlehem, some wise men came from the East. 'Where's the royal child?' they asked. 'We saw his star rising, and we followed it here.'

King Herod heard about this, and he was anxious. He gathered all the Chief Priests and Doctors of the Law together. 'Where is this brat going to be born?' he asked them. When they told him, he summoned the wise men in secret and asked them to report back to him...supposedly so he could go and pay his respects.

They set out obediently to where the star shone directly above a humble farm building: they went slowly and quietly in and there was Mary with her baby. You can imagine how surprised she was to see them! They were joyous, placing their hands together, bowing: and laying out—as you know—their gifts of gold, frankincense, myrrh.

Afterwards, they had a dream. Did they all dream the same dream? Either way, the dream said *don't go back to Herod.*

321

Then Joseph had a dream. An angel was standing in front of him. 'Wake up!' he said. 'Leave for Egypt immediately—all of you. And stay there till I come for you again. Herod wants to kill your baby.'

Now Herod was extremely annoyed when he realised these wise men had given him the slip. He sent out his guard to kill all the children of two or less in the town: that's the kind of evil paranoid wretch he was.

He died, of course, and then the angel came back to Joseph. 'You can go back to Israel,' he said, 'it's safe now.' But Herod's son was on the throne in Judaea. Another dream guided him north to Galilee, and Nazareth.

LUKE:

Before all that, Caesar Augustus had issued a decree for a census. Mary was still pregnant, but when her time came there was absolutely no room for them anywhere. Hence the farm building. The Master was born among farm animals.

We're told there were some shepherds nearby watching over their flocks through the night to protect from wolves. An angel came to them, lighting up the air around them! 'Good news—' he said, smiling at their disbelief. 'Today a saviour for the nations has been born! You'll find him in a farm building over there.' The shepherds rubbed their eyes and looked at one another. 'Well, let's go and check this out.' And they did. And they were on fire with what they found.

Eight days later the baby was called Jesus, and they took him up to Jerusalem to 'present him to God,' as every male child was.

And there was an old man called Symeon who lived in the belief that somehow Israel, for all it had been through, would one day see the light. And that very morning he had an impulse to go to the Temple where Jesus' parents had just arrived. He saw the child immediately, and he knew. And he said these famous words:

Lord lettest thou thy servant go in peace
according to thy will
for mine eyes have seen thy salvation...

Mary and Joseph were amazed. The old man blessed them and told them something of the destiny of their child, that he'd set many on the downward or upward path...and serve as a revelation *which will be disputed*—and a sword *that will also pierce you to the heart*. This was his prophecy.

And Hannah, a devout 84-year-old woman who was also nearby, told everyone about this child.

Symeon reminded us: 'And the innermost thoughts of people will be brought into the light of day.' How right he was, and is.

MARK:
And before all that, Isaiah said 'Look, I'm sending my messenger ahead of you to prepare your way; the voice of a man calling out in the wilderness 'Prepare the Lord's way—make the path straight.'

And this was John who appeared there offering baptism for the release of our sins. Everyone flocked out to him by the River Jordan; he was all the rage.

323

He was a wild man: he wore a camel hair tunic with a leather belt, and he lived on locusts and wild honey. And what he said to everyone was *'He's on his way—'*

MATTHEW:
'The Kingdom of Heaven is near—'

MARK:
'One much greater than me is coming and I'm not even good enough to untie his sandals. I have baptised you in water, *but he will baptise you in fire.'*

JOHN:
This is what he said when they sent out priests from Jerusalem to ask him who he was. He told them the truth:

'I am not the Christ.'
'So are you Elijah?'
'No way.'
'The prophet, then?'
'Not him either.'
'So who then?'
And he said: 'I am a voice crying in the wilderness, that's all.'

MARK:
Then Jesus walked down from Nazareth, and John baptised him there...

MATTHEW:
But John argued with him: 'Are you coming to me?' he asked him. 'It's I who needs to be baptised by *you.'*

MARK:

And as his head came up out of the water, the sky split open and he saw a great white dove coming down towards him—

MATTHEW:

And there was a voice from all around which said 'THIS IS MY SON, MY BELOVED CHOSEN ONE, WHERE ALL MY JOY IS LIVING.'

They pause.

LUKE:

John used to berate the crowds. He'd shout 'You children of snakes, who is warning you to run from the fire that's on its way? You've got to prove you're sorry by what you do. And don't think of telling yourself you have Abraham for a father—God could summon up children from these stones! Hear me: the time is now: the axe is ready at the trees' roots and every tree that fails to bear fruit will be hacked down and thrown into the fire!'

'So what are we to do?' they asked him. John said: 'Let someone who's got two shirts share with a man who hasn't got one—and a man who's got food, likewise.' He advised tax collectors not to exploit anyone. He told soldiers not to bully anyone.

MARK:

But then he was arrested.

LUKE:

He'd spoken out against Herod Tetrach marrying his brother's wife—

BOTH:

—so he was thrown into prison.

JOHN:

When Jesus walked by, he used to say 'Behold the Lamb of God'; just gazing at him. And later, before he was imprisoned, people would say to him 'Are you aware that everyone is going to that man you baptised?' And he would say 'No matter. If a man has gifts, they come from above. I told you myself I was not a saviour. Only a bridegroom has a bride. But his friend beside is happy for him. My cup is filled. *He must wax and I must wane.*'

LUKE:

And so he did. His head on a plate at a diabolical feast, brought in to please a woman a king was too weak to refuse. Salome. Read between the lines.

MARK:

Then Jesus went out into the desert—the Sinai. As we would say, *the Spirit drove him there.* For forty days.

MATTHEW:

He had no food, he was starving...

LUKE:

...but he was guided there.

MARK:

Then he was harangued by Satan.

MATTHEW:

Satan said 'Come on now. If you're really the Son of God, *order these stones to become bread.*'

LUKE:

Jesus met his eyes: 'Man cannot live on bread alone...'

MATTHEW:

'...but on every word that comes out of God's mouth.' So then Satan took him to the Holy City and made him stand on the cornice of the Temple. He said: 'Now, if you're really the Son of God, Jesus, jump off! Jesus, jump! Don't the scriptures say the angels will catch you?'

LUKE:

Jesus met his eyes again: 'It's laid down that you don't put God to the test. So don't even try.' Then Satan took him to a high mountain...

MATTHEW:

...and showed him all the world's kingdoms. And said 'Jesus, I'll give you all of this if you surrender your will to me.'

LUKE:

...and our Master replied: 'You will only surrender to God, Satan. He is your only Master.'

MATTHEW:

That got Satan thinking...and he left off.

LUKE:

...until another opportunity might present itself.

MATTHEW:

And the angels looked after him...Jesus, that is...

LUKE:

...until, victorious in the Spirit, he made his way back to Galilee.

MARK:

Then as he was walking there he saw Simon (who he called 'Peter') and his brother Andrew who were fishing. He called them and said 'Come and be with me.'

MATTHEW:

Walking on he saw two more brothers—James and John in a boat with their father untangling and arranging their nets. He offered the same invitation and gentle command...

JOHN:

They came from John, when he said Behold the Lamb of God. They followed him. They asked Jesus where he was staying. He said 'Come and see.' Which is what Philip said to Nathaniel when he asked 'Can any good come out of Nazareth?' Meanwhile, Jesus had already seen him under a fig tree.

MARK:

They went into Capernaum, and on that first Sunday he went into the synagogue and spoke. And what he said amazed them, because he spoke like someone who knew what he was talking about!

LUKE:

He stood up to read from Isaiah:

The Spirit of the Lord is on me,
He anointed me to bring good news to the poor.
He sent me to proclaim deliverance to prisoners,
and new eyes for the blind...

...and when he'd finished he handed the scroll back and said
'Today, in fact now, you will see this promise coming true.'

MATTHEW:

Then went round the whole of Galilee talking about the
Kingdom, its presence, its connectedness, its goodness. It was
good news he was bringing! And it was healing—he touched
everyone who came to him; every kind of outcast. Large crowds
were drawn to him. All of Syria spoke of him.

MARK:

There was a man there with a demon in him who shouted
'What's your business with us, Jesus? Have you come to destroy
us? *We know who you are!*' Jesus turned immediately and said
loudly 'Come out of him now!'

It was always the same. He would refuse to let the demons
speak. Afterwards, he would take space on his own for a while.

JOHN:

Then there was a wedding at Cana. Mary (his mother) was
there, and his disciples were all invited. You know the story: the
wine ran short. His mother tells him. 'Not now!' he says, a little
impatiently. 'My time hasn't yet come.' What was he thinking?
Mary draws breath and says 'Just do whatever he tells you.' But
he says 'Fill these stone jars with water.' They do so. Then he says
'Draw now, and serve the Master of the Feast.' Then the man

tastes it, and it's the best wine. He calls out to the bridegroom 'Look at this!' Water into blood.

LUKE:

He's standing one day by the Lake of Gennasaret, the crowd pressing on him. He notices an empty boat by the water, gets into it, and sits down to continue speaking. Then he says to Simon ' Take her out into deep water, and lower your nets for a catch.'

Peter remonstrates. 'Master, we tried all night and didn't catch a thing. But I'll do it anyway.' And they land a ton of fish; so many, the nets bulge to breaking point. 'Hey, come and help us!' they call out to their mates; and they fill both boats with writhing silver. Then something breaks in Peter: he falls at Jesus' knees. 'Leave me; I'm a sinful man,' he says. Jesus smiles at him: 'Don't worry, Peter. From now on you'll be catching *people.*'

MATTHEW:

Then he went up into the hills with them; sat down, and as they joined him he said these beautiful words:

'Poor people are free in spirit because the Kingdom of Heaven is theirs!

People in grief are free: their pain will ease—

And those that hunger after justice, I say, will be satisfied.

Those who forgive will have forgiveness given to them

And the pure in heart are happy because they can only see God.

Likewise those who have been punished for being right—
theirs is the Kingdom of Heaven.

So think of yourselves as free when the time comes for people
to treat you badly because of this, because of me.

Remember the Prophets, and know your reward is in heaven.

You are the salt of the earth, you are the light of the world! Let
your light shine.

Don't imagine I'm here to abolish the Law—I'm here as its
fulfilment. As long as heaven and earth are here, the Law has to
be fulfilled because it is God's.

Believe me, if you're no better than the Doctors or Pharisees
you certainly won't be entering the Kingdom of Heaven!

Thou shalt not murder; you know that: but anyone who is
angry with his brother is answerable too.

Leave your altar offering, and go and make friends with your
brother first.

Come to terms with justice as quickly as you can—don't make
it worse.

You've heard *Thou shalt not commit adultery.* But actually
anyone who lusts after a woman has already done that in his
heart.

If your vision leads you into evil, then throw your vision

away—it's not a true seeing. It's much better that you lose a part of you than the whole of yourself—that would be hell.

If a man divorces his wife for anything but infidelity he forces her to commit adultery! Do you see that?

Again, you know *Thou shalt not swear falsely*. But I'm telling you not to swear at all, by anything: the power is not yours.

You've also heard 'An eye for an eye and a tooth for a tooth.' You have, we all have. But I'm saying *don't react to evil—give more than it can ever give you.*

And you've heard 'Thou shalt love thy neighbour and hate thine enemy.' But I'm saying love your enemies and pray for those who are foul to you, so you can become like children, free to be with your Father and my Father...who makes the sun shine and the rain fall on everyone.

If you just love the people who love you, that's easy, isn't it? Matthew, don't even tax collectors do as much? If you're only gracious to your friends, then so what?

Friends, we're called to something higher,
which is to be as God is—to know the Way of Heaven.'

> LUKE *(echoing)*:
> 'Be compassionate like your Father. Don't judge, and you won't be judged either. Forgive and you will be forgiven. Give and you will receive, and as you give you will receive, measure for measure.'

MARK:

When he came to Capernaum again, the news spread fast and people came in such numbers they filled the doorway of a house he was in. He was teaching them the Word, then four men approached him carrying a paralytic on a stretcher. And because they couldn't get to Jesus, they peeled back the roof and lowered him in!

The Master saw their faith and said simply (to the paralysed man) 'Your sins are forgiven.' But some of the Doctors of the Law who were there thought 'How can he say this? This is blasphemy! Only God can forgive our sins.'

Jesus knew what they were thinking, and he challenged them. 'So which is the easiest thing to say, *Your sins are forgiven* or *Get up and walk*? I'm going to show you that the Son of Man *has* the authority to forgive. And he turned to the paralysed man and said 'Get up now—you can go home.'

And he did! Everyone was silent, in awe.

LUKE:

He went home praising God.

MARK:

Then Jesus left and went walking by the sea. Later he was at a man called Levi's house and a number of tax collectors and outcasts joined them all at table. (Many of this underclass had decided to follow him). And the Doctors and Pharisees said 'Why on earth is he eating and drinking with people like this?'

The Master heard them, and he said 'Listen, it's not the

healthy who need a doctor, is it? I'm here for the sinners, not purists like you!.'

LUKE:

Then they said 'John's disciples are always fasting—yours eat and drink! What do you say to that?'

Jesus said 'Well, you can't make a bridegroom's friends fast for as long as he's with them, can you? But when he's taken away from them, that is the time they will fast. Those days will come.'

He gave them a parable too:

'No one tears a piece from a new cloak to mend an old one. Not only will it make a hole, but the piece won't fit on the old cloak anyway. And no one puts new wine into old skins, or the new wine will burst them. New wine must be *in new skins,* yes?

Anyway, no drinkers of old wine care about new wine, do they? 'The old is just fine for us,' that's what they say.

MATTHEW:

Jesus continued as they sat with him and listened, his voice resonant in the clear upland air:

'Don't parade your virtues in public because you want to be seen—you'll get no reward that way.

When you give to the poor don't do it like the hypocrites do in the synagogues, saying 'Look at me.'

Don't let your left hand know what your right one is doing: in other words, give privately. God will see you!

When you pray, don't be like them performing their prayers. When you want to, go into an inner space and pray to a God that lives in secret...He will see you.

Don't lean on hollow repetition like some magic formula... put your heart into it—God knows what you want before you even ask him!

This is how I'd suggest you pray:

JOHN:
Our Father and Mother in Heaven

MARK:
Your Kingdom come again

LUKE:
Your will be done

JOHN:
As above, so below—

MATTHEW:
Give us the nourishment we need

LUKE:
And forgive us our wrongdoings,
as we have forgiven our friends...

MARK:
Don't let us stray from the path,
save us from evil...

335

JOHN:

Yours is the true reality, the power, the glory
always and forever. *Ameyn.*

MATTHEW:

We promise. And he continued:

'If you fast, don't look miserable—just remember your Father
in secret...*He is seeing you.*

Don't hoard up money *where moth and rust destroy and thieves
break in and steal.* What's the point? You need treasure in
heaven, not here!

For where your treasure is, there will your heart be also.

The body's light is in the eyes. If your seeing is sound your
whole body will be bright. But if your seeing is dark, then your
body will be also.

If your light is in darkness, seriously, *how great the dark will be.*

No one can serve two masters. You can't be a slave to God and
Mammon either.

So don't worry about your lives, what you eat or drink, or
about your bodies, and what to wear. Life is more than food,
yes? The body more than clothing.

Look at the birds: they don't sow or harvest but God feeds
them.

Can any one of you add a moment to your lives by worrying?

Look at the lilies in the fields—they don't work at all!
And not even Solomon in all his pomp looked as good as any
of them.

God knows what you need.

Put Him first, and everything you need will appear.

Let tomorrow look after itself. Today's trouble is enough!'

LUKE:

He also said: 'Good trees don't bear rotten fruit: rotten trees
don't bear good fruit. We know our trees by the fruit they
produce.' We don't go to thorn trees for figs, or brambles for
grapes, do we?

Someone who's good does good from the goodness that fills
their heart. With a bad person, it's the reverse. But in either case,
what fills the heart comes out at the lips!'

MARK:

It happened one Sunday too that he was walking through the
cornfields with his disciples, and they nipped off some ears of
corn as they walked. Some Pharisees who saw them said 'Look
at that. Why are they flouting the Sabbath?'

Jesus answered them: 'Did you never read about what David
did when he and his companions were starving? He went into the
Temple and handed out the sacrificial loaves. The Sabbath is *for
us:* not the other way round. The true self is a master on *every* day.'

337

Meanwhile the Jews who had come down from Jerusalem were saying things like 'He has Beelzebub in him' and 'He casts out demons through their Prince.' Jesus confronted them: 'So how can Satan exorcise Satan? A house divided against itself cannot stand, you know that. You have to start by tying up Satan!'

'Hear the truth: People will be forgiven all manner of things—acts, and bad talk of all kinds. But whoever curses the Holy Spirit is never forgiven because the Holy Spirit exists outside time.'

LUKE:
Jesus came to Capernaum, and a centurion there had a servant he treasured who was very sick. He saw The Master and begged him for help.

MATTHEW:
Jesus asked: 'Am *I* to come and heal him?'

LUKE:
The centurion (or so I'm told) had sent some Elders on his behalf saying how deserving he was of kindness etc. having supported their synagogue. Jesus went with them and had nearly reached the house when he got a message sent by some of the centurion's friends.

MATTHEW:
He then said these words you have not forgotten:

Lord, I am not worthy to receive you
but only say the word, and I shall be healed

338

—well, his boy primarily. Later he explained 'I'm also a man who receives his orders from above, with soldiers at my command. I say to one 'Go,' and he does, to another 'Come,' and he does, and to my servant 'Kindly do this—' and he does it.

LUKE:

Jesus then surprised everyone by saying 'Well, in all Israel I haven't found such faith...you see *he believes it will be done, and it is.*' And then when they got back to the house, they found the boy had rallied and was as right as rain.

JOHN:

There was a man called Nicodemus—a Pharisee and a Council member—and he came to see The Master secretly after dark. 'Rabbi, some of us know you are a teacher from God—no one could do healing like you have if that wasn't true.'

Jesus looked at him and said 'Hear the truth, Nicodemus. Unless we are *born again* we can't see the Kingdom.' Nicodemus took him literally. 'How can anyone be born again at my age?' Jesus smiled and said 'Listen: unless we're born both of womb-water *and of spirit* we can't come into God's Kingdom. Flesh is flesh—you know that—and spirit is spirit. So don't be surprised when I tell you that we have to be born a second time. Think of the wind—it blows where it wants to and you hear it, but how it comes and where it goes, well, do you know? Everyone who has been born a second time is like that.'

Nicodemus looked bemused.

Jesus continued: 'For goodness sake, you are a teacher to this nation and you don't know this?' I only speak from what I've seen: but you people reject our testimony. If you don't believe basic things like this how are you going to believe it when I tell you more advanced things? *No one has gone to Heaven who hasn't already been there.* And just like Moses lifting up that snake in the wilderness, *so will the Son of Man be lifted up.* Everyone who has faith in this will come alive eternally.'

MATTHEW:

Jesus continued:

'Don't judge: you will be judged if you do, and by the standards you apply!

How come you note the little mote in your brother's eye and fail to see the wooden beam in your own? Hypocrite: attend to your own eye first, then you'll be able to see clearly enough to really help your brother.

Don't give sacred things to dogs, or throw your pearls in front of pigs: or they'll trample them, and maybe tear you to pieces as well.

Ask, and you'll receive. Search, and you will find. *Knock, and the door shall be opened unto you.* Everyone that asks, receives: every seeker finds, and everyone who actually knocks on the door finds that it opens.

In every way, treat people as you'd want them to treat you. The Law and the Prophets all amount to this.

*Enter in by the narrow gate...*the way to destruction is a wide open road where many people are walking. The way to life is

through a narrow gate, and a difficult road—and many don't
find it.

True life is a hidden place!

*Beware of false prophets who come to you in sheep's clothing but
underneath are ravening wolves.* You will know them by what
they do. A good tree cannot bear bad fruit...

It's not enough to call me Rabbi or Master: you have to do
God's will to come into the Kingdom that is heaven.

If you can hear what I'm saying and act on it, you're like a
careful man who builds his house on rock. When the waters
rise, his house doesn't fall. But if you hear what I'm saying and
ignore it you'll be like the impulsive man who builds his house
on sand. What a fall it has!'

Jesus finished and turned away. People sat where they were
without moving, trying to let it all sink in.

JOHN:
This was when The Master withdrew from Judaea and went
back to Galilee. His journey took him across Samaria to a town
called Sychar, where Jacob's spring is.

It was midday, hot, and tired from walking, he sat down just
as he was when a Samaritan woman arrived to collect water. He
asked her: 'Lady, can you give me a drink?'

Now you know that Jews and Samaritans were not friends in

any sense. Surprised, she said 'What makes you ask me, sir?' And Jesus answered 'If you knew how generous God is, and who it is that's asking you, you would have asked *him* and he would be giving you living water.'

The woman looked at him quizzically. 'You have no bucket,' she remarked, 'and this well is deep. Anyway, where do you get your living water from? Are you greater than our ancestor Jacob?'

Jesus met her eyes. 'Everyone who drinks ordinary water is thirsty again. But the water I can give you is like...a spring mounting into eternal life.'

'Sir,' she said, 'I want it.'

Then he said 'Go and get your husband and then come back.' She said 'I have no husband.' 'You're right,' he said, 'you've had five and you aren't married to the man you live with now. You've told me true.'

'Sir,' she said, 'I see you have the second sight. You know our father worshipped on the mountain here, but you Jews say the only place to worship is in Jerusalem.'

Jesus said immediately 'Believe me, a time is coming, a new time when we won't be worshipping in either place. We think we are superior to you. But the time is very close when those who *really* worship will be doing it in spirit and in truth wherever they are, and within.' He pointed to his heart. 'God *is* spirit.'

Then she said 'I know the Messiah is coming. When he's here, he'll tell us everything.' Jesus said quietly 'I'm telling you.'

Then the disciples came back from town and were astonished to see him talking to an outcast female; but none of them said anything, they just stood around.

Meanwhile she went into town on fire with what had happened, and told everyone about it.

The disciples were begging Jesus to eat. But he said 'Don't worry, I have food you don't know about.' 'Has anyone got him anything to eat?' they were asking each other. Jesus said 'My food is in doing His Will. You say *four months to harvest time,* don't you? I say the fields are whitening right now. One man sows, another man reaps. I've sent you to harvest a field you haven't even planted: you're here for the harvest, the harvest of time.'

The disciples looked at one another. Another of his flights of metaphor! He was a hard man to understand sometimes.

Meanwhile many of the Samaritans believed what the woman had told them, and asked Jesus to stay with them, so he did, for two days. And their hearts were open.

MARK:

He began to teach by the sea. But the crowd that gathered was so big he got into a boat, and sat down as they stood by the shore. He told them parables, stories to open their minds and speak into their imaginations: not simply laws to abide by. He was an artist in this. He could talk to anyone...

He often began by saying 'Listen to this!' Here's one everyone remembered:

343

'Imagine a sower going out to sow. As he drops his seed, some of it falls by the path. The birds come for it. Some of the seed lands on a rocky patch where there isn't much soil. It grows immediately because the soil is shallow: but now the sun comes up, and look, it's scorched...it withers. No roots. Other seed falls among thistles which then grow tall and choke it: there's no yield. But some of the seed finds rich soil, and grows up beautifully.

Now don't take my sower too literally: he's not as careless as he sounds!

He who has ears to hear, let him hear.'

He spoke in images that everyone could understand, pictures from life. That was his poetry.

'What can we say God's Kingdom is like? Imagine a grain of mustard seed. It's smaller than any other seed! But when it's sown in the earth—yes, it spreads everywhere and outwards and up so the birds can come and sit in it and shelter. That is what the Kingdom is like: it's a plant that takes over.'

Jesus always explained these stories to his disciples, to make sure they understood them. He couldn't be sure that anyone did otherwise.

One evening, one of the Doctors of the Law, moved by what he'd heard, came forward. He wanted to join them in the boat as they were leaving. 'I'll follow you wherever you're going,' he said to Jesus.

His reply came:

'Foxes have holes
birds have nests—
but the Son of Man has nowhere
to rest his head.'

He was a traveller, through and through.

MATTHEW:
Another man said 'Let me go and attend to my father first.'
Jesus met his eyes and said 'Come. Let his death go. Let the dead
bury their dead.'

Out on the inland sea, the wind blew up: dark clouds had
come in. Soon it was like a storm. Rain, wind, waves. But Jesus
slept. The disciples were panicking: 'Master! Wake up! We'll be
overboard!' He opened his eyes. 'Why are you so scared? Where
is your faith now? Listen.'

Then, the story goes, he got to his feet and commanded the
wind to be still: and it began to drop. Soon there was calm all
over the water, just a gentle rocking of the boat; then stillness.
Evening light. They were amazed. 'What kind of man is this?
He's no ordinary man, I told you.'

MARK:
They landed in Gerasene country on the other side, and as soon
as they had, a disturbed looking man came out from among the
graves to confront them. He was a wild man, but not like John:
no one could tame or chain him and he was in great pain. He'd
wander the shills shouting and self-harming himself with stones.

345

Seeing Jesus, he ran towards him. Jesus saw him coming and immediately began speaking the words of deliverance. 'Please don't torment me anymore!' the man said. 'Who are you?' said Jesus. 'I'm called Legion,' he replied, 'because there are many of us.'

'So I can see.'

There was a herd of pigs feeding on the mountainside. Legion's spirits wanted to go there...and they did. They grunted, they roared, then they went crazy...charging down to a cliff above the sea...

MATTHEW:
The herdsmen were terrified. They took to their heels and went to the first town telling everyone what had happened. The whole town turned out to come and see for themselves.

MARK:
There was Legion sitting there, looking exhausted but completely calm.

MATTHEW:
This was too much for them. 'Please leave us!' they said to Jesus and the disciples as they stood around. Jesus nodded—his work was done. They turned towards the boat.

MARK:
And Legion said 'Take me with you!' But Jesus said no. 'Go home now—it's time for you to do that. And tell your people what God has done for you.' Of course he did that, saying it was Jesus.

LUKE:

Around this time he went up into the hills to pray. He spent all night in communion, and in the morning he called everyone who was with him and explained that there were twelve in particular who had to carry this forward: he called them 'apostles' (meaning 'close witnesses').

MARK:

They were Simon (who he called 'Peter'), James and John his brother who he called *Boanerges* or 'Sons of Thunder', Andrew, Philip, Bartholomew, Matthew, Thomas (Alphaeus' son), Thaddeus, Simon the Zealot—and Judas.

LUKE:

There were two men called Judas: James' son, and the zealot from Kerioth—his betrayer-to-be.

But there were women too—Susanna, Joanna...and one in particular who had his affection in a way that some of the men (especially Peter) couldn't understand. It was a men's group, but Mary Magdalene was always there—at least for The Master. They only slowly became aware of her.

She had a kind of reputation in the town, but she was beautiful so that was probably jealousy. She needed some help from Jesus, and he gave it willingly. She loved him: there was no question about that.

One evening, a Pharisee had invited Jesus to his table, and he'd just sat down when she came in, inexplicably upset, holding an alabaster jar of very special ointment. She stood right beside him. Her tears streamed down her face; then she did something extraordinary. She bent down and kissed his feet, wet with her tears, and then dried them with her hair. Then she spread oil on them from the jar. Jesus let her do it all: we can't say what he was thinking.

The Pharisee, who was a purist as they all were, could hardly contain himself. Jesus could see exactly what he was thinking. 'Simon,' he said 'can I suggest something to you?' 'Of course, Rabbi' Simon replied.

So Jesus told him a story, while Mary sat down near him.

'There was a man who had two people owing him money: one fifty pounds, the other five. Neither of them could pay him back, however: and he decided to release them both from their debt. Now which of the two do you think would feel the most for him?'

'The man with the greater debt I imagine,' Simon said.

'You're right.' And turning around to Mary, he said to him 'You see this woman? I came here, but you didn't give me water for my feet. She made my feet wet with her tears—she dried them with her own hair. You gave me no kiss. She has showered me with them. You didn't touch my head—look at what she did to my feet. So I want *you* to know that she has released her burden through love, great love. The man who owes little and is lightly forgiven feels nothing by comparison.'

Jesus took her hand 'You know the truth of this' he said to her. 'You know what has saved you. I know it, too.'

JOHN:

Jesus crossed the Sea of Galilee. But crowds were now drawn to him everywhere, so he went up into the hills again. A substantial number followed him up from some way behind. Slowly they reached him.

Jesus said to Philip: 'Where are we going to get bread for these people?' Philip looked at him, knowing perfectly well there was none up here. He said 'We could spend all the money we have and they'd only have a mouthful each.' Andrew said 'There's a small boy here with five barley loaves and two dried fish. But what's that in a crowd like this?'

Jesus said 'Just ask everyone to settle down.' They did, on the grass, and the story says 'there were about five thousand of them.' Jesus takes the loaves and says a blessing. Then he starts breaking small pieces off—the bread, then the fish—but still they keep coming. Still they keep coming, these small pieces, till everyone has something, and still there's more until there are even crusts left over. Jesus looks over the crowd, all peacefully eating and asks the disciples to collect whatever is left so that nothing is wasted. From so little can come so much—but at the same time *we mustn't waste anything*...that's what he seems to be saying.

Meanwhile the crowd were proclaiming him, and more than that (it's said) *wanting to make him king*. He already was a king, but they couldn't see that yet.

Jesus withdrew again.

MARK:

His power was immense. And he was sensitive, he felt

everything. There was a woman in the crowd who was suffering from internal bleeding and she thought *If I can just touch even the hem of his cloak, then maybe...*

She did, and she was right: she stopped bleeding! Jesus felt the power go out of him, and swung round. 'Who touched my clothes?'

His disciples remarked 'Well, there are people everywhere here, Master.'

Jesus looked round to see who'd touched him. The woman—we don't know her name—was nervous and still in shock about what had just happened. She came up and told him all of it.

Jesus breathed, then smiled and said 'You know your faith has saved you. Go in peace and be rid of your pain.'

It was always their faith, again and again. No one was healed without it. 'Do not be afraid' he said repeatedly.
'Only have faith.'

Matthew:

These were some of the instructions he gave his inner circle (you've heard their names):

'Go out into Israel: here's your mission, as mine is. Wherever you go, tell people *the Kingdom is near.* I want them to experience it.

Heal the sick, as I have done. You can do it.

350

Take no pay for what you give—you were given it freely.

Take no money, or changes of clothes, or provisions. These will all be provided.

When you come to a place, find out where its good people are and stay with them. Greet every house you enter. Bless it.

If anyone doesn't welcome you, just leave, and shake the dust from your feet.

Realise I'm sending you out like sheep among wolves. *So be cunning as snakes and innocent as doves.*

Be on your guard. You won't be loved everywhere, that is for sure. And if you land up in court don't be anxious about your defence. When the moment comes, the words will be right there in your mouth. It's the Spirit that speaks through you then, always remember that.

You will be hated for using my name. It draws out the poison from everyone.

But don't be afraid of that. Nothing is hidden that won't be revealed, nothing secret that won't be known.

Speak out in daylight what I tell you in the dark.

Every single hair on your head is numbered. You are of infinite worth.

And listen: don't imagine I've come here to only bring peace—

I've also come to bring a sword that divides the old from the new. The Kingdom does not belong to family and family ties.

Whoever wins his life will lose it. And anyone who loses his life for the Kingdom will gain it in abundance.

Anyone who welcomes you welcomes me! Everyone will have their reward.'

MARK:

When he went back home then, a different kind of welcome was waiting for him. Sunday: he's teaching in the synagogue, and people who know him look at him and say 'So where did Jesus get all this from? He's the carpenter, isn't he—Mary and Joseph's boy? Aren't these his sisters too?'

Jesus says to them wryly 'A prophet is only ignored in his own town.' But it was depressing too, and he was *unable to do there any miracle of note*...just a few sick people. He couldn't get over their lack of faith.

MATTHEW:

At the same time, he'd say:

'Father, thank you for hiding these things from sophisticated intellectuals and revealing them instead to ordinary people. Thank you for choosing to do it this way.

Everything I have was given to me by Him: only He understands me—and only a man who is awake can understand Him.

Come all you burdened workers,
I will give you rest.

Put on my yoke: learn from me
learn from gentleness and humility.

My yoke is easy: my weight is light.'

LUKE:

And once, you know, his mother and his brothers came to see
him but they couldn't reach him because of the crowd. But he
was told they were outside, waiting for him, wanting to see him.
But he said 'Are they my only family? *Everyone* who hears God
is a mother and a brother and a sister to me!'

JOHN:

And he also said 'Hear the truth: you don't really come
looking for me because you've seen miracles but because
something has woken up in you. I don't want you to work for
ordinary bread (or any other kind of food you like) *but for eternal
life.*'

They asked him then: 'How do we do the work God wants
us to do?'

And he said 'All God asks of you is a life of faith in what he's
giving to you all the time. That's why I'm here.'

They said 'If that's true, what sign can you show us which
would prove what you're saying? Our ancestors had manna in
the Sinai. The scriptures say *He gave them bread from heaven to
eat.*'

Jesus said 'Listen. It wasn't Moses who gave you manna—it was God, and it's God who is giving you that bread right now. This is the food that gives life to the world!'

'Lord,' they said, 'give us that bread every day.'

Jesus said 'I am that, and you are you when you are in me. When you're awake, you'll never be hungry or thirsty. The problem is you've seen this, but you don't believe in it.'

He paused for a moment. 'I won't turn away *anyone* who comes to me. I haven't come here to do what I want to do but what my Father wants me to do. And He wants everyone to awaken—that is the Judgement, that *is* the Last Day. Everyone who sees this will have eternal life. I've come here to *raise you up,* for that.'

There were muttered protests. And again they were saying— as Mark has told you—'But this is Joseph and Mary's boy. How can he possibly say things like this?'

Jesus tried again. 'No one comes to me unless he's guided by God. What do we read in the Prophets? *All men shall be taught by God.* That is, directly. Everyone who has heard Him recognises me. No one knows the Father in any other way. You have *to be with Him* to know this.

So anyone who has faith has eternal life—and I am that faith, for you. This is the Bread of Heaven: eat it, and you won't die.

And after a moment he added quietly 'And know that the

bread I have to give you is also my own body.'

People hearing him were incensed. 'What on earth is he talking about?'

Jesus was telling them a mystery they couldn't understand. He was saying: if you don't absorb the Son of Man utterly, flesh and blood, then you have no life in you. You are not spiritually awake. But to them it was cannibalism, it was blasphemy. They took him literally.

Jesus was saying 'Your ancestors ate a different kind of bread and died. But if you eat this bread...'

Even the disciples were anxious. 'This is too risky. How can anyone feel comfortable with it?'

Jesus turned on them 'So this shocks you? So what would you say if you saw the Son of Man ascending to where he came from? His spirit, rising? Don't you see *it's the spirit that gives life?* The body on its own is useless.

These words I'm saying to you *are* spirit and *are* life. But some of you just don't get it.'

Quite a few of his outer circle drifted away after this. Then he asked his disciples 'Are you going to abandon me as well?' And Peter said 'Where would we go? You have the secret. We know God sent you.'

Jesus looked away. 'Even so, one of you will.' But he said no more about it at the time.

MARK:

Jesus was in trouble with the Pharisees; they were on his case. They looked for anything they could get at him with. For example 'How come your disciples eat without washing their hands first?'

Jesus blazed: 'How right Isaiah was when he talked about people like you! Hypocrites! *These people honour me with their lips but their heart is far from me. Their worship of me is empty—they make dogma out of the concepts of men.* So: you neglect God's commandments—instead you live by a man-made religion!'

Then he got the attention of people who were listening to him again and said 'Listen: there's nothing outside you that can come in and defile you. On the contrary, it's what comes out of you that can do that.'

Later, his disciples asked him about that. Jesus was still angry. 'You too?' he said. 'Don't you see that whatever comes in, comes through your stomach and not your heart? Then you excrete it. It's what comes *out of your heart* that defiles and defines you. Every evil thing we have in us comes from within.'

He knew that, because he knew demons.

MATTHEW:

He knew the Kingdom of Heaven too and was constantly trying to tell us what it was:

'The Kingdom is like treasure buried in a field. When someone stumbles on it, he covers it up, and he's so excited he goes and sells everything he has just to buy that field!'

And again:

'The Kingdom is like a merchant looking out for beautiful pearls. He discovers one of enormous value—then what does he do? He goes and sells everything he has and buys it!'

So, as he said, if a Pharisee could be schooled in the Kingdom of Heaven then he'd be richer than even he knew.

LUKE:

One time he was praying quietly he put a question to his disciples. 'Who do people think I am?' And they said 'John the Baptist come back, or Elijah, or one of the prophets.' Jesus said 'And you? Who do you think I am?'

Peter got there first: 'God's anointed!', he exclaimed, his face eager with anticipation. Jesus looked down then told them simply not to talk about this to anyone. He seemed troubled.

'You see, the Son of Man, because of who he is, suffers inside—and he will suffer here with these Elders and Priests and Doctors of the Law who will sentence him to death for his audacity...but on the third day, he will rise.'

What did they make of this?

They *didn't,* or at least not for a while: it was unthinkable.

JOHN:

The Master always used to say 'My teaching *is not mine*: it comes from God. And anyone who tries to do His Will (and not merely their own) can easily find out whether my teaching comes from God or whether I've made it up myself. A man who teaches on his own authority is looking for recognition for himself. But a teacher that looks for recognition for the real source of his teaching is a true teacher.'

He paused, looking at his listeners for their response.

'And what's more, he keeps the Law as well. How many of you do that really? Is there anyone here who does? I don't think so. And yet you complain that I heal on the Sabbath!'

They couldn't refute his logic. And it was ordinary people who believed what he said who also knew Doctors, Priests and Pharisees for who they were...

MARK:
Some time later Jesus invited Peter, James and John and took them privately up a mountain...

LUKE:
...and as he paused there to pray, his face began to shine; then his clothing as well, then all of him, all around him—it was like a brilliant light

MARK:
...it was a whiteness, an unearthly white

LUKE:
...and then they saw two men like light beings talking with him

MARK:

...Moses, and Elijah

LUKE:

...and they were talking to him about Jerusalem, and what he would do there.

MARK:

Then Peter woke up from the shock of seeing this. 'Master, it's a good thing we are all here. Let's make a shelter for all three of you, shall we?'

LUKE:

He didn't really know what he was saying. He just felt he had to do something!

MARK:

But then the light came down around all of them, like a cloud, and a voice spoke in their inner ears and eyes.

LUKE:

'THIS IS MY SON, THE BELOVED ONE. LISTEN TO HIM— ALWAYS.'

MARK:

The next moment, looking round, they were gone, and Jesus was alone.

LUKE :

The three men held their peace and told no one what they'd seen.

MATTHEW:

And it was then that Jesus started to make it clear to his company that he would go to Jerusalem, and what would happen there to him. Peter couldn't handle it. He reached either side of his Master's arms and said 'No, Lord, please—*this shall not be your fate.*'

Jesus broke free, and almost hissed 'Get behind me Satan. *You are a snare in my path.*' Poor Peter, he didn't know what to say.

But Jesus said: 'If any of you really want to follow me you need to put yourself aside, take up your cross, and walk.

You choose to save your life—you lose your life. But if you lose it for this, you will find it.

How can anyone gain by winning the whole world, and yet betraying his own soul?

And what can any of you give that is as precious as your life?

This is the Kingdom, this is the edge. Some of you standing here will be there that day when the truth forever shines.'

JOHN:

Jesus went up to the Mount of Olives where he'd find rest and solitude. He was down in the Temple next morning when they brought in a woman who'd been caught having sex with a man who wasn't her husband. Her hair was dishevelled; she looked frightened. They challenged Jesus in strident voices telling him that according to Moses she should be stoned!

Jesus knew exactly what their game was, and he just looked at the ground. Then he bent down and wrote with his finger in the dust. He pretended not to hear them.

Their voices grew louder, putting him to the test. What would he say? Finally, he stood up and said quietly 'Let any of you who has never strayed cast the first stone.'

Then he bent down again and continued writing. This caught them completely off guard—and in truth they left, one by one, till he was alone with the woman.

Jesus said to her: 'Well, where are they? So no one has passed sentence on you?'
'No one,' she said. 'Neither do I,' he said. 'Go now, and stay on the path.'

She turned to thank him but he only raised his hand as if to stop her. She bowed quickly and left.

MARK:

Jesus healed so many people, daily and spontaneously: there is no record of how many. A man brings his son to him—he's epileptic, and as soon as Jesus sees him he starts to fit, foaming at the mouth, writhing and convulsing on the ground. Jesus asks his father how long this has been going on. His father tells him it was since he was a child. 'If you can do anything...' he is saying.

'*If* I can?,' Jesus says. 'Anything is possible if you have faith.'

He never stopped saying that because the healing was also for everyone who witnessed what he did. What he called 'this faithless generation' and sometimes 'this wicked and perverse generation' weighed on him wherever he went. He carried it everywhere. He carried it to the end.

Meanwhile as they went into Capernaum he was aware they had been arguing on the road about which of them had the greatest ability! He called them to him and said: 'Listen. If any of you want to be the first you also have to learn to be the last of all, the least of all, and the servant of all. Do I make myself clear?'

Then he picked up a child that no one was taking care of, and put him down in front of them.

'Whoever in my name welcomes one such child also welcomes me, and Him who sent me. Do you see?'

Later he addressed the disciples as if they were children too.

'How hard it is to enter the Kingdom! We make it so difficult. It's easier for a camel to pass through the eye of a needle than a wealthy man with all his money and attachments—his status is too vast.'

'Then who can be saved?' they asked him. And he said 'Well, for most people it is impossible: but not for God. Anything is possible for Him. And so, for us.'

MATTHEW:
The Pharisees kept asking him for a sign, both wanting and not wanting to believe him.

This was his answer: 'In the evening you say 'Red sky at night, it's going to be fine' and in the morning 'Red sky in the morning, it's gong to be stormy.' Who can tell the weather from the sky but *not* read the sign of the times? Jonah's sign is the only thing I will say to you.'

Later, the disciples were arguing about their lack of bread. Jesus reminded them of their lack of faith, and told them they were better off hungry than eating the yeast of the Pharisees...

LUKE:

He also said to them privately: 'Your eyes are privileged. I tell you many prophets and kings have wanted to see what you're seeing, and haven't.' And when a lawyer asked him what he needed to do to come into eternal life, Jesus pointed him to the Source:

'What is written in the Law? What does your reading tell you?' He was telling him that it was there, and had been there in essence from the Beginning.

The lawyer quoted to him: *'You shall love the Lord your God with all your heart, soul and strength—and you shall love your neighbour as yourself.'*

'That's it,' Jesus said. 'Do it, and you will live.'

JOHN:

The Master tried to make it clear that what he was saying was *through* himself, for everyone—it wasn't him, it was what he represented *in* everyone; in who we can be in our 'I,' our true being:

363

'I am the Light of the World. Anyone who follows this path will not be walking in darkness but will have the light of life!'

The Pharisees accused him of exactly this, of course—of testifying for himself. And Jesus replied 'What if I am? I know where I came from and I know where I'm going. Which you do not. You judge so easily. I judge no one. And when I do judge, the judgement is sound because I'm not alone—*He is in me.* I have two witnesses!'

'Where is your Father?' they asked him. Jesus answered: 'You know neither of us. If you knew me you'd know Him as well—and in yourselves. Then you would be the Light as well!'

But they told him he was a Samaritan, and possessed. He was trying to tell them about the 'I am' in all of us that is older than Abraham, and is God within us. But they could not understand him.

MARK:
Peter said to him 'Didn't we give up everything and follow you...?' Peter was confused. Jesus was confusing. He made his mind spin—from fish to men, from mountain path to miracle. His heart was open, but his mind...how does one think about such a man?

Jesus was saying 'There isn't anyone who's given up his house and his family or his fields for the sake of this who won't receive a hundred times as much in return...and remember: *the first shall be last, and the last shall be first.*'

They were on the road travelling towards Jerusalem, Jesus

ahead, the disciples in consternation. Jesus is telling them his
fate. His words drift back over his shoulder, like his hair. James
and John catch up with him and ask him to grant them a wish.
They want to sit right beside him in his glory.

Jesus says 'You don't know what you're asking for. Can you
suffer what I'm going to suffer?' 'We can' they say, almost in one
voice. And Jesus said 'Then you will. But the rest—and the
reward—is not mine to give. It never has and it never will be. It
all comes from Him.'

A little further on: 'Look at the pagan rulers and the despotic
power they have. Yours is a completely different power. It is to
serve—that is your way to greatness. A woman knows this
already and more deeply...'

They were thinking about which woman he was meaning.
Then they heard a blind man calling out to be healed.

MATTHEW:
Jesus was saying 'If any two of you agree in making a prayer,
it will be granted because when two or three are gathered in my
name *I'm* there, with them.'

Then Peter was asking 'Master, how often can I let my brother
wrong me and forgive him? Seven times? What do you think?'
Jesus laughed: 'Not seven—but seventy times seven! Listen to
this:

'There's a king who wants to settle accounts with his retainers.
The first they bring owe him a fortune—at least a hundred
thousand pounds. He has no way of paying his debt: so the king

365

orders him to sell everything including his wife, and to pay him from the proceeds. The man begs him for patience, promising to pay him everything.

The king feels sorry for him, releases him, and cancels his debt. But then as the man goes off he runs into one of his servants who owes him five pounds, grabs him by the throat and says 'You owe me—pay up!' The servant begs him to be patient, but he refuses—and then he has him imprisoned.

His fellow servant goes to tell the king what's happened. The king summons the man and confronts him in no uncertain terms: 'I cancelled your debt! So what about your servant, eh?' In fact the king was so angry he then had him imprisoned anyway.

Jesus added: 'That's what God will do to you if you don't forgive each other!'

LUKE:
Remember the lawyer Jesus was talking to? He asked Jesus this question: 'Who is my neighbour?'

And Jesus told him this: 'A man travelling down from Jerusalem falls into the hands of thugs. They rob him, strip him, wound him—then make off leaving him half-dead. A priest who is travelling on the same road sees him, but passes by on the other side. A Levite also sees him; too busy to stop, he walks on by. But a Samaritan—yes, one of those—finds him, and immediately his heart opens. He tends to his wounds, puts him on his own mount, and takes him to an inn. In the morning, he gives the inn keeper some money and says 'Look

366

after him, will you? I'll be back in a few days.'

So who do you think was a neighbour to that unfortunate man?'

JOHN:

Jesus spoke about being a shepherd because anyone could understand that. He said:

'Listen. Anyone who breaks into a sheepfold is a thief. But a man that comes in through the gate is a shepherd: and the gate is opened to him. And the sheep recognise his voice. He calls his sheep: he has names for each of them. When he's driven his sheep out, they follow him. They wouldn't follow a stranger, would they?

They looked at him, trying to absorb what he was saying.

'*I* am the sheepfold gate. Anyone that comes through me will be safe. A thief only breaks in to snatch what he can. I come to show you Life. I am the Shepherd. And I give my life for my sheep.

A hired man won't do this! What does he do when he sees a wolf coming? He runs. The wolf pounces. Well, he doesn't really care about the flock, does he?

I am your shepherd. As the Father knows me, I know my sheep, and they know me. And I lay down my life for my sheep.

I have other sheep, too, not of this fold. I will lead them too; *and there will be one flock, one shepherd.*

I do all this because I choose to; and I have the authority to do it.'

Of course the Pharisees loved all this and pronounced him mad, while inwardly they were anxious because this was the real thing and people were realising it. Meanwhile, despite their best efforts, others were saying 'Well, how can a demon open a blind man's eyes? Tell us that.' And of course they couldn't.

Meanwhile, Jesus was pacing up and down in Solomon's Arcade. The Jews there surrounded him and said 'How long are you going to keep us guessing? *Are you* the Christ?'

Jesus said 'I've told you—but you have no faith. Everything I have done is a witness to this, can't you see it? You aren't part of it because you don't believe in it. My own recognise me. I know them, they follow me. My Father gave them to me, and no one can steal from him! *I and the Father are one.*'

They reached for stones to throw at him. Jesus asked them calmly: 'You've seen what I've done. So what exactly have I done wrong?' 'You are claiming to be God!' they shouted. Jesus stayed calm, looking at them.

'But doesn't your Law say *I said you are gods?* So are you accusing me of blasphemy because I've said *I am a Son of God?* If you don't believe me then believe in the work, then you might understand what I'm standing for in all of you!'

They didn't: they only tried to arrest him. But they couldn't do that either.

MATTHEW:

After Jesus has scolded the disciples for trying to push away the children from him, a young man came to him and asked him what he could do to have eternal life.

Jesus looked at him sideways 'Why are you asking *me* for a definition of good? Only God is good! But...you must keep the commandments.' He listed six: murder, adultery, theft, lying, honouring our fathers and mothers, and loving our neighbour in loving ourselves.

'Sure,' the young man said, 'I've done all those. What more?'

Jesus looked at him again, traveller to rich kid. 'If you want to be free, go and sell what you have and give it to the poor. Then come and join me'

The young man's head dropped. Bad news, and he couldn't do it.

What is the most precious thing you have to give?

LUKE:

Jesus was in Bethany where Mary and her sister Martha lived. (Mary's brother was Lazarus). Martha always made Jesus welcome: all that Mary wanted to do was listen to him. Martha got irritated; she called Jesus to intervene: 'Tell her to help me, will you?'

But Jesus smiled, unpredictable as ever. 'Martha, you're lovely, but you're fussing. Mary wants to listen, and that can't be taken away from her.'

For The Master, such moments were like parables too. What is the point of duty if it has no understanding? He knew human nature and what manifests through it, as he knew his own. Mary was a lily of the field who had the passion to be herself—as he also knew.

JOHN:

Then Mary's brother got very ill, and the sisters sent out Jesus a message. Lazarus was a friend. But Jesus was strangely unconcerned: he said he could see through Lazarus' illness, and all was well. So he didn't hurry. Perhaps he was resting, too. Then after a couple of days he said 'Let's go'—but the disciples said 'To Judaea? They've just been trying to stone you there!'

Jesus was cryptic. 'But there are twelve hours in a day. If you walk in the day, you're safe because you're in the light. It's when you try to walk in the dark that you stumble.' And then: 'It's time for us to go and wake Lazarus.'

The disciples didn't realise he'd died—but Jesus knew and told them they'd been spared the pain of it. He'd been dead four days when they arrived.

Martha went out to meet him, saddened and frustrated but still affirming her faith. Jesus met her eyes and said 'Your brother is still with us. Can you believe that?' She said she could. Then she went back to get Mary and whispered to her privately. Mary came out quickly, flanked by the visitors who assumed she was going to Lazarus' tomb.

But she was going to Jesus. And with great feeling she told him if he'd been here Lazarus wouldn't have died! It touched him, and

370

he began to tremble till his whole body was shaking. 'Where is he?' he asked quietly. She showed him. Then he let go: he began to cry as she did. They cried together as they stood there.

Even the visitors were moved, wondering what he could still do. He was walking towards the cave tomb, still shaking. Then he gathered himself and looked ahead.

'Take the stone away,' he said. 'But Jesus, there will be a smell—it's been four days now!' Jesus answered her: 'But Martha, what did I tell you?'

He took a moment in prayer, thanking God for having already heard him, and then he said loudly 'Lazarus, come out!'

Silence. And then he did, slowly, grey-faced as he was, tottering forwards, wrapped in bands of cloth. Mary gasped, and then embraced him gently with Martha. They sat him down immediately then and started to release him. Jesus stood by and drew breath, the crowd lingering behind him unable to approach him because the energy around him was so strong.

LUKE:
And so it was when he blazed as well! He seemed enormous. No one could contradict him. Even the Pharisees seemed spellbound. And it didn't matter where he was, he was never compromised. Even at a midday meal he was invited to he remarked 'Well, these days you people clean the outside of the cup or the plate *but not the inside,* you know? You worry about my hands, but how clean are your hearts? In any case, if you gave the wealth you're always accumulating to charity your hearts *would* be clean.'

371

'But you Pharisees that pay all your tithes like good boys but overlook the claims of justice and the love of God? And you that want the best seats in the synagogue and grovelling respect in the street? My God, you are like unmarked graves!'

'Master,' one said, 'you are insulting us too.' He was a lawyer.

'I am,' Jesus said. 'Think of the unbearable burdens you lay on people that you wouldn't even touch with your smallest finger.'

He went on. Everyone had stopped eating.

'You, tomb-builders to the prophets your fathers killed! What did God say? *I will send them prophets and apostles they will kill and they pay for.* Like a minimum living wage—no, like slave labour! All of their lives are held to your account—you don't realise that, do you?

You've removed the key of knowledge
but you stand outside the door
obstructing people who are trying to come in!'

Then he got up to leave, his plate unfinished. Imagine their reaction: they were furious and determined to try and catch him one way or the other, to make him incriminate himself.

Meanwhile he openly warned everyone against them telling them to fear God instead because 'every single hair on your head is numbered.'

He also told them about a rich man who was smug with his abundance and told himself to *eat, drink and be merry* till God told him what a fool he was because he was just about to die, and then what? What treasure did he have in heaven? He had nothing!

His parables became more urgent, and more obvious.

JOHN:

Meanwhile the Chief Priests and Pharisees called an emergency meeting of the Council. 'What are we doing?' they said. 'This Jesus is performing wonders everywhere! If we just leave him to it, everyone will turn to him and then the Romans will be on to us. We can't take that risk!'

But Caiphas, who was as canny as he was a wolf in sheep's clothing, said 'Are you crazy? Don't you realise this is exactly what we want—a scapegoat for the nation! That will guarantee our safety. The Romans will see it. We'll make sure of that!'

Caiphas was an anti-prophet, but he prophesised none the less: that Jesus would die not just for Israel *but for the whole scattered family of God.*

LUKE:

As Thomas tells us, Jesus said 'I came to set the world on fire.' And he did, in everything he said with his words and his actions. He was a lightning rod and that is how people saw his light, his passion beside a priesthood who worshipped God in name but not in fact. The old woman who was bent double that he healed on the Sabbath personified this—their hypocrisy and the heartlessness of their observance. Jesus exposed them: they had nowhere to hide. As he said: 'If your donkey fell over or into a well on a Sunday, which of you wouldn't rush to pull him out?'

They had no answer.

And when they complained about the company he kept and the women who went round with him, he told them straight. 'If any of you with a flock of sheep lost one, wouldn't you go looking for it? Any shepherd will tell you. He looks everywhere till he finds it, then he shoulders it home and tells his friends. It's like this in heaven: there's always more joy over one lost sheep than ninety nine purists who have nothing to say for themselves at all!'

Then he told them about the story of the Prodigal Son which has the same meaning. Look at the father's passion when his son returns to him, and what he says to his resentful elder son: *this is what God is like, the God of Love. And this is what he came for, to show us that love: not the love we thought we knew, but something that means *all* of us, and always.

JOHN:

And that's where Mary Magdalene came in. She was always wanting to reach him; and she did, and he let her. He didn't care what the disciples thought—he *did* care, of course, but what they had was on a different level that the others couldn't touch. You've heard the story about the jar of precious spikenard from Luke. How many times did Mary anoint him? She knew what was coming before anyone else did—she knew it in her being. This great act of love and grief I place beside Judas, because it is his antithesis. So of course he complains about the waste and the money that could be given to the poor. He didn't care about the poor as much as he thought, but he did care that Jesus was not as he wanted him to be. So who was this woman pouring adoration on him? It was irritating. He was jealous, too: obviously.

Jesus said 'Judas, let her be. She can keep the rest for the day of my burial. You will always have the poor; but you won't always have me.'

Judas turns away. Mary stays where she is. Jesus is in between.

MARK:

So they left for Jerusalem, and when they got near, Jesus sent two of them ahead...

MATTHEW:

He said 'Go to the village over there. The first thing you'll see is a donkey tied up. Just tell anyone who asks that I need it, and will return it.'

MARK:

So they fetched it, and Jesus mounted it. This was the beginning of the end.

MATTHEW:

And it was a prophet who said *Behold, your king is coming to you humbled and mounted on a donkey and its foal.*

MARK:

People were spreading cloaks on the road and greenery they'd cut from the fields. A shout went up 'Blessed is he who comes in the name of the Lord!'

MATTHEW:

And so they came into Jerusalem. The whole city was buzzing. When people asked who this was, they got their answer. 'Oh yes, *him.*'

LUKE:

Is it too late to tell you about Zacchaeus? When Jesus came to Jericho on his way, Zacchaeus wanted to see what he looked like. But he was small. He was rich, but he was small. So what did he do? He climbed a tree.

Jesus passed underneath and looking up, saw him immediately. He called up to him 'Zacchaeus, come on down—you've got to look after me today!' Zacchaeus was delighted. Jesus, always spontaneous, recognised the same quality in him. And where bystanders were critical, Zacchaeus said promptly 'I'm telling you now that I'm giving half my fortune to the poor, and anyone I've defrauded.' He couldn't stop himself. The Master's heart lifted.

And now he's in Jerusalem, being taunted by the Pharisees who are making fun of his disciples. And he's saying *'If these keep silent, the very stones will cry out.'*

MARK:

And what is the first thing he does when he gets there? He goes to the Temple: and there in the precincts are the moneychangers with their stalls, selling doves...

MATTHEW:

And what does he do? He becomes pure flame. John, what did you say?

JOHN:

He grabbed a scourge and drove them out shouting. He swept their coins like so many crumbs off their tables, turned them over sideways and cried 'Away with all of this! How dare you make God's house a seedy mall!'

The disciples looked at each other amazed. It was like a whirlwind. And it was surely tempting fate.

The Temple guard weren't happy about this at all. 'What the hell do you think you're doing, Nazarene!' He fixed their eyes.

'Demolish the Temple, and in three days I'll rebuild it!'

Was he insane? 'It only took forty six years to build—' one of them said acidly. 'So how are you proposing to do *that*?'

But Jesus stared beyond them nearly forty years. He saw Rome breaking it to pieces.

MARK:

Evening came and they withdrew from the city. In the morning, they passed the fig tree Jesus had cursed in frustration. He told them their faith could move mountains, even as his own was being put to the test.

When they came back to the Temple, the Chief Priests were waiting. 'What makes you think you have the right to do these things?' they are asking him.

Jesus replies 'I will ask you for something. If you answer me I'll tell you by what authority I'm acting. John's baptism—was it sanctioned by heaven, or humanity? Answer me.'

They were caught. They knew if they said 'By heaven' Jesus would ask them why they didn't believe in him—but if they said it was purely by the people, the people would be furious because they knew John the Baptist was a prophet who had more integrity than all of them put together.

So they said 'We don't know.' Jesus smiled. 'Then I won't tell you either.'

MATTHEW:

He told them a parable instead that was clearly aimed right at them, about a landowner's vineyard leased out to farmers, and the servant he sends to collect the rent. What do you imagine happened to him? Did they pay up graciously? Oh no: they beat him up. And another sent in his place. And another. (How naïve was this landowner?). Finally he sends his beloved son thinking they would surely realise who he was. (Answer: very). Instead they kill him, wanting his inheritance.

So what do you think God will do with these farmers?

Meanwhile Jesus is telling them what they really don't want to hear, which is about their own authority being taken from them and given back to the people...

LUKE:

...while he is the rejected cornerstone that swings among them like a division bell.

So they try again to trip him up.

'Rabbi,' they ask him, 'are we justified or not in paying tax to Caesar?'

Jesus sees the trick immediately and asks to see a coin. He fingers it and looks up. 'So who's portrait is this?'

'Well, Caesar's,' they reply.

'Well then, pay Caesar what is due to him. *And pay God what is due to God.*'

His answer impeccable, as he was. Not that that stopped them trying, circling round him, refusing to be a victim.

He blows their question about marital law out of the window as he gazes into the afterlife where we no longer marry, and where God is a God of the living, always. How could they answer this? His light filled their eyes.

MARK:
Meanwhile the poor widow who put what she had in the offertory chest didn't escape Jesus' minute attention: and how what she gave was immeasurably more because it was herself.

MATTHEW:
And later, on the Mount of Olives, he was trying to prepare them for the time to come and the Lie of History that was waiting—anti-Christ to the Kingdom.

'Be careful no one deceives you, because sadly many will use my name and people will be led astray. You will hear much about war, too—many wars. Humanity cannot escape them. And Nature will throw in famine and earthquake and tidal wave against our houses built on sand. But these are only the birthpangs!'

LUKE:
'The world will disown you because its faith is not yours. you

will be hated as I am now—but at every moment, you can state your faith and that is your faith and your choice to be who you are. And remember what I said: the words will also be given to you in your own defence. The Holy Spirit will breathe through you in all its eloquence.

You will be betrayed: you will know that place. The world is on fire and you are gold tested by fire, by dark flame.'

MATTHEW:
'You will see desolation *standing in a holy place,* as Daniel told us—and the world will enter its Iron Age of winter. The New Age of awakening can only come after when the world has been scoured to the bone of all its shadow. You'll see it in the sky— the stars know it: but then it will come like lightning inside lightning.

This generation will remain till all these things have taken place: my words will remain. But only the Father knows the time.

Remember Noah? People were living as they do right up to that moment, and it will be the same as that flooding water.

So watch. Watch and pray. It will come when you least expect it.

What will the Kingdom be *then?*

Think about those five wise and foolish young women. The wise ones took oil for their lanterns while they waited for the bridegroom—the other girls forgot. Then the bridegroom arrived in the middle of the night—chaos! And by the time they'd gone to get their oil the wedding had begun, and it was too late.

Remember those girls. Don't miss the boat.'

LUKE:

Meanwhile Judas was having thoughts. This Jesus was a disappointment. This movement wasn't a revolution: it was a one man band and all he could talk about now was his death. Well then, so be it. It's going to take a lot more than this to change things around here. Where is his pride? His political fight? It's all words. Stories and more stories that don't change anything. I'm going out into the night. I'm leaving this behind. Besides, I need the money. Living like this has bankrupted me. I've got nothing.

MARK:

So the day came—it was the Festival of Unleavened Bread. The disciples asked Jesus where he wanted to eat. He sends two of them with this intriguing instruction: they will be met by a man carrying a jug of water who will show them to a house with an upper room. I've often wondered who he was.

JOHN:

They were at supper there, gathered round the table, when Jesus did something completely spontaneous. He got up, wrapped a towel round his waist, and began to wash the disciples' feet one by one, moving round them, kneeing down. What had he said? Now he was embodying it. The disciples let him do it, wondering. A silence fell in the room. Just the sound of the water. He came round to Peter, who broke it:

'Surely you don't mean to do this, Master?'

And Jesus said 'I certainly do, and you will see why.' But Peter refused. He couldn't bring himself to accept this complete reversal any more than Judas, in his own way. But Jesus insisted 'If you don't let me wash you, you have no part in me.' Peter said 'Then wash all of me!' He meant it, he was emotional.

Jesus looked up 'Anyone who's clean doesn't need to wash—only the dust off his feet. And you are clean—well, not all of you.'

MATTHEW:
That set them all going. So who wasn't? Jesus knew, and of course so did Judas. They all started to say at once 'Not me, Master! You know me.' Their voices rose.

Jesus said 'One of you has dipped his hand in the bowl with me...and the Son of Man is on his way.'

Then Judas, who was near the door, slipped out. They would never see him again.

LUKE:
Then Jesus took some bread, blessed it, lifted it up, and broke it: and time stopped.

'This is my body which I'm giving for you. Do this whenever you remember me.'

Then he raised a clay wine cup:

'And this is my blood—this is the New Covenant between

382

you and the Father, new and everlasting.'

Did Judas linger for a moment outside the door? Did he hear this? Perhaps it only made his steps more determined.

MARK:

They passed round the cup. Then they all sang a psalm at Jesus' suggestion.

MATTHEW:

Then he told them: 'Tonight you will all renounce your faith in me.' He didn't mean Mary, he meant them: twelve men. They were deeply shocked. Peter spoke up immediately in denial. 'I will never do that!'

Jesus looked at him: 'Peter, you will do it three times.'

Peter was vehement. They walked along, confused and dismayed. Where were they going anyway? Jesus took them to a garden beyond the Mount of Olives right at the edge of the city. It too was full of old olive trees. Then he told them to sit down while he went to pray. Peter, James and John went with him. Then Jesus told them 'My heart is so heavy I could die. Can you stay awake for me?'

MARK:

Then he went a short distance, and threw himself on the ground. He prayed aloud like a shout. He tried to find enough calm to speak. 'Father, father, everything is possible with you. *Take this away from me,* can you? But, what you will—I am empty.'

Then coming back he found them all asleep. Asleep! At a moment like this! Ah yes, *the spirit is willing but the flesh is weak.*

MATTHEW:

He left them, to pray again. The movement of his words, his lips, the same. And again, as the pain passed through him. And once more: 'Not my will Father but yours.' He let go. And he let them sleep like the children they also were.

LUKE:

*The sweat on him was like drops of blood streaming to the ground...*I wrote that because I was already thinking of his crucifixion.

JOHN: 'I leave you my peace: my peace I give to you.' Jesus said so much to them before they left that room and within hours it was a distant dream...'*that the love you had for me may be in them and I be in them also.'*

Then Judas arrived with soldiers, Priests, Pharisees, the Temple police. Judas was to kiss him as a sign that he was their man, but I didn't let him do that. Jesus gave himself up because he was ready—ready as he could ever be.

'Yes, here I am,' he said. And some of them stepped back— but not before Peter drew his short sword and swung it at the High Priest's slave, poor Malchus, shearing off his ear.

'No!' said Jesus, with all the force of his being. 'Those who live by the sword shall die by it!' Even then, he was teaching. Then he spoke to them:

'I see you've come to arrest me like a common criminal even after all the time I've spent in the Temple. But this is happening for one reason only—prophecy.'

Then the disciples ran.

MARK:
But there was one young man who went along with them. They tried to arrest him as well, but he struggled and then ran free, naked. Who was he?

They took The Master to the High Priest. Peter followed at a distance and then sat in the courtyard of his residence, by the fire there. Jesus was inside as they did all they could to marshal evidence against him that would stand—but it didn't, and they knew it.

MATTHEW:
Meanwhile Jesus was silent. Caiaphas tried everything to get him to speak, finally cajoling him to say he was the Christ.

Jesus finally spoke: 'The words are yours. But I tell you this: *you will see him coming.*'

This was enough for Caiaphas, 'He has blasphemed!' Jesus looked at him wearily. He knew what was coming.

The abuse begins. He is spat at, slapped, and taunted. 'Prophecy to us, Messiah! Which one of us hit you?'

All of their resentment and jealousy at a greater man erupts. They couldn't touch him before, but now they had permission—it was official.

LUKE:

Meanwhile Peter was denying him in the courtyard. One of the girl servants was insistent—then someone else saw him and said 'You're one of *them*, aren't you?' Peter lifted his arms and opened his hands. Then an hour or so later someone remarked on him sounding like a Galilean. Peter wasn't a Galilean, but that wasn't the point and he knew it...even as he denied knowing Jesus for the third time. The cock crew.

He saw The Master's face in his mind: and he wept, furiously; banging his fist on his knee.

MARK:

Then they take Jesus to Pilate, his hands tied.

MATTHEW:

Meanwhile Judas saw the light and brought back the money they'd given him. They were indifferent. But they bought a field with it, the Field of Blood, that was no use to anyone.

MARK:

Pilate, not really understanding what all this was about (but bound by duty) is asking Jesus 'Are *you* the King of the Jews?'

Jesus is still silent. Finally: 'The words are yours, not mine.'

And even when the trumped-up charges are read out to him twisting the meaning of his words, it is the same. Pilate really does not know what to do. This whole business is very strange. Why has this clearly very spiritual man so alienated his own people?

MATTHEW:

At that moment he gets a message from his wife who was clearly sympathetic. *Do nothing to that innocent man,* it says. *I dreamt about him last night and the dream deeply upset me.* Pilate is even more uncertain. But he can't be seen to be. He doesn't want a riot on his hands either.

JOHN:

'What have you done?' he asks him. Jesus tells him 'My kingdom is not of this world.'

'So you *are* a king then?' What *is* this man saying?

Jesus: 'It's you who says so.' But he says more: he tells him he came into the world for one purpose only, to bear witness to truth, and that everyone who cares about truth listens to his voice.

But Pilate can't feel that. He knows what power is, and he knows how to play the part of someone who is in control. But *truth*?

'What *is* truth?' he asks him.

Then he goes out again to the crowd of Jews and tells them 'I find him guilty of no crime.' But he won't insist on it. His hands are also tied.

LUKE:

That's right, and as Matthew also says, he's frightened. This is all getting out of hand. They want him crucified—their voices are rising into an ugly chant. There's only one way he can handle it.

MATTHEW:

Which is to wash his hands of it. He actually does this in front of the assembled crowd and confirms his place in history as a coward for all time.

Do you imagine his wife slept with him that night? I imagine she wished she could slap him.

MARK:

Jesus is being flogged like a common criminal. It is outrageous.

Then the soldiers take him to the palace and dress him up in a purple robe with a crown of thorny twigs, and take the piss out of him. What an idiot!

Satan's revenge.

MATTHEW:

Then they take him out for crucifixion...

JOHN:

...and button hole a man called Simon, a Cyrenean who had just arrived in from the country—they make him carry the cross. Imagine his surprise.

LUKE:

The crowd swirls ahead. Jesus is silent, bruised and bleeding—this great lover of people abandoned to a travesty. People follow in a trance around the Roman guard. Can this really be happening? And the women are already ritually wailing—while the women that know and love him can only cry in silence.

One woman—whose name you know—walks as close as she dares to behind him, her heart breaking.

Golgotha lies ahead—The Skull—the place where there is only death.

MARK:
They offer him wine drugged with myrrh. He refuses.

MATTHEW:
He tastes it, but spits it out.

MARK:
Then they crucify him: and divvy up his clothes.

LUKE:
Two men, one to his left, one to his right, also crucified. We're told he later said 'Father forgive them, because they don't know what they're doing.' Only a great soul would even think of such a thing, let alone say it.

JOHN :
Meanwhile the sign above his head reads 'King of the Jews.' Pilate has refused to change it.

MARK:
People passing scorn him—'He saved others but he can't save himself.' I wonder where they are now...

MATTHEW:
Darkness begins to fall across the country. It will last for three hours...

LUKE:

One of the men says 'If you are the Christ, save yourself—save us!' The other intervenes 'You have no courage? This man was innocent. *Jesus, remember me when you come into your Kingdom.*'

JOHN:

Meanwhile, and most of all, the women standing there: his mother, his aunt, Mary (Cleopas' wife) and Mary (his own). *And I was standing there too when he told me 'Here is your mother now' and 'Here is your son,' as she was weeping.*

MARK:

No one can hear about what he said before he died without a chill passing through them from head to foot—because he cried it out loud.

MATTHEW:

...in all his humanity.

MARK:

Eloi, Eloi, lama sabachthani...

MATTHEW:

'My God, my God, why have you abandoned me?'

And someone stupidly remarked that perhaps he was talking to Elijah. Another ran and fetched a sponge he filled with vinegar. But I tell you this: when he cried out, *the Temple curtain in the city was ripped in two from top to bottom. The ground shook. Tombs cracked open. The dead walked...*what else can we say?

LUKE:

He cried out 'Father, into your hands...'—and he let go. He emptied himself totally, he emptied his spirit utterly.

The women gasped.

Only one man spoke in that silence, a centurion that was there. He saw it, he had eyes, he said it. And that was all.

JOHN:

With almost his last breath, he said *'The work is finished.'*

MARK:

The crowd dispersed: the entertainment was over. And then Joseph came forward—his uncle Joseph he'd shared so much with when he was young, travelling with him. He came for his nephew now, to wrap his broken body in bands of linen.

MATTHEW:

And he had him taken to his own rock-cut tomb; and sealed its entrance as the two Mary's sat there. They stayed, they held a vigil. Not even the guard could have told them to do otherwise.

They were the watchwomen.

LUKE :

It was Monday morning in the dim light of dawn when they came back with the spices and ointments they'd prepared for his body...

And then imagine: the entrance stone, rolled back! By who? Why?

MARK:

They ventured inside...and there, sitting on the right, was a young man in a white robe. They were terrified. But he met their eyes. 'Are you looking for Jesus who was crucified?' he asked them. *'He's not here: he has risen.'*

They looked at one another.

MATTHEW:

The watchmen outside were paralyzed: they couldn't move. Then the angel said 'Go and tell them he's on his way to Galilee.'

LUKE:

The women went to tell the men, but they didn't believe them. But Peter ran to the tomb anyway to see for himself.

JOHN:

Mary stayed there: disbelieved, bereft, her beloved dead, her life as she'd known it over.

She peered inside again. Two beings sat where his body had been on its shelf of stone.

'Why are you crying?' they ask her. And she tells them why: they have taken his body, his beloved body away! Perhaps she felt his body had been stolen deliberately by his persecutors; it was a reasonable enough thought.

She turns. There's a man standing there. She assumes it is the cemetery gardener.

He speaks. She answers him. She only wants to know where his body is...

'Mary,' he says.

Oh my God. She meets his eyes, his unforgettable shining eyes. 'It's you!'

She moves towards him and he steps gently back, smiling.

Then he tells her to go and tell the others.

MARK:

My account breaks off there, although there is a piece that was added on later. What did the women fear? That they would not be believed. And they were right. They're still right.

MATTHEW:

Some of the guard went and told the Chief Priests what had happened. They were bribed, and told in no uncertain terms to tell anyone who asked that Jesus' devotees had stolen the body themselves while they were asleep.

JOHN:

Jesus came to them that evening as they hid behind locked doors. He filled the room with soft pulsating light. 'Peace be with you' he said, lifting up the palm of his hand one nail had pierced.

Then he breathed towards them slowly and completely and said *Receive the Holy Spirit.* This is the work now. You can also forgive.'

LUKE:

On that same day two of them were walking to Emmaus, a village just south of Jerusalem. They were talking about everything that had happened when a man came alongside them. He asked them what they were on about.

'Haven't you heard? You must be the only person who hasn't—'

(That was Cleopas, by the way—his wife Mary was at Golgotha).

Cleopas went on with his tale of belief and disbelief. The stranger lamented their lack of faith and asked them if they knew what the Prophets had said—which he then summarised for them, in essence, as they walked. He was clearly a very well-informed man.

They got close to the village; the stranger said he was going on. They pressed him to stop over; twilight was approaching. It was only when they were eating later that he broke the bread, and they realised. They saw him *as he vanished from their sight.*

MATTHEW:

Meanwhile the eleven disciples made their way to the mountain where Jesus had arranged to meet them. It is said that he spoke of his authority there, and urged them to spread the Word: reassuring them that he is with us until the end of time. Of *that* I am sure. He's each one of us who lets him be. He's in our hearts and minds.

LUKE:

When these two disciples went back to Jerusalem and told the others what had happened, Jesus appeared again with the same greeting. And slowly the incomprehensible became clear to them—that he had died *but he had not died.* This was a mystical fact. He even wanted something to eat!

He told them to stay in the city until they received the power of the Spirit.

But more, much more was the knowledge that all they had experienced with him, all they had seen before his appalling and unjust death, *was real.* It was not a dissolving dream. And it could only now begin to be understood from inside their own awakening being...

He took them a little closer there every day.

JOHN:

And once more, it's said, he came to them. Simon Peter had gone back to fishing, to a life he'd had and left. What else could he do? A few of us were with him—and we went out in a boat.

We caught nothing, but as dawn was breaking we saw a stranger on the beach. He called out to us 'You caught anything?' 'No!' we answered. It hadn't been a good night.

'Try casting on the other side!' the stranger was calling.

And then it happened. Fish everywhere. And one of us said to Peter: 'It's *him.*'

Peter threw himself into the water to swim ashore. The others came in a small landing boat behind him.

And there he was, for the last time, sitting on the beach beside a little fire: this lover of life. He looked up 'Bring some of the fish then!' And so we sat eating.

The upper room had become a beach, and this was not the night, it was the morning.

Then Jesus spoke directly to Peter:
'Do you love me more than all of this?'
'Master, you know I do.'
'Then feed my people.'

Then he asked him again. And a third time (once for each denial).

Peter was getting emotional.

And again he said 'Feed my people.'

And in that moment Peter's life came full circle to where they'd first met.

His ministry was only just beginning.

'Follow me,' Jesus was saying, just as he had then.

We were all standing. And when I stepped forward, and Peter asked about me, Jesus not only told him that was *his* business, *his* choice, but said what he says to all of us:

'For yourself, follow me.'

John points forward, then raises his left hand as a blessing. The lights slowly dim. Applause.

*

ACTS—CANONICAL

Jesus loved Mary Magdalene more than the others and many
times would kiss her on the mouth
—Gospel of Philip

*With Acts we have Luke, physician and storyteller, to thank for
most of what we know beyond the crucifixion of Jesus and the early
days of the Christian family in shock, disorientation, devastation—
and faith. I have chosen some key moments accordingly. These are
accepted (hence 'canonical') accounts.*

*There are also the apocryphal stories which far from being simply
charming or incredible (I believe) extend our awareness; again I
have chosen some accordingly.*

AFTERSHOCK

*L*ORD...they are asking him
  still wondering
if he is going to be a king of this world, after all

so finally he has to remind them
that only the Father knows the time

and that also
they now have work to do!

Aftershock awakening.
The Holy Spirit hovers like a raincloud
ready to pour down—

and he's lifted into it, disappearing
as they gaze on wide-eyed
at two men in white, near them
who ask them what they're doing?

Jesus can travel this tunnel of air
in either direction, they're telling them
meanwhile they can only be here
with all there is to do
even to the ends of the earth...that is
at least as far as Rome.

PENTECOST

THEY REGROUP (was it the same upper room?)
They fill in the gaps—Matthias for Judas,
and finally some of the women as well
not least Mary the mother; and James too
family, because they're all family now
in grief and longing, and with a task

no ordinary death can imagine.
It begins like a wind, filling the whole house
and then a flame like flowers that are tongues of fire
a bouquet separating to a flame per head
resting there above each of their crowns
burning into the roof of their mouths
to speak—and speak strangely
as had never been seen, heard
or understood...but anyone hearing
heard their own tongue

Parthians, Medes, Elanites
Mesopotamians, Judeans, Cappadocians
all being spoken to—Jews, Cretans, Arabs
all being told about the wonder of God
drawn in awe into that wonder

Only some, who couldn't speak the language
heard nothing: so their only explanation
was *they must be drunk*

and on new wine—well,
so the joke is on them...

It was new wine in abundance, unending.

FAMILY

1 c. 35 A.D.

WHAT DO WE KNOW? What do they tell us?
They held all things in common
because they were family
because they only had each other.

They broke the bread, shared their food gladly
they even sold off what they had
to make sure they each had enough.

World within a world
of rendering unto Mammon,

of competition and capitalist tax
where money is more important than people

of communism in everything but name,
and because it was for God

it is a dream that will never fade.

2 c. 1819, North Italy

WHEN THE MONEY ARRIVED, it's said
Shelley—the so-called atheist
who read the Bible daily—
would tip it out onto the floor
then divide it up equally

among all those present
with a coal shovel.

SANHEDRIN

THERE WILL ALWAYS BE a Sanhedrin
trying to silence what is new.

Listen to them, threatened by the truth
huddling closer, like crows having to share an umbrella.

The new is the lamb
even in the mouth of a tiger;
the air is transparent all around it.

The old exists to dismiss it—

                    or be dismissed.

We know their game very well
obstructors of the real thing, at best a foil.

History waits for the outcome
that has already been decided

meanwhile the lamb goes on bleeding
speaking the name of Jesus, cursed from behind.

A PARABLE

Ananias and Sapphira

SAYING ONE THING, but doing another, you die.
Poor unfortunate couple: he says he'll sell a property
for the common fund, but she gets him to hold back
on part of the proceeds—which is a lie.

Actually, they were free to do as they liked
as Peter points out, *just don't lie about it*
Now why would they do that?
It's too late to ask—

Ananias falls down dead.
Sapphira has one last chance, her own
but she tells the same lie under duress
—and *boof,* there she goes!

Don't be like Ananias and Sapphira,
let your mind be crystal, your heart a rose.

GAMALIEL

HERE'S A WISEACRE, a sage in the midst of them
his advice: *be careful how you deal with these Christians*
reminding them of Theudas—
four hundred followers, all scattered with his death.
Then there was Judas the Galilean—same story...
Gamaliel offers the scales: if this Jesus thing is false
we will know—and if it isn't
we will be fighting against God.

How well he seems to know even as he sits on the fence
and the whole thing creaks under him—
how skilfully, guided by his unknown angel,
he softens the blow

before the hammer of ages falls.

THE STONING

STEPHEN IS FRAMED, he's been set up
nevertheless as the Sanhedrin gaze at him
he appears to have the face of an angel.

He gives a flawless answer, it can't be faulted
but he's no politician: he's not thinking of himself
he's only thinking of the truth.

And so he accuses them of what *they've* done
then he bears witness to Jesus in a vision
sitting in a universe we've lost.

Stoning is all they can do to him
to remove their pain from their inner ears
and the stain on their conscience as it mixes with his blood.

Stephen doesn't even stop there:
he asks forgiveness for each of them,
forever freed from their evil dream
where they'll live with what they've done
repeated over and over, in its curse and its closure
till Kingdom come.

NOT FOR SALE

WHEN SIMON the magician
caught wind of what the scene was
he wanted some of it—
in fact, he wanted all of it

until Peter tells him
in no uncertain terms
that it is Not for Sale.
It still isn't—

even in the Aquarian Marketplace
where you can train in anything
and buy it for a handsome fee:
but call it what you want

it never works unless
it is what it always was
the holy of holies
not trademarked by anyone.

Pray for Simon then
in his bitterness of gall
and chains of sin—
he could be you: he thinks maybe he is.

AS THE SPIRIT MOVES

STRANGE how things happen
as our intuition or something else dictates.
Something else tells Philip to get out on the road
between Jerusalem and Gaza: he will find out why.
Imagine: an Ethiopian eunuch, treasurer to a queen,
returning from pilgrimage, sitting in his chariot,
by the side of the road, reading Isaiah?
How likely is that?

Go and talk to him. Philip does.
Asks if he understands what he's reading?
He doesn't. He's scanning a verse
about a man who is entirely defenceless.
Who is he? he asks Philip
who tells him the whole story, and more.

Further along, they find some water.
The Ethiopian wants to be baptised.
He wants to die, he wants his inner life
To be who he is again.

It can happen to anyone, at anytime
the life that is inside a life.
Think of Saul—he's next.

Meanwhile Philip is spirited away
as far on ahead up the road as Azotus,
leaving the man rejoicing,
his head still wet
a new life opening like his eyes.

What happens next?

CORNELIUS

CORNELIUS IN CAESAREA, at about the ninth hour,
sees an angel coming into his house, who asks him
to send a messenger to Jaffa for Simon Peter
(he can see exactly where he's staying).

Cornelius obedient.
Meanwhile Peter, on the roof of his house
about to pray and hungry for his supper
has a vision of everything he's allowed to eat.
It blows his mind.

Cornelius' men arrive. Peter invites them in.
Next day they travel there: Cornelius is waiting,
sees Peter, and prostrates himself at his feet.
Peter helps him up immediately, and remonstrates
'I'm only a man after all.'

And he is what he has seen:
that God has no favourites
so when he goes to speak to Cornelius' guests
his mind and heart are open
much like his host
and even more his master,
who teaches us repeatedly
the Kingdom is for everyone.

P.S.

BUT NOT for Herod or anyone
who thinks they can claim or own it.

How many now?

Out he comes in all his regalia
to speak to the Tyrians and Sidonians,
enthroned on a dais.

They flatter him of course, as insincere as he is
'It is a god speaking, not a man!'
It is Henry VIII, Hitler, Gaddafi, Mugabe
and the story is the same.

It's just a matter of time
before revelation is at hand
for all of us who are blind
to where the glory belongs.

And so a fist of light
zaps him down.

PETER

WHAT A JOURNEY. That first call by the lake,
then *take her out into deep water*
—to the depth of his faith—
before being told 'you'll be catching people!'
by the lord of your own faith. His face
ever present, loved and loving
mysterious beyond all manifestation
as they climb the mountain of Transfiguration,
but also as sharp as a lash or razor
'Get thee behind me, Satan!'
and all for wanting him spared *his* fate.

Then the washing of the feet
that he could seem to demean himself like that,
but nothing beside the three times betrayal
exactly as he'd seen it. Clairvoyant Christ
with a mind brighter than the sun
his body, his being are vanishing in
but not before he's done what he came here to do
here, and below, all the way down
returning to a beach at dawn
where Peter has returned to fishing...
to the life he'd lost, the only one he knew

to be as solid as the rock He wanted him to be,
and that's where it began: *Feed My sheep*
so he was given the key. And what came between them
that can pass from one man to another
like an invisible substance: awoken from grief,
that poured around his head at Pentecost

411

into the depths of his speech—
that spoke to the Sanhedrin, to Simon and Ananias
that raised Aeneas the paralytic and Tabitha
and Cornelius, grounded in his own humanness,
slowly became Christ in him...

Christ-Peter, Peter-Christ, delivered
from prejudice and from prison
to be the man he was seen as—as we can only be
when our soul is seen, and the seeing
is a threshold of light and a crossing
through the awakening of all we've been.

How many times will
we have to live our lives again
before we are free?

THE SAINT

A.D. 60

Paul, as told by Luke...

I NEVER KNEW a man who had so much trouble
his whole life brought out against him
as the substance of his own confession
to the Sanhedrin, to Festus, then Felix and King Agrippa
and now Caesar by his own request!
(Agrippa said otherwise he'd have been set free).

412

His friends had begged him not to go
in Tyre and Caesarea, but what did he see?
The Master still riding in on a donkey?
The invitation of his destiny?

Now he's sailing with the wind against him
under the lee of Cyprus, then the open sea
to Myra, before hugging the coast again
as the storm breaks (his warning unheeded—)
just off Crete, the ship unable to sail into the wind,
for the force of it, bound in cables...like him in chains...
before they start throwing the cargo overboard,
the storm absolutely raging—

And still he could see clearly, despite no food
he couldn't calm the storm but he gave them hope
out of his own: *no loss of life, only the ship* he says
—as the angel of his inner ear had told him.
He urges them to stay on board, he tells them to eat
before they finally run aground:
                                        Paul
and all the other prisoners spared
like the parting of the Red Sea
swimming ashore, clinging to the wreckage...

Malta: a warm native welcome,
but when he gathers sticks for the fire
a snake slithers out and encircles his wrist
so they think he must be a murderer,
but when he shakes it off into the flames
they change their minds: they think he's a god!

Saul and Paul, he's both, and neither
how long does a sinner have to make amends?
He's healing Publius' father: the island follows.
They load up the ship. In the end, nothing but respect.

Three months on Calypso's island; we sail on
his bearded face as always facing forwards
eyes keening to the light and the breeze...
no Odysseus returning, no Penelope waiting
only Christ in his heart beside him.

I never saw a man so alone
who loved the presence of his friends.
I was as glad to be one of them
as the only earthly balm he had—
and not chained to his right arm, but free.

ACTS—APOCRYPHAL

THECLA

Iconium, 185 A.D.

1

S ITS THREE DAYS and nights
where she can listen to the great man preaching
by an open window...later seeking him
as a lamb in the wilderness looks about for the shepherd.

She's beautiful, and she becomes a virgin:
this nonsense outraging her fiancée
who rouses the people, and gets Paul into prison.
(He'll be flogged, then told to go away).

Meanwhile Thecla has bribed the jailer
visiting her beloved in prison

where she's found *bound with him in affection*
(like Jesus with Mary? What can we say?).

Thecla's in hot water,
in fact they want to burn her
but God is having none of it—

Rain and hail above
and an earth tremor below
snuff out the pyre like cigarette smoke.

She joins Paul in secret outside the city,
vowing to follow him wherever he goes.
He's really not sure: his PR is raw
but he finally agrees—to Antioch.

2

ALEXANDER IS WAITING there to fall in love with her,
meaning he wants her absolutely for himself.
Tries to bribe Paul who will have none of it,
denying she is in any way his...

Thecla's not interested anyway, and lets him know.

Alexander's wounded ego demands revenge
persuades the governor to put her in the arena.
Here she is, naked, surrounded: her hands in prayer,
then turning, sees a great pit of water

and shouts aloud: *This is my baptism!*

Light flashes, a cloud of fire comes down
the water is safe, she can't be harmed
but Alexander has another sadistic idea

'Let's tie her to two of my bulls,' he says
(his balls, if they could—) meanwhile
goading the poor animals under their bellies,
so they'll rip her apart in rage.

They jump in pain—but Thecla's firecloud
singes through the ropes and sets her free.
The governor's eyes are opened, and Alexander the Bastard
has to chew his pride in misery.

Our heroine is more than vindicated.

3

SHE STILL YEARNS for Paul, though
—loving as only a woman can—
discovering he's gone on to Myra.

Reaching him, she tells him everything.
He appoints her to return to Iconium
full circle, as a missionary there...

knowing she can never be with him
on his road of thorns and chains,
his Roman road of fate.

They separate.

Later she moves to Seleucia,
enlightens many; finally dying peacefully
in her own bed, *in a noble sleep.*

Do they ever think of each other
across all the miles between?

PAUL AND THE LION

WALKING OUT at night, towards Jericho
it came out of the valley, imagine—
but Paul and two women were praying
so that mother and daughter didn't realise.

Paul opens his eyes: sees the lion at his feet!
'Lion, what do you want?' he asks
'I want to be baptised,' the reply.

Now it's not every night you meet a talking lion
or come home to find one in your apartment
bearing its message of reality...

Paul knows there's a river nearby—
the lion is following him down to it
Paul in fear and wonder, prays out loud
then takes him by the mane into the water.

Three times: presses his head down,
then shaking himself out like a dog,
says to Paul 'Grace be with you—.'

Paul, astonished: 'Likewise with you!'

He will meet him again, in the arena
and the lion will remember
the very moment the man does—
eye to eye, as everything else falls silent.

ANDREW TO STRATOCLES

Patras, 2nd C. A.D.

BROTHER OF AEGEATES, who will seek his death
because his wife Maximilla is no longer his
—deciding to be one-in-herself, bride of Christ—
this timeless invitation of priest and therapist:

Bring forth what you have
I know him who is silent, I know him who yearns
already your new man speaks to me...
seeing what he could be and is—

and has been from the beginning
before his personality took him
away from being himself
to survive, to please, to play many parts

before this moment could claim him whole.

MYGDONIA

Third century A.D, North India

TO BE FREE OF A HUSBAND, a role, a function
imagine what opened in the name of the Lord
for Mygdonia, through Thomas...this shaft of light
this inner excitation of something named yet unnamed
that bursts into flame—

                    her sex like a Roman candle
her body becoming light

                       and she is free, free to choose

to never be controlled by Charisius again.

Poor Charisius, he's not a bad man either
only desperate to get her back
abandoned, suicidal, as he implores the saint
threatens him, then defends him again—

But Misdaeus, the king, will have his way
because Thomas—a sorcerer!—will not obey
anyone but his own king...and Mygdonia
has decided anyway

her resolution sealing his fate
his martyrdom to the four directions—
by four men, on a hill outside Madras, with spears.

CHRISTOSOPHIA

after Jacob Boehme

A MAN AND A WOMAN—imagine
simultaneously together and apart
erotically entwined, and single
each on their own path—each
because of each other.

Rilke dreamt it: 'to be guardians
of each other's solitude...'
Jesus and Mary lived it
so briefly, so fully
flashing across the sky of love—

that it's taken this long
to begin to understand
what they achieved:
an equal transformation of being,
an alchemy beyond opposition.

JAMES

Acts also prepares us for the letters of James (Jesus' brother) and John in his old age, radiant and clear-sighted. James' testament is unique and again I've added to it to give a sense of who he was and how he was seen.

HE WAS MY BROTHER. Flesh of my flesh. Both older and younger, and there was always something different about him. He didn't look up to me: he looked through me. And our father, too. With mother it was different. She was so close to him, and with something she knew that she could not say. A kind of troubled sixth sense. I see that now. But he was always off wandering and exploring. And he'd talk to anyone. The animals, too.

We were a clean simple family. My father worked hard—he was always in demand. We all did, at the chores. Nazareth was peaceful then, and after Egypt our parents wanted that more than anything. They wanted roots, and us to grow well. Jesus was the restless one. Always asking questions...and then sometimes so dreamy you could barely reach him.

Then he was studying and travelling. We saw less of him. We thought he would become a rabbi, that was the obvious thing. But Jesus was never predictable. He was living and learning but he was waiting—he was waiting for his time.

There were other teachers: Theudas, Judas, one even called Jesus...they gathered people, they spoke to them out in the open: they came and went. Whatever they said, there was still Herod and Rome. Our country was never our own, though we liked to pretend it was. There were limits we could not go beyond.

But not this Jesus, not our brother. That was the very edge he began on when he first spoke of the Kingdom—a place that was everywhere and nowhere, beyond anyone's jurisdiction, and open to anyone.

It was God's country he was talking about, outside of the Temple and Rome, forged at the heart of Creation itself. This was the God we spoke about, but also the God we had lost...this God of the Beginning in which all things were good. And this God, Jesus saw, was in each of us, sometimes under layers that needed to reach the light of day.

He was that light of day! It was in his eyes. He called you with them: light called to light in a way the darkness all around us couldn't grasp. And his light was a fire, too. I watched it grown in him like his own stature.

He was away, as I said, studying; and then with his uncle Joseph—we saw less of each other. I studied the Old Testament too, especially the Book of Wisdom. But then the day came when he was back here and he began to speak, he began to heal. That day at Cana, and then at Capernaum...many days there. He always said a prophet is never known in his own town, and most people in Nazareth weren't even aware of him. Then when they were it was 'Oh, you mean Joseph and Mary's son—really?'

You know that story. You know little of me but that doesn't matter, there is little to tell. I was his brother, and everything came alive in me because of him, and everything that broke open in me was because of him also.

That is why I wrote this letter, or sermon as it is, with the help of my fluent scribe. In those terrible days when he was taken from us the brothers looked to me. For all he'd said about family, I was his brother and that is also what I meant to them. It was my moment to step forward and acknowledge him.

I was his brother, and he was within me; so may you hear his voice here inside my own.

HIS LETTER

for Christians scattered everywhere

BROTHERS, LIFE WILL always have its trials, but when they come, try to be positive about them. Your faith is only tested to make you patient! And patience is what will make you complete.

If any of you are needing wisdom, you must ask God for it— you know, He gives it freely without ever holding back. But you *must* ask with faith because if you don't you're like waves thrown up by the sea when the wind blows. You're in two

minds, and you can't expect anything clear in that
unreceptive state.

It's right that a poor man can be proud of his status while a rich
man can be thankful for his humility, because as we know
wealth lasts no longer that the flowers in the grass: up comes
the hot sun, and they wither...what looked so beguiling is
transient. It's the same for a wealthy man: his business may
continue, but he? He disappears.

So remember if you can: happy is the man who stands firm
when trials come. He's proved himself, and the prize of life is
his, the crown that the Lord promises.

When you've been tempted, never blame God. God is beyond
all that: he never tempts anyone. Anyone who's tempted is
seduced by his own desire. Which then, you see, creates sin—
like a child, but here the child is death's.

Don't get this wrong: everything good, everything that feels
perfect, comes from above *from the Father of all light.* He
doesn't vacillate, and He's not mutable.
He chose to make us His Children through what is true, so
that we would be Creation's first fruits.

Take note of this too: *be quick to listen, but slow to speak...*and
slow to let your anger rise too! God's rightness is never served
by our anger or any of our impurities or bad habits. Only the
Word that's been planted in you can heal your soul.

*But you must do what the Word tells you, and not just listen to
yourself.* To listen to the Word and not act on it is like seeing

yourself in a mirror and then turning away, forgetting what you look like! A man who can look steadily into the law of freedom making that his habit—rather than listening, but then forgetting—will be happy in everything he does.

No one can think they're spiritual while they go on deceiving themselves, unable to control their own tongue...anyone who does this has got totally the wrong idea. Pure unspoilt spirit in our Father's eyes is coming to the help of abandoned women and children when they need it, and keeping yourself free from the world.

Brothers (and sisters) don't try and hold your faith while making distinctions between classes of people. Suppose a beautifully dressed man comes into your synagogue wearing a gold ring and at the same time a shabby down-and-out, and you show the wealthy man the best seats and the poor man the floor by your foot-rest, then what? Can you see what you've done?

Remember it was those who are materially poor that God chose to be rich in faith and to inherit the Kingdom he promised to those who love Him. But you have no respect for the poor! But listen: isn't it always the arrogant rich who are against you? Isn't it always *them* when you're dragged to court? Isn't it they who insult the name you are devoted to? So keep to the highest law of scripture—*love your neighbour as yourself.* As soon as you fall into the trap of snobbery you buy into these superficial discriminations that mean you break the Law.

You see even if someone seems to hold to the Law but breaks some of it, he is still breaking *all* of it. The Law is always whole in any and every moment. It was the same man who said *you mustn't commit adultery* and *you must not kill.* If you murder someone you don't have to sleep with someone else's wife as well, do you? One wrong means it's all wrong. But for yourselves, talk and be as if you are only going to be judged by one law: the law of freedom...because there will be judgement without mercy for those who have no mercy, but those who have compassion need have no fear of being judged.

Think about the man who's never done a single good deed but claims he has faith. Will his faith save him? If one of your brothers or sisters is in need of food or clothing and you say to them 'Be well. Wrap up warm and eat plenty!', but you do nothing to help them, what good is that? Faith is like this: if it doesn't go alongside actions it is dead.

This is how you need to talk to people like this: 'You *say* you have faith and do good things—let me show you my faith, but *only* through what I've been doing. Then show me yours.'

You believe in the One God—that is well and good, and I believe you; but, you know, demons *also* recognise this and they're scared! Don't you realise, silly man, that *faith without action is useless?* Surely you remember that Abraham was justified because he was willing to sacrifice his son? There you have it: faith and action together: his faith perfect because he was tested to the limit. Abraham put his faith, his whole trust, in God...that's why he's called 'God's friend.'

You can see now that it's only by doing something good, and not just believing, that a man is justified. Here's another example—remember Rahab in Jericho welcomed those messengers and showed them a safe way to leave?

A body dies when the spirit leaves it. Faith is a corpse when it's separated from good deeds.

Brothers, only a few of you should consider being teachers. Those of us who teach are more highly judged!

After all, we all get things wrong, again and again—the only person who could reach perfection would be someone who never said anything! It's a question of self control. We put a bit in a horse's mouth: the whole animal responds. Or think of ships: no matter how big they are, even if a gale is driving them, they can still be steered. So the tongue is only a tiny part of the body, but it can claim to do great things. Think how small a flame can set fire to a forest—the tongue is like that. Among all our body parts, the tongue is a world unto itself—it raises or infects the whole body. Catching fire from hell, it sets fire to the whole Wheel of Creation! Wild animals, reptiles and fish can all be tamed by a hunter, but no one can tame the tongue. It can be like a pestilence too, full of lethal poison. Look at the world around you: read the news. We use it to bless but we also curse: out of the same mouth. Brothers, this doesn't work: does any water supply offer fresh water and salt water from the same pipe? Can a fig tree yield olives? Or a vine, figs? No less can salt water ever be fresh.

If there are any really wise people among you, then let them show their wisdom by how they live. But if you still have bitterness and jealousy in your heart, or self-seeking ambition, then don't make claims for yourself or obscure the truth with lies—this isn't wisdom that comes from above, it's merely earthly and egotistical. Wherever you find jealousy and ambition you also find disharmony and dissension. The wisdom that comes from above is always essentially pure: it also creates peace, is kind and considerate: it's full of compassion demonstrably by what it does, and there's no hint of hypocrisy or partiality in it. When peacemakers work for peace, they sow a seed that bears sacred fruit.

Where do these wars between you first start? Aren't they seeded in your own inner conflicts? You want something you haven't got—and you'd kill for it. You have an ambition you can't satisfy—so you fight to try and achieve it by force. You don't have what you want *because you don't pray for it.* When you do pray and don't get it it's because you haven't prayed correctly. In other words, you've asked for something simply *for yourself.*

You're like unfaithful wives: don't you realise that trying to make the world your friend is making God your enemy? Anyone who has put the world first discovers this. Surely you don't deny scripture where it says *the spirit He sent to live in us wants us for itself alone?* But he's given even more than that: 'God fights with the proud, but he gives all he has to the humble.' Let go to God then; and let go of the world. The nearer you get to God, the closer he will be to you. Clean your hands, clear your minds—don't sit on the fence! Look at where you are and grieve it: then the Lord will lift you up.

Don't bitch about each other round the corner. Anyone who judges a brother is compromising the Law. And who are you to do that? There's only one judge, and it isn't you!

'Today or tomorrow,' you say, ' we're off to this or that town—
we're going to spend a year there trading and making some
money. But you never know what tomorrow will bring...you're
no more than a mist that's here a little while, then gone. The
most you can ever say is 'If it's his Will, we'll be here to do it!'
How cocky you seem! Certainty like this is always an illusion.
Everyone who knows what's right to do and doesn't do it is
missing the point, and living in sin.

And as for you wealthy creatures: start grieving now. Your
wealth will go rotten, moths will eat all your fashionable finery.
All your gold and silver will tarnish, and the same rust will eat
into you too. It's a burning fire you've stored up for your last
days: you will see it. Working men mowed your fields, and you
cheated them—look at the money you withheld as you
shouted and bullied, and see that *their* cries have reached the
Lord of Hosts. Here on earth you've had a life of comfort and
luxury...in a time of slaughter you went on feasting to your
heart's content. It was you who condemned innocent men you
trampled on without remorse as you climbed the ladder of
your own success.

Brothers, be patient till the Lord's coming. Think of a farmer
and how he waits for the autumn rains, and then the spring
rains before the ground yields its best. Don't lose heart,
because the time will be soon. Don't grouch about each other
so you end up being judged yourselves: *the Judge is already
waiting at the gates.* Take the prophets as your example and
remember it's those who have staying power who are blessed.
Remember Job and what he went through, and what the Lord's
purpose was with him.

Above all don't swear by heaven or earth. Don't swear by anything, you do not have the power. If you mean yes, say yes: if no, say no. Stay in your truth, then there's nothing to judge.

If any of you are in trouble, pray—if you're happy, sing! Sing a psalm. If you're poorly, send for the elders to anoint you and pray for your healing. Their prayer of faith can raise you up, and forgive you in the Lord's name. Talk about your sins, your wrongdoings, to each other: be honest and open and pray for each other, too. This will heal you: heartfelt prayer is potent, always. Elijah was as human as we are—he prayed for it not to rain and there was drought for three and a half years, then he prayed again and how it rained! The land was fertile again.

If any of you stray off the path into untruth, and someone guides you back; you can be sure he's saved your soul from death and a plethora of mishaps...bless him.

JOHN 1 (THE FIRST LETTER)

A WITNESS

S OMETHING we've heard
that has been since the Beginning,
that we've seen with our own eyes
seen and touched with our hands,
the Word incarnate that is life
was made visible
—and we witnessed it.
This is our testimony
the eternal life that's with the Father
and is tangible now for us.
We're telling you
what we've seen and heard
so that you can be one with us
as we are with Him
and his son Jesus Christ.
We're writing this for you
to make our joy complete.

1 WALK IN THE LIGHT

So this is what we've learnt
and is the message we have for you.
God is light—there's no darkness in him.
If we claim we're in union with him
while we're living in darkness
we're lying, because this isn't how it is.
But if we live in the light
(as He is in the light)
we're in union with one another.
Do you see? And Jesus' blood
is purifying us all, from within.

2 SEEING THE SHADOW

We're deceiving ourselves
if we claim we have no sin in us
we're refusing to admit the truth.
Sin is our shadow, we walk with it
and if we own it
the God who is faithful and just
will forgive and purify us
of all our wrongdoing.
To claim we've never missed the mark
is like calling God a liar
proving his Word is not in us.

I'm writing this, children
to help you stop missing it
but if any of us do

we still have an advocate in the Father,
Jesus the Just—the sacrifice
who dissolves all our sin
and not only ours
but the entire world we're in.

3 THE LAW OF LOVE

WE CAN only know God
by keeping his commandments.
Anyone who says 'I know him'
failing these
is a liar, in denial.
But when any man obeys God
his love comes to perfection in him!
We can only be sure
that we're in God
when a man who claims this
is living as Christ did.

Dear friends,
this isn't a new commandment
but one we've been given
since the Beginning
which was the message given *to* us.
But in another sense
what I'm writing to you now
that's being carried out in your lives
as it was in his
is a new commandment
because the Night is over

and the Real Light is shining.
Anyone who clams to be in the light
but who hates his sister or brother
is still in the shadows.
But anyone who *loves* is living in the light
And doesn't need to be afraid of falling
unlike the man who is hating
not knowing where he's going
because it's too dark to see.

4 BE DETACHED

Children, I'm writing to you
your sins have already been forgiven in his name.
Fathers, I'm writing to you too
because you've come to know the one
who's been here since the Beginning.
Young men, I'm writing to you
overcoming Satan. Children,
you already know the Father.
Fathers, you know the one
who's been here since the Beginning.
Young ones, you're strong—
God's Word has made its home in you.
Don't long after this transient world
or anything in its that's passing...
the Father's love is beyond this
and nothing this world has to offer
—the pumped-up body, the lustful eye
pride in all your possessions—
could ever come from *Him*.

And this world
with all its lusts for
is coming to an end;
but anyone who does God's will
stays alive forever.

5 BE AWAKE

LITTLE ONES, these are the Last Days
you were warned an Anti-Christ must come
and several have already appeared!
We know this is the end of time.
These Christ-rivals even come from among us
but they were never really one with us
if they were, they'd still be here.
But you, you have been anointed
and you can receive true knowledge.

It's not because you don't know the truth
that I'm writing to you
but because you do:
no lie can come from it.
The man who denies that Jesus is the Christ
is himself Anti-Christ
denying the Father as well as the Son,
because you can't have the Father without the Son.

Keep alive in yourself what you learnt in the Beginning
because as long as that is alive in you
you will live in the Son
and in the Father

and what is promised
will be there for you:
Eternal Life.

This is all I'm concerned about:
the people who are trying to lead you astray.
But you still have the anointing
and you don't need anyone to teach you:
the anointing opens you to the true gnosis.
You're anointed with truth, not a lie!
And it has taught you this: *stay in Him.*
Live in Christ, my children
so that when he comes
we can have confidence
and not turn away in shame.
You know God is rightness—
So then you recognise that everyone whose life is right
has been guided and created by Him.

6 LIVE AS GOD'S CHILDREN

THINK OF THE LOVE He feels for us
by letting us be His Children
—and that is what we are.
Because the world can't acknowledge Him
it doesn't us, either. So here we are.
What the future is, we can't say
all we know is when it's revealed
we will be like Him
because we see Him as he is.

7 THE HOPE

So here's the hope. But anyone
who holds it must purify
to be more like Him.
There is no other way.
Anyone who sins
breaks the Law—
they are one and the same.
You know he came to dissolve this
because there's only truth in him,
and anyone who lives in God
stops missing the mark.

Otherwise, he's unknown
never seen or understood.

Children, don't let anyone tempt you:
to live divinely
is to be as he is—wholly;
to sin without caring
is to be on the other side.
Satan was always like that:
it was to undo all he'd done
that the Son of Man appeared.
Everyone born of God
has God's seed inside him
which means he always wants to be
on the right path.

8 WHO ARE WE?

SO THIS WAY we can see
who the children are—
are they God's or Satan's?
Anyone refusing to live well
and not loving his brother
is no child of God's!

This is the message
you've heard from the beginning
that we are here to love one another
not to be like Cain
slitting Abel's throat
for one reason only: *he wasn't him.*
You mustn't be surprised the world hates you
we've passed out of death into life,
and we can be sure of this
only because we love.
If you refuse love, you are as dust
to hate your brother is to be his killer
and killers, you know, don't live forever.
He gave his life for us—
this has taught us love
so we can do the same
for our sisters and brothers.
If a man is rich
and sees his brother is in need
but does nothing about it,
how can the love of God
ever live in him?

Children, our love is not just talk
but something *that is what love does,*
only by it can we be certain
that we are living in truth
quietening our conscience in his presence
whatever accusation comes at us;
because God knows all of it; all of us.

Dear friends,
If we aren't condemned by our conscience
we don't need to be afraid in His Presence,
and whatever we ask Him
we can receive,
because we keep his laws
living as he wants us to.
His commandments are true
that we believe in the name of Jesus
and that we love one another,
as he told us to.
Whoever keeps to this
lives in God, and God lives in him.
We know it
by the Holy Spirit he's given us
in all its presence and love.

9 TRUSTING

BUT IT'S NOT every spirit you can trust
test them, to see if they are God's!
There are many false prophets among us.
You can tell any spirit from God by this:

440

he will acknowledge the name of Jesus
but any spirit that denies this
is not from God, but the other side
that we also call 'Anti-Christ.'
Anti-Christ is in our world now.
Children, you've already overcome
people like this
because you are from God, and you have
one in you that's greater than anyone
in this world or ay other.
As for them, *they are of the world*
and so they speak it's language
and the world hears them.
But we are God's children
and those who know Him, hear us
—the others refuse us!
And this is how we can tell
the spirit of truth from a spirit
that never augurs well.

10 LOVE AND FAITH

So, my dear ones,
let us love one another
since Love is His
and everyone who loves
comes from Him.
The loveless can never know God
because God is Love,
His love for us revealed
when he sent his son

to give us life again.
This is the love I mean
not our love for God
but His for us
through Jesus
absolving us
of all we've done wrong.

Dear friends,
since God has loved us like this
we too should love one another.
No one has ever seen God,
but as long as we love one another
He, Father and Mother, will live in us
and His love will be complete.
We know we're living in Him
as He is in us
because he lets us share his Spirit.
We saw and we witness
that he sent his son
to save this world.
Whoever acknowledges Jesus
has God living in them
as he or she is in God.
We've put our whole faith
in God's love for us!
God is Love
so anyone who lives in love
lives in God
and God lives
deeper and deeper within.

Love will find its perfection in us
when we can face the Last Day fearless
because even here
we have become as He is.
In true love there is no fear,
perfect love casts out fear
fear anticipates punishment,
and anyone living in fear
is not yet fully in love.
We are for love, then
knowing He loved us first
so anyone who says he loves
but hates his brother,
you see, is lying
because a man who can't
even love his visible brother
can never love God
(who he has never seen).
So this is the commandment
to love, and what it means.

Whoever believes Jesus is the Christ
has come from God
and whoever loves the Father
that created him
loves the child he fathers.
We know we love God's children
if we love God
and do what he asks us:
this is what loving God is
and it's not difficult

because anyone who is His
has already overcome the world
in this victory
that is our faith.

11 FAITH

WHO CAN OVERCOME the world?
Only someone who knows
that Jesus is God's son.
He who came by water and blood
—not water only
but water and blood—
with the Spirit as a witness
because the Spirit is truth,
so there are three witnesses
the Spirit, the water, and the blood
all three of them as one.
We accept human witness
but God's is absolute
and this is his testimony
given as evidence for Jesus his son.
Everyone who believes in him
has this witness inside of him,
anyone who doesn't
imagines God to be a liar
because he can't trust
in his or any father.
This is the witnessing:
God has given us eternal life
and this life *is* his son—

anyone who has him *has life*
anyone who doesn't has dust.

I've written this for you
so that you who believe in the name of Christ
may be certain you have eternal life.

12 IN THE END

WE KNOW that if we ask Him for anything
and it's in harmony with His Will
He will hear us—
knowing that whatever we ask
He will hear us—
we may even know it has already been granted.

If anyone sees his brother or sister sin
he only has to pray
and God will breathe life
—not on a deadly sin, mind;
there's a sin that really is death.

Every kind of wrongdoing is a sin
but not all sin is the end.

*

SUMMA

Anyone who essentially comes from God
does not sin—
because the Son of God
protects him,
and the Evil One
can't reach him.

We know we belong to God
but this whole world lies
in the power of evil!

We know too that Christ has come
and has given us the power
to know the True Divine.

We are in that
as we are in Christ:
this is eternal life.

Children, be on your guard
against false gods
and idols of the heart.

MAGDALENE

For where your heart is, there is the treasure
—*Jesus in The Gospel of Philip*

Mary, as we know so well, has been all but airbrushed out of the accepted accounts, her impact and true character minimised as well as her true gravity and presence. This is an attempt to redress that imbalance drawing from a number of sources as well as my own imagining...

H IS EYES...the river,
my eyes...the clear golden sunlight,
meeting...where are we?
Out of time, here. It doesn't matter,
and it matters completely.

I know you burns through the page
sun to its magnifier—
but it's a raising too, a raising up

and it is gentle: his eyes
the sound of the river, his flowing hair, beard.

It's as if I've caught him wondering.
He's already caught me completely.

His Nazarite face, and mine out of Egypt.
The ascetic and the whore
—how wrong can you be?

Eros was our beginning, it had to be
but where we were going
and how we've come to live inside each other,
God alone knows
in a place beyond right and wrong.

Where had we come from?
He, from the Essenes and further beyond
me (apparently) after my father had died
and I'd been promised in marriage to Babylon,
our caravan attacked by robbers...

adopted by Joseph of Arimathea,
or sold into slavery and bitter rage?
Whichever you want to believe
Mary of Magdala, or Myriam of Tyana.

How many ways are there to where we come to?
Either way, the past was finished
as I met his eyes. My life was only just beginning
as Mary, as you know
and will never completely know me

because he is the mastery and I am the mystery

which means *we live beyond personality,*
where there is always space for you
to enter in, and find yourselves through us.

What can I tell you?
Eros was our beginning,
and we knew all a man and woman can know
even in that moment.

How could we not?

Human, always, brought together
for a purpose we could not see
only suffer and exult in
as the river knows...

His love was that he knew love
in all his humility and being,
the first man to treat me like a woman
not a hireling, an object or a slave.

They say he helped me,
they say I had seven demons
that any woman can understand,
and that any man can confess to.

I had darkness, the darkness of our time
I had craving—I clung
I had ignorance—I judged
I had a secret wish to die

I knew the enslavement of the body
and the false peace of the flesh,
and I knew rage...

and the voice of Satan clings to each
tempting you to be it and submit
stop, why lie to yourself, you are mine
before the soul says *No!*
you never saw who I truly am—
then goes on its way rejoicing.

He knew this, in the desert
and the hollowed out depth of his being;

but he did not know the love of a woman,
the love of a man with a woman,
not then.

And so I came for him
as he came for me.

He raises his eyes, there by the river
and he looks at me again
then says in silence what he will one day say
to me in that garden after the longest night

'Mary!' And you know what I replied:
I spoke his name.

I spoke his name as I speak it now
forever inside my heart
where we can never be parted.

450

I was always his, and he was always mine
from that moment, there could be no other;
he was my king. But he had no vanity
like Solomon or any other since.

He was my king, and I was his companion
as far as anyone could see—
and inside that I was his *koininos*
which you may translate as *soulmate*.
Queen.

We transformed each other.
How could we not?

Only if you see him
as *only* the only Son of God.

He knew the darkness all around us
of time brought to its nadir,
and he knew the reality of light
as it was in the beginning...

What does a being do, knowing that?
He acquiesces, or he acts.

And I was with him,
I was with him sitting silently
as he spoke—my being was with him,
my love, and the in-between of us...

We were not married—we had work to do.
And this was our marrying,

where the black and gold serpents rise
then turn and face each other,
in an upturned figure of eight
adorning the spine's staff.

Caduceus.

I knew how it was for him
with him, with all his healing
his joy, his radical laughter—
and I knew his despair and grieving.

He loved us all.
How can a being do that?

Only when we're empty of everything
We believe is ours, and is 'I am'
that fills the secret hole
against the darkness and the cold
that treads the path of kings...

My kingdom is not of this world.

And I knew the anointing,
I grew with in my being
from Isis, in the river of time

and it was this gift for him
to give him everything, as he gave
to give him my energy, my love, a love
that only Isis could dream of;

not for a New Year in gold
but for the darkest gates of death
death after mockery, betrayal, desolation.

I brought him this,
I taught him to trust his heart

I held him in the aroma of our love,
he kissed me often on the mouth (it's true—)
and called me *the Woman who understands the All.*

He was *Idihaya*—the Single One,
and I was the Woman...I've told you.

He knew I would outlive him.

He knew he would outlive himself
but not in any way even he could understand,
until his teaching became him.

What did he teach us?
In every word and gesture?

Emptiness,
that complete emptying out of self
that only a lover can know—

Abundance,
supreme generosity of spirit
that the Father showed him in everything
(like his own prodigal son—)

Oneness,
beyond duality, mine or yours,
man or woman, day or night
above and below, winter and summer
autumn and spring—all seasons
forever seasons of the spirit
turning in the wheel, created
by the Father and Mother of creation

Christ and Sophia, Father and Mother
Father-Mother and Holy Spirit,
nameable and unnameable

He knew if we made ourselves *one*
then we would enter in.

He wanted us all to enter *in.*
He wanted us to live.

So he gave us his body,
he gave us his heart and soul.
He gave us his eyes...
he gave me his eyes.

He gave us the day and the night
as one path of light.

And then he died.

I watched him die.

And the tearing in my heart was beyond words

forever, beyond pain.

And I was Mary again, beginning
without him.

Beloved man, broken
humiliated, emptied, given...

and we had no idea what to do.

All I knew was to wait.
I was the Woman who Stays.

The tomb guards didn't even think
of asking me less.

We all stayed, that night
when the brothers had gone.
Peter, Andrew, all of them.

Then in the first light of morning...

Set your seal upon my heart
for love is stronger than death

I had proof then, as if I needed it.
I needed it!

And I ran, as he told me to
with the most amazing news.

And they did not believe it.

(Peter came running anyway...)

The tomb was open and empty
and the garden was dew-morning-bright.

He was speaking to us in silence
as he did with his eyes...

I wept for their lack of understanding,
and therefore of him.

But how could they? My knowing was alien
as the gold bangle on my wrist—
far easier for them for me to be
a fallen woman rather than a priestess;
and if not in their eyes
then in those around us, certainly
which is why Peter claimed
'Women are not worthy of this life.'

He wanted Yeshua closest—they all did,
that was the least of my worries...

I knew, and I had to hold out hope
and more than that, faith—
and still more than that, knowledge.

I told them *his grace will be with all of you*
I told them that he'd prepared us
and it was true—
but they were only as ready as they knew.
Only John truly understood.

MAGDALENE

So we were one in our grief, but not *One*
and not at one either. I tried
but history is always its own blindness
measured as far as we can see

an underworld under the trinity
all the way before we awaken;
and the way can only be transformation.

How long did I stay? Jerusalem was dangerous,
I had to leave, there was nothing for me there
but the memory of pain.

We all went our various ways as he told us to,
carrying the Word like seed...his body,
and his presence grown all inside

and still growing, from the Light.

Some say I went to France,
some to Cyprus
some even to the farther shores of Britain
where Joseph journeyed for tin...

I went to Silence, as you may read;
I was full with him.

Then I was silenced.

But it did not stop me speaking
inside your hearts and minds

and far beyond those days and nights.

I've never been forgotten.
He willed it so,

the same way he came to my well
thirsty to drink.

Our child is future time
when the time is right
and you will see us standing together
as we did
with a Rose between us;
then you will see
that all he meant was Love,
being all we are
when the rest has been crucified
and transcended.

REVELATION

Revelation is legendary as the mighty prophecy of The Bible, of Apocalypse, of Armageddon. It has been held in awe and fear—some people have even claimed you can go mad trying to understand it.

The key (we believe) is to see it in context, written in response to the dire situation that was Rome at the time of its dissolute emperor Nero. We can be fairly certain that Revelation was in fact written by a Roman convert to Christianity, someone well-to-do enough to be sent into exile (Patmos) rather than simply disposed of as many Christians were in the persecution.

This book is fuelled by bitter experience. To clarify Rome, I have included the figure of a Roman historian familiar with Tacitus, who tells it all in detail. Like Ezekiel before him, the writer vaults into the realm of pure imagination and 'seeing.' The vision of the Lamb (Christ) is juxtaposed with the Beast (the emperor), famously named with the number 666; the final battle that is Armageddon will see his eventual defeat.

The split between heaven (Christ and the angels) and apocalyptic earth can then be healed: the vision of the New Jerusalem descending is that healing. Despite everything, there is a new dawn beyond rage and despair—a new day, and a new life for you and me.

INTERIOR OF A CAVE, at first indistinct. It is darkness. Your eyes are closed. You bring your awareness to a point between your two physical eyes. Then you begin to see the cave and its rough sloping ceiling reaching inwards...and a man sitting there, an old man with uncut beard and hair.

He begins to speak, deep in your mind.

THE TIME IS CLOSE.

He is coming on the clouds,
everyone will see him...
including those who crucified him;
the whole earth will grieve for him.

I give you my word.

I am also John. Through our bond in Jesus I am your brother and I share your sufferings at this dreadful time. I was sent to Patmos for preaching God's word. It was His Day, and a huge feeling came over me like a wave. I heard a voice as if behind me, strident as a trumpet:

'Write down all you see and send it to the seven churches....'

I turned sharply round, and as I did I saw seven lit gold
lampstands and an enlightened man in a long robe tied at the
waist with a gold band. His hair was white as snow, his eyes
intent as fire: his feet polished brown like bronze, his voice like
waves breaking.

I can still see him as clearly.

In his right hand he's holding seven stars, and then out of his
mouth where his tongue was comes a double-edged sword...his
face becomes so bright it is blinding.

I started to feel hot and faint, then the room was rotating as I
fell.

He lays his hand on my shoulder, his voice suddenly gentle.
'Don't be afraid, *it is I,* the First and the Last, the Living One. I
am Life, and the truth of who you are....I was dead, but now I
will live forever. I hold the keys of death, and your underworld.

Now draw in words all you see of what is happening, *and
things that are still to come.* And see it symbolically: the seven
stars are the angels of the churches ,and the seven lampstands
are the churches themselves.

Tell them this:

I know about you: I can see how hard you work and what
you're putting up with. I know your aversion to evil and how
you tested those pseudo-apostles with the claims they were

461

making. However: *you have less love than you used to.* Remember how you were: this is your turning.

I know your trials, and how poor you are although rich in spirit: and the rubbish you've had thrown at you by those Satanic synagogue goers. Don't be afraid of what is coming: you will be tested, but only for a matter of days.

I know how you've kept the faith, with this demonic Emperor-worship all around you, King Satan enthroned; and when beloved Antipas was murdered for his witness. But some of you still eat from old recipe books, which is not the food you need now.

I know how generous you are too. I know your devotion. But you're giving space to a woman who does not have your best interests at heart. I've watched and waited, but she isn't changing. She will have trouble until she sees that *it is I who search your hearts and minds and give what each of you need and deserve.*

And you: you are supposed to be alive, but you're dead! Wake up—revive what little you have left! How enthusiastic you were when you first heard the message—what happened to all that? Remember it now while you still can before the thief comes in the night that is my disguise.

I've opened a door that no one will be able to close. You've kept my commandments as they—in all their apparent superiority—will recognise. And I will keep you safe in this time of Great Transparency which is coming...which is in fact already here. Hold on to what you have inside, knowing it is your prize.

462

But you: what can I say? You're neither hot or cold—you're lukewarm, and I can't hold you in my mouth. I spit you out. You think you're rich, but actually you have nothing...you try to ignore your naked humanity. I'm warning you: the true gold, tested by fire, is what you need. New clothes: and new eyes—I'm telling you what you need to hear, not what you want to hear. I'm standing at the door and knocking. Can you hear me?

The sound of knocking.

You will feed from the tree of life in Paradise.
The crown of life will be your prize.

I will give you the hidden manna and the white stone
with a new name, only known
by the man or woman that receives it.

You will have authority. You will have the Morning Star.

I will give you a white robe, and your name
will remain in the Book of Life.

I will make you pillars in the sanctuary
of the temple of the New Jerusalem

and if you open the door to me now,
I will come in and sit beside you.

The knocking stops...there is an intense silence. Somewhere the sound of waves, just audible, breaking far below.

Then out of the shadows steps a Roman historian, middle-aged, with short greying hair, in a cloak.

He speaks as he moves, as if dictating a letter, gesturing with his right hand, turning and walking and pausing.

Life had become no longer reasonable. Maybe it never had been—maybe we were fooling ourselves. But Rome was a pretty easy place to be; it was tolerant, we were tolerant. You could mostly live as you wanted and practise what you wanted as long as you didn't make a nuisance of yourself. There were many gods after all, and we were a plural society. We had all the confidence an Empire could afford; we were the centre of the world, after all.

Emperors could be more or less likeable or admirable: usually they cared, at least to some degree, about being liked by the people...but mostly their intrigues and dramas didn't concern us any more than your own leaders do now. We had our own lives, our own anxieties, and our own attempts at happiness. At the very least, we had our humour. We loved life too; we loved our wives, we even loved our slaves though history will deny it, of course. Values change, and history is the story of those changes.

Nero changed everything: his single appalling trajectory and descent not only increasingly threatened our prosperity and stability as a city, it did something more disturbing. Nero was the underbelly of the city itself that perhaps we'd taken for granted—he was its seething unconsciousness, he was absolutely its lack of conscience. And it had all started so well (apparently) with his homage to Claudius, his uncle, whom he secretly despised. But then look at his father, after all—like father, like son! Nero was a country bumpkin (they say Jesus was, too) so the chip on his shoulder was as huge as his ego and his lack of experienced love. He craved our love, and for a while he would do anything for it, but it was always for his own aggrandisement and he made it his own ruin because he believed it gave him the permission to do anything he wanted.

Nero wasn't an emperor—he was merely desperate to be someone. He was a better singer than he could ever have been any genuine figure of authority: he was an artist, an *artiste*, rather: a massively ambitious amateur: and he was a complete narcissist. We—the Roman people—were food for his table, supplies for his ego-state, especially when it wavered. Which of course it did, more and more frequently, and then he was paranoid because he knew in truth he was hated; and the more he became hated, the more of a monster he became. He was a hideous overblown child, a thumb-sucking soul-sucking psychopath living entirely out of his lust for recognition and nourishment. His feasts from noon to midnight in the Field of Mars, and by the artificial lake he created lined with brothels ready to welcome him ashore: his rape of Rubraea (the vestal virgin): the horror of his mock-marriage to that poor boy Sporus (who he had castrated for the part); the incest with his mother Aggrippina, even inside a public carriage...then his murder of her, after every other attempt to make himself look guiltless had failed. Then he kicks poor Poppaea, his wife, to death while she's sick and pregnant with his own child.

But then—oh then—he turns on his own city *as if it was himself.* Neropolis! And what does he do? He sets fire to Rome! He orders his own guard to take out burning torches into all our narrow familiar streets! He torches our city! And he watches: he watches it all from the height of his own depravity, and picks up his lyre to sing that poem about Troy's burning as if it wasn't really happening for real at all. And so The Beast was born.

In your day, he would have been sectioned: but you can't

465

section an emperor: you have to dispose of him, sometimes by any means possible.

The Beast was born, and he made the whole of Rome seem beastly. The Forum, the amphitheatre, the market places, the temples and the taverns with all their repetitive rituals and lewd graffiti (as if all Romans really cared about was their cocks, which was also true!)—he made it all as disgusting as he was himself: vain, utterly self-centred, and insane. As a friend of mine put it: 'He was a mansion in a house of vice.' And of course he set the tone for those who followed after him—Galba, Otho, Vitellius—all ruthless opportunists in their own way. Farewell Caesar and Augustus! Nero was the template, his behaviour the benchmark.

Meanwhile those Christians had to pay the price. Someone, after all, must be to blame for it. What perfect suspects they were, refusing to worship in public, keeping themselves to themselves or sometimes openly making the sign of the cross. People knew something of what they were about with their worship then assumed they must be cannibals and practising incest behind closed doors with all their talk of brother and sister and love one another. They weren't always the friendliest of people either, it has to be said—and hardly surprising since they'd been persecuted—but their aloof disdain did not help their cause. And everyone knew they hated the Jews as well. No love lost there—or gained, for that matter. They wouldn't take part in games, theatre or processions: they wouldn't put garlands on their outside door during festivals. All they saw were false gods all around them. Well, they were harmless: which is why they made perfect scapegoats. What could the consequences ever be?

So this is what Nero did to them. Our old friend Tacitus puts it succinctly:

First, Nero had self-acknowledged Christians arrested. Then, on their information, large numbers of others were condemned—not so much for incendiarism as for their anti-social tendencies. Their deaths were made farcical. Dressed in wild animals skins, they were torn to pieces by dogs, or crucified, or made into torches to be ignited after dark as substitutes for daylight. Nero provided his Gardens for the spectacle, and exhibited displays in the Circus, at which he mingled with the crowd—or stood in a chariot, dressed as a charioteer. Despite their guilt as Christians, and the ruthless punishment it deserved, the victims were pitied. For it was felt that they were being sacrificed to one man's brutality rather than to the national interest.*

Who knows, but they were on our conscience, their cynical murder one of many last straws. And in the greater scheme of things they were a sacrifice to a consciousness that was only beginning to dawn above the whole edifice of our culture and its lower three chakras. They had stepped, or tripped, even unknowingly (and illiterately) into the heart, humanity's heart, where all were equal in the sight of their God and no human hierarchy existed. They—it must seem obvious now—were the future. And they were a revolution that had waited for millennia to happen.

And for that revolution, that evolution, to happen, the world in a different way would also have to burn—not as Nero burnt it, but inside our very souls. Their eyes, always so clear and bright, were that burning. They knew the fire as they would know it for centuries still to come, among themselves, even...

Well, the great ones prayed for their enemies: but they were human, they cursed their enemies too. It wasn't long before their

*Tacitus, The Annals of Imperial Rome, transl. Michael Grant (Penguin 1956) p. 365-6

religion would become illegal but in the meantime there was also a place they could be sent outside the city walls where they couldn't cause any trouble—and that was Patmos. Goodness knows how they lived there, and there was (as you can imagine) nothing on earth to do.

Some of them must have been quite well to do, otherwise they would simply have been bumped off in Rome. Some of course were Roman anyway, which was also the point—Roman Christians, converts, and people of standing as well as intelligence. I can't say for sure how any of it worked: I remained in Rome until the time of my death. But it was never the same place, and never the same world, again. We saw the seeds sown of what became our own judgement. Perhaps, after all, we tolerated the intolerable; we reasoned the unreasonable, and in the design that watches over our lives it was, as one of our own kind would later say, our Decline and Fall.

He dissolves into the shadows as the old man returns into your awareness, sitting with his eyes closed...his forehead slowly illuminated. There are writing materials in front of him. He speaks again...raising his right hand in a mudra, thumb and fourth finger aligned; and moments opening his eyes.

His expression follows what he is describing.

A

CHAPTERS 4–10

I'M SEEING a door open in heaven, and the same voice speaking to me: 'Come up here—I'll show you the future.'

A great energy came into me.

Through the door, a throne: and a figure sitting on it in light that is clear as diamond and blood-red as ruby...and around him, and his raised seat, a rainbow of green, emerald-green like virgin forest. And around this throne in a circle, twenty four others like the hours of day and night, and twenty four elders in spirit sitting on them, with gold crowns on their heads like kings.

And from the throne, flashes of lightning! And thunder, rolling...seven flaming lamps blazing there, the seven angels of God.

And between me and the throne—a sea, a sea like glass, like crystal so it was simultaneously near and far.

In the centre around the throne itself: four animals, or animal beings, with eyes in the front and the back of their heads; all seeing like God

the first, lion-like
the second, bull-like
the third, with a human face
the fourth, an eagle in flight—

all winged, surrounded by all seeing
all singing, constantly singing like a mantra

Holy holy holy
is the Lord God almighty
as he was, is, and is to come

—and every time they sang this, the twenty four elders leaned forward to worship the one who sat on the throne, removing their crowns and saying

You are our Lord and our God
this Oneness you are
full of grace and power
maker of all that is
that exists by Your Will—

I gaze again at the throne: and the figure sitting there is holding a scroll, which has writing on both sides, and is sealed with seven seals.

Then there's a powerful angel who is asking out loud 'Is there anyone here who is worthy of opening this scroll and breaking its seals? Is there?'

No one moves. There is no one. It made me cry to see that! But then one of the elders leans towards me and says 'No need to cry: the lion of Judah, the essence of David, has triumphed— *he* will open the scroll and break its seals.'

Now I'm seeing, between the throne and the elders, a lamb that has been sacrificed...with seven horns, seven eyes like the angels God has sent out all over the world tonight.

This lamb (this man), steps forward to take the scroll from the right hand of the figure on the throne—and as he does so, the four animals bow down, and the elders bow down: each of them holding small harps and a golden bowl full of incense that is the essence of the prayers of all the saints. And they're singing:

470

You are worthy to take the scroll
and break its seals
because you died for us, and with your blood
you bought us for God—
people of every race and nation;

you made us priests and kings
to serve the Lord and steer the world.

And now a rumbling like many feet, and a seething of wings—
and innumerable angels gathering in, I mean thousands and
thousands, all shouting

'The Lamb is worthy of all power, wisdom, strength, glory and
blessing!'

And now everything in Creation is joining in: *'All praise to the*
One on the throne!'

The four animals reply: *'Amen.'* And the elders bow again.

Now the lamb is breaking one of the seals and one of the
animals thunders *'Come.'*

A white horse appears, its rider like Sagittarius holding a bow.
He's given a crown of victory: he rides away to victory.

The lamb breaks the second seal. Again the voice, *'Come.'*

A second horse, this one red, vermilion, and its rider is being
told to take peace away and get people killing each other! He's
given a massive sword.

Then the third seal, broken. Again, the voice, and now a black horse with its rider carrying a set of scales to weigh food in as an animal voice announces sardonically: 'A ration of corn for a whole day's labour, and three of barley; but don't you dare touch the oil or the wine!'

Then the fourth seal, and again the voice with its command.

And now this horse, so pale it could be a ghost; and its rider is emaciated, skeletal, that some have called 'Plague.' And he's given licence to kill as well.

He breaks the fifth seal, and underneath the altar I'm seeing all the souls of the people who have been killed because they witnessed him and the Word, and they seem to be shouting 'Master, how much longer before there's retribution?' Each of them are being give a white robe in the spirit, and being told to be patient *until the roll is complete*, which made it sound like destiny.

Then the ground starts to shake...and the sun is being eclipsed—black sun, no light...but in the sky, look, the moon is turning red...and the stars are dropping like meteors, shaken like figs off a tree! Look at the sky! It's disappearing like a scroll rolled up...

All this while the sixth seal is broken.

Everyone is taking to the hills and mountains to hide in the caves and among the rocks. They're saying 'Hide us, we can't bear to be seen! Hide us from His Rage.'

For the Great Day of his anger has come, and who can survive its napalm?

Now my eyes expand over the earth, and I'm seeing four angels standing at its corners—north, south, east and west—holding the four winds back to keep them from blowing.

Then there's another angel rising in the east where the sun comes, carrying a seal, and he's calling to the angels 'Wait! Wait before you do any damage until we have sealed the foreheads of God's servants!'

I hear they number 144,000: twelve thousand from each of the twelve tribes.

Now I'm seeing a multi-racial multitude of people from every nation, and they're standing in front of the throne like a peaceful army dressed in white robes, and holding palm fronds in their hands. And they're shouting *'Victory to the Lamb!'*

All the angels are bowing in front of the throne touching the ground with their foreheads and saying 'Amen.'

One of the elders starts speaking to me: 'Do you know who these people are and where they've come from?' I tell him surely he can tell me. He says 'These people have come through the great persecution, and because of their purity, they're standing here.' He continues 'They are protected now: they will never hunger or thirst again, and neither the sun or the scorching desert wind will plague them. He will only lead them to fertile ground and running water and all the tears will disappear from their eyes.'

473

I gazed in wonder, as one of their kind.

And now he's breaking the seventh seal. Silence. Everything stops. Everything goes still.

Half an hour or so passes.

Now something is happening again. Trumpets. Trumpets are being handed to the seven angels who stand near the throne. Another angel has a golden censer that's like a scoop or shovel, and he steps forward to the altar. He's given a pile of incense to light, with the prayers of the saints; the smoke is rising in billowing clouds, it smells divine. But then he's filling it with fire from the altar—he turns—and he throws it down on the earth! And there's lightning, thunder, and the earth is shaking, quaking.

Can you hear it?

Now the seven angels are standing in a line. They lift the trumpets to their lips. The first blows into his:

and hail, fire
mixed with blood
drops onto the earth beneath
and the trees, the grass is scorched—

The second angel blows:

and a mountain of fire, on fire
is falling into the sea!
And the sea is turning into blood...
ships are sinking...

The third angel blows:

and a huge comet is falling from the sky
blazing, burning, into rivers and springs

this is the star called Wormwood
because it's bitter, and it turns the water
into itself; you can die from drinking it.

The fourth angel blows:

and sun moon and stars are blasted!
There's no light for part of the day or the night.

And now I'm seeing an eagle flying overhead and calling

'Trouble, trouble, trouble
for all the people of the earth
at the sound of the trumpet!'

The fifth angel follows:

and I saw an angel that had fallen who was once a morning star

and he's being given a key to the shaft
that leads down into the Abyss...

He unlocks it; and smoke pours upwards
darkening the sun and the sky...

and out of the smoke, locusts, dropping
become like scorpions on the ground

told to attack anyone who was unsealed—
not to kill them, but to give them pain

months of pain, so they long to die
as they were.

Locusts, like horses armed for battle!
Crowns on their head, faces that seem human
hair like women, teeth like lions
                              imagine

body-armour like iron, and their wings whirring
like a charge of horses and chariots—

tails like scorpions, ready to sting

led by the Angel of the Abyss
whose name is Abaddon and Apollyon

destruction and *ruin* in Hebrew and Greek.

Then the sixth angel stepped forward, his trumpet raised to
his lips:

and a voice from the four horns of the golden altar is saying

'Release the four angels chained
in the great river Euphrates!'

These angels had been positioned for this moment

to destroy a third of the human race
with thousands upon thousands in their army

horses, and riders with their breastplates of flame
hyacinth-blue and sulphur-yellow

the horses with their lions' heads
fire, smoke and sulphur coming out of their mouths...

Three plagues from the three of these
wiping out unregenerate humanity.

Such power in their mouths
and their tails, their tails like snakes
their heads like battering rams...

But even the people that survive
will refuse to abandon their idols
or stop worshipping their devils
or renounce their killing
their dark arts, their lust
and their thieving.

You know who they are...

Another potent angel is descending from heaven
wrapped up in a cloud, a rainbow over his head;

477

his face like the sun, his legs pillars of fire.

He has a small scroll in his hand, unrolled
his right foot in the sea, his left on land
and he shouts so loud
it's like a lion roaring!

Seven claps of thunder respond!
I am getting ready to write,
and then I hear a voice saying

'Keep those thunder-words secret;
do not write them down...'

Then the angel raises his right hand in heaven
swearing by the One who lives forever and ever
and made earth and heaven with all there is
the earth with all it bears, the sea with all it holds,
and says

'The time of waiting is over
when the seventh angel blows his trumpet,
God's secret intention will be fulfilled
just as he spoke to his prophets...'

Now I'm hearing the voice that spoke to me from heaven
speaking again:

'Go and take the scroll out of that angel's hand,
standing on sea and land—'

I go to take it, and he says to me

478

'Take, eat.
It will turn your stomach sour
but in your mouth it will be
as sweet as honey.'

So I do as he tells me;
as it is as he has told me.

Then again:

'You are to prophesy, this time
about many different nations, countries
languages, and world leaders.'

CHAPTERS 11–16

NOW I'M BEING GIVEN a reed, straight as a rod, and I'm being told 'Go and measure God's sanctuary: the altar, and the people who worship there...but leave out the outer court because it's been given to non-believers, and you know they are going to trample on the holy city for three and a half years.

What is measured is spared.

The rest is Rome; home of the Beast.

I will send my two witnesses, dressed in ashes.

They are the symbolic olive trees, and the lamps that stand before the Lord of the World.

There will always be names for them:

Moses, Elijah
Joshua, Zerubabbel
Peter, Paul (that was Saul).

Fire will come from their mouths and burn up anyone who tries to harm them!

They can lock up the sky so it doesn't rain!

They can turn water into blood! They can send plague into the world as often as they like!

And then this: when they have witnessed, *the Beast will kill them.*

Their bodies will lie on the main street of the city that is Sod Them All, and Egypt, land of the slaves; the imperial mind in which our Lord is crucified.

Men from every nation will stare at them and forbid them to be buried!

They will celebrate their death with present-giving, and meaningless expressions of relief!

These two prophets have been a pain in the arse of the world...

However: after three and a half days, the Almighty breathes life into them, and they stand up!

Everyone is absolutely terrified.

A loud voice from above says 'Come up, dear ones' and in sight of everyone they are gathered up in a cloud.

It's mental.

There's a violent earthquake. A tenth of the city collapses. Seven thousand people are killed. The rest can only thank God they have been spared!

And now the seventh angel raises his trumpet:

and there are voices in heaven announcing
that the kingdom of the world has become
the kingdom of the Lord, forever.

The elders bend and touch the round with their foreheads, giving thanks and announcing the time of judgement and retribution for all the witnesses, all the prophets, all the saints.

The world will tilt on its axis where it was weighed to evil.

'The time has come to destroy those who are destroying the earth'

Heaven opens: the Ark of the Covenant is visible.

Then lightning
                thunder
                              earthquake
                                            hail

whiting out the screen of your mind.

And now a great sign: blazing with light, and in the light, a woman, a beautiful pregnant woman standing in the moon: the moon full of the sun's light, and she's clothed with it, her nakedness clothed, and twelve stars on her glittering crown.

Then she's in labour; she's crying aloud.

Then a second sign: a huge seven-headed dragon with ten horns, each head crowned with the power of evil. And its tail a dragnet full of stars it drops towards the earth.

It stops in front of the woman giving birth, its seven tongues hanging out, only wanting to eat the child as soon as it appears (which of its disgusting heads will have the first bite?).

The woman leans back and leaves...it's a boy, he's a king, *set to rule with an iron sceptre*...and he's taken straight up to God as she wraps herself in what she has, and runs, into the desert, where a safe place awaits her during these hellish days.

AND NOW THERE IS WAR IN HEAVEN—Michael and his angels attack the dragon!

The dragon lashes back, its heads and tail sweeping like an angry cat...but Michael drives him back, and then out, yes!

Primeval serpent,
this world's deceiver,
Satan by any other name
                    is hurled

—along with all his twisted accomplices—

down to the earth's surface, burning up as he descends, howling with pain

as a voice from above shouts out *'Victory! And for Christ! By his blood! And for all those martyrs who surrendered! Their power!'*

Let the heavens rejoice!

But for you on earth, trouble is coming. You have a raging devil to contend with now because he knows his days are numbered.'

The snake-devil lands, and as soon as he does, he goes after the woman!

Which way did that bitch go?

Ah, but look: she's given a great pair of eagle's wings...and she runs, she runs, she takes off and flies!

She flies towards the desert and her safe place.

Satan-serpent stopped in his tracks vomits water like a gushing river after her!

He farts with fury!

But the earth opens up like a great sink hole to swallow the foul water—

Diabolical dragon then slouches off to make war on the rest of her children who live for Christ in their hearts.

I'm standing on the seashore now, the island behind me. I'm looking into the waves, then a little way out to sea when the water parts and up rises this disgusting monster: it has seven heads, ten horns, each horn crowned again as before, and its heads all have blasphemous names like NERO, GALBA, OTHO, VITELLIUS: their fat ugly faces flashing briefly into view.

The Beast is like a leopard, paws like a bear, mouth like an amphitheatre lion—dragon has given him the power. One of his heads appears to have a fatal wound, but had recovered: and after that the whole stupid world had marvelled and followed this dinosaur.

Look at them kneeling as he passes saying 'Who can compare with you? How can anyone defeat you?'

The Beast mouths its blasphemies as it goes in procession, against God, against whatever it wants to malign. It can do whatever it pleases; it has free rein. Everyone will worship its purple, stunned by its filthy charisma...only those whose names are in the Book of Life have the power to resist.

Listen:
Captivity for those destined for captivity;
the sword for those who will die by it.

Now the ground breaks open behind me as a second beast emerges. It has two horns like a ram—but it sounds like a dragon. It is the Beast's servant, the Beast's PA, getting subscriptions for him everywhere. It can even work miracles, pseudo-miracles, this secretarial beast...as it organises the creation of a statue for the first. It even breathes life into the statue so that the damn thing speaks!

'I am a stupid emperor, can't you see?
But if you do not worship *me*
I'll have you put to death immediately—'

And in the meantime he has everyone branded on the right
hand or the forehead like a slave. You literally cannot function
in the world unless you have evidence of this.

Name: emperor. Number: 666.

Now I'm seeing Mt. Zion in these rocks ascending...and
standing on the mountain is Christ, who has a multitude with
him, all of the 144,000 with God's name written on their
foreheads. A sound is coming out of the sky like the ocean and
it's full of harp strings all resonating. There is the singing of a
new hymn in the presence of the animals and the elders, in a
language that can only be learnt and spoken by the saved.
These are the pure ones who follow Christ in truth wherever
he leads them.

There's another angel, flying high overhead now, announcing
the Good News of eternity to all of us who live here—every
nation, race and tribe. He's calling *'Hey! Fear God and praise
him because the time has come: worship the Creator.'*

A second angel behind him is calling *'Babylon has fallen,
Babylon the Great has fallen! You have drunk the wine of God's
anger!'*

A third angel follows: *'All of you who worship the Beast will*

*have to drink God's wine! Fire and brimstone! It tastes like
torture! There is no respite for those who worship the Beast!'*

And a voice is saying to me in my inner ear:

*'Write this down:
If you die in Christ, you die happy!
You can rest forever in the good things you've done.'*

A white cloud, and a man sitting on it, with a gold crown and a
sharp sickle in his hand. Then another angel appears out of the
sanctuary and shouts to him:

'Put your sickle in and reap: this is the harvest of time, and it's ripe!'

He set to work, this harvester-reaper.

Another angel who is also carrying a sharp sickle comes out
and shouts across:

*'Put your sickle in and cut all the bunches of grapes from the
vine—they're ripe!*

He is meant the earth's vine. Now the angel sets to work as
well; and the whole earth's vintage is loaded into a winepress

the winepress of God's anger

trodden until the wine came up like blood to the horses'
bridles, for miles around.

So much anger, however...

Seven angels are bringing the plagues that are the last of it all, because with them, His anger dies.

And perhaps, my own.

I see a glass lake suffused with fire, and beside it, all those who had fought against The Beast and won. They all had harps and they were all singing 'The Song of Moses' from Exodus.

As they finished, the sanctuary itself, the Tent of the Testimony, opens: and out come those angels dressed in white with golden sashes round their waists.

One of the four animals gave the angels seven gold bowls filled with Holy Rage. It was so intense that the smoke filled the temple, and no one could go into it until this expression was complete.

A voice is shouting: 'Go and empty the seven bowls of God's anger over the planet!'

It is a terrible, searing cry.

The first angel empties his bowl on the earth:

and all those who had worshipped the Beast
broke out into disgusting sores.

The second angel empties his bowl over the sea:

and the water turns immediately to blood
as everything in the water dies—

The third angel empties his bowl into the rivers:

they turn into blood, too
                           red rivers, red springs

and the angel of the water is saying

'You are the Holy One, the Just One
and this is the punishment for those
who killed the messengers, and it is right—'

Even the altar itself agrees.

The fourth angel empties his bowl over the sun:

it scorches like a sauna
but with fire, not water
and still the idiot multitude cursed
not understanding any of it—

The fifth angel empties his bowl over the Beast's throne:

and the lights go out all over the empire
men biting their tongues for pain...
but still they're cursing!

The sixth angel empties his bowl over the Euphrates:

all the water dries up, and here's the way
for the Kings of the East to come in
(those Parthians the Romans love to fear—)

and now from the fangs of the dragon,
the mouth of the Beast, and all his false witnesses
three horrible spirits of halitosis emanate...

like frogs! Demon spirits, though
able to work miracles for show
and going out to the kings of the world

to call them together for ARMAGEDDON.

This is how it will be. *I will come like a thief in the night.*
Remember?

The seventh angel empties his bowl into the air:

and a voice shouts from the sanctuary
'The end has come!'

Flashes of lightning, peals of thunder
the most violent earthquake in the history of man

erupts through Rome-Babylon
split into three along its fault line—

as other cities collapse like so much trash

islands vanish in a tidal wave

even the mountains disappear

and great hailstones the size of cannon balls

489

are falling on the people,
as they curse on...

B

CHAPTERS 17–18

NOW ONE OF THE ANGELS comes to speak to me. he says:
'Come over here and I'll show you the fate of the famous
courtesan *who rules enthroned beside abundant waters*...the one
who all the kings of this world have fucked with, and who's
made everyone in this world drunk with the wine of her
adultery!'

We're talking about a place and a culture, not an individual
woman. But here she is:

He takes me quick as a flash in spirit to the desert; then I see it.

A great scarlet beast, again with seven heads and ten horns;
seven hills, ten kings; one beast, one filthy incestuous
emperor—

and she's riding him like an emperor, in purple and scarlet,
glittering with gold, jewels and pearls; and she's holding a
golden wine cup full of a disgusting broth made of sweat,
semen and vaginal secretions:

and on her forehead is a name

BABYLON THE GREAT

mother of all whores and the dark arts of lust

—*she has no heart!*
Her heart is a hollow cavern of pain!
She has betrayed her heart to the trade—

She is drunk on the blood of the saints
and all the martyrs of Jesus

and I'm absolutely stupefied
(what woman could be so diabolical?)
The angel is saying he will explain.

'The Beast we have seen was Nero: he is dead. His evil spirit
will rise out of the Abyss *but only to go to his destruction.*

And the people of the world who were seduced by the Beast
will think it an extraordinary thing; he was dead, but the curse
of him lives on.

The seven heads are also emperors. Five of them have already
gone to Hades, one is here now: one is yet to come, and will
stay for a short while.

The Beast meanwhile is going to his destruction.

The ten horns are kings who have not yet been given their
power, and will have it only for a single hour because of the
Beast. They are all for the Beast and will go to war against the
Lamb.

But the Lamb is the Lord of all, and the King of kings. Do you understand?

He cannot in the end be defeated.'

The angel continues as I listen, standing beside him in spirit:

'The waters you saw are all the people of the world. But the time will come when the Beast will turn against the courtesan, strip off her clothes and leave her naked, eat her flesh and burn her remains in the fire.

God knows all of this in advance, and arranges it accordingly in ways we simply don't realise.

The courtesan, a symbol, is Rome—and all that Rome symbolises.'

Then another angel arrives, irradiated with light. And he's shouting at the top of his voice:

'Babylon has fallen! Babylon the Great has fallen! She's derelict, she's the home of everything unnatural. Everyone has been under her spell, every merchant's wealth has come out of her lust!'

And another voice is saying:

'Come away from her, so you avoid her taint and her punishment. Her sins have reached heaven and God knows all her crimes: she's to be paid in her own coin. And paid double.

Every single one of her killing shows and orgies will become a

492

torture and a grief. Like will be met with like.

Meanwhile, she's smug on her throne. And one day, it will all go tits up.'

There will be grief for her from everyone who's consorted with her. They will see the smoke as she burns, but will also keep a safe distance from her agony.

All the traders will join in when there's no one left to buy their stuff...

All the fruits you set your heart on
have failed:

gone forever, and never coming back
is your millionaire life of luxury and ease.

They will wonder at her catastrophic demise.
As you will also, in your own time.

All the captains and sailors will throw dust on their heads as they watch the great conflagration; and heaven will applaud as everything explosive in her ignites...

and all the blood that was ever shed.

A huge angel picks up a huge boulder like a millstone and hurls it into the sea, saying 'It will be like this. So may it be. Babylon will be like Atlantis, never seen again.'

And all the blood that was ever shed.

493

Never again in you, Babylon; never again.

My joy is in your burning.

The flames reach the sky.

And behind it, a new dawn invisibly beginning when the rage is done.

And after this, the sound of a huge crowd in heaven singing *Alleluija* and *Victory*.

And the elders and the animals lean forwards, and kneel down.

Now a voice from the throne:

'Praise God, all of us
who great and small revere him!'

And they answer *'Alleluija. God's reign has begun. Now to the marriage of the Lamb. His bride is ready: she's in dazzling white linen, pure as love—'*

The angel tells me: *'Write this:*

Everyone invited to this wedding is happy.
Everything you've written is sent from God.'

I'm bowled over, and I go to kneel at his feet, but he says gently *'No, don't do that. I'm in service just like you and all your friends who are witnesses. It's God alone you must kneel to.'*

C

CHAPTERS 19–20

NOW HEAVEN OPENS and a white horse is standing there: his rider is Faithful and True.

He's a judge with integrity, a warrior for justice.

His eyes are flaming alive, his head crowned; his name is known only to himself

...and his cloak is soaked in blood.

He is the Word of God.

Behind him, dressed in dazzling white, are the armies of heaven on white horses.

There's a sharp sword in his mouth called *discrimination*. He is the channel of Divine Fire, holy rage.

An angel is standing in the sun and he's shouting to all the birds: *'Come gather at the great feast! Flesh of kings, generals, heroes, riders, all kinds of men; business men, citizens, bureaucrats and slaves, small and great.'*

Then the Beast with all his huge army gathered to fight the white rider...

but pretty soon the Beast is taken prisoner, taken alive with the false prophet who worked under him, and they are thrown into a burning fiery lake that strips the skin and viscera from their bones...

All the rest are killed in battle: and then the birds descend on their bodies.

It's a great day to be a vulture.

Another angel descends with the key to the Abyss and an enormous chain. He pins down the dragon and binds him with it, wrapping it round and round his venomous scaly skin.

Then he throws him into the Abyss.

He slams the entrance shut over him.

(This is for a thousand years. He will be released again then, but only for a short time...).

Now I'm seeing thrones—and those who are given the power to judge sitting down on them. And the souls of all those who had been beheaded for witnessing Jesus and preaching his Word—refusing the Beast—come back to life again out of the spiritual world, and reigning with Christ.

This is known as the first resurrection: the rest will follow in a millennium.

These are the elect for our world.

When this next thousand years are over, *Satan will be released again.*

He will deceive all the nations and mobilise Gog and Magog for war again.

His armies will be fighting in every nation and they will besiege the camp of the saints, the city God loves...

But fire will come down from heaven and erase them.

Then Satan will himself be thrown into the burning lake of sulphur like the spectre that he is, and his shadow will groan in agony with all his satanic companions.

You may name them. You will know of them.

Their torture will know no end.

A great white throne, now...and earth and sky are vanishing...

and the dead are standing there
great and small
as the Book of Life is opened
and the other records too
with all they've done...

The sea is giving up the dead!
Hades is emptied of the dead!
They are all gathering,
and are all judged by what they have lived...

Then death and the underworld itself are thrown into the
lake—

that is the second death
that takes anyone whose name
is not in the Book of Life.

D

CHAPTERS 21-22

AND NOW THERE IS
a new heaven, and a new earth
the first has disappeared
there is no longer any sea...
and the Holy City
the *Civitas Dei*
is descending
beautiful as a bride
dressed for her husband-to-be.

A loud voice is calling:
'You see this city?
Here's where God
lives among us—
he will make his home here
we shall be his people
his names is God-with-us.

He will dry the tears in our eyes,
there is no more death,
no grieving or sadness
now the past has gone.'

The Oneness on the white throne says:
'I am making the whole of creation new.
Write this, John of Patmos,
what I'm saying will come true.
What I'm saying is already accomplished
because I am the Alpha and the Omega
I am the Beginning and the End
and I will give the water of life
to anyone who is thirsty, for free;
anyone who wants to live
is a son or daughter to me.

But cowards, liars, killers?
Ah, the lake must take them
until they learn how to live.'

Then one of the seven angels who held the bowls of plague
comes to speak to me. He says :

'Come, I will show you the bride.'

He takes me in spirit
up a very high mountain
and from there he shows me
THE NEW JERUSALEM
coming down out of the air
with all the radiant glory of God

glittering like crystal-clear diamond;
high walls, twelve gates
at each gate an angel
and over the gates
the names of the twelve tribes
where all our story began;
three gates for each of the directions
the walls on twelve foundation stones
each of then named with an apostle.

The angel is carrying a gold measuring rod in his hand to show
me its perfect proportions, its golden mean.

The plan of the city is square: its length the same as its breadth.

He's measuring it all to show me...

Twelve thousand furlongs in length, breadth, and height.
Its walls, 144 cubits high!
(that's 200 feet in your language)

The walls are diamond
the city pure gold, like polished glass
its foundations faced
with diamond, lapis, turquoise
crustal, ruby, golden quartz
malachite, topaz, emerald
sapphire, and amethyst.

Twelve gates: twelve pearls
each gate a single pearl,
the main street of the city all gold,

transparent as glass. And I see
there is no temple in the city
because God is the temple
the Lamb is the temple

—and the city has no need for sun or moon
because it's lit by divine radiance.

The pagan nations will live by its light!
The kings of the earth will bring it treasures!
Its gates will never be shut
by day or by night
it will always be an open place.

And nothing unclean can come into it
no one who's loutish or false
only those in the Book of Life
who are actually alive.

The rest can't even see it.

The angel is showing me the river of life
rising from the white throne of God
and running crystal clear down the city centre
flanked by trees, trees of life
that fruit twelve times a year
and its leaves are the cure for anything.

The throne in place,
we will see him face to face
his name written on our foreheads.

The angel says to me:
'What you've written is true, you will see.'

I say, treasure what you find here.

I, John, heard and saw all these things...and again I moved to
kneel at his feet, and again he said *Don't do that. I am in
service just like you. It is God we must worship.*

And he said: *'Don't keep this matter secret, either. The Time is
close. Meanwhile, let everyone continue as they are. Very soon, I
will be with you again, bringing everyone what he or she truly
deserves. Because I am the Alpha and the Omega, the First and
the Last, the Beginning and the End. Happy are those who have
cleansed themselves so they can enter in. The rest you know.'*

And with that he left, and I was alone but not alone; and the
island of my exile was a blessing

where the water of life is for free.

*The cave is slowly illuminated with dawn light, as he finally
stands and moves, emerging.*

Then slowly it returns to darkness again, like a door closing.

GENESIS CODA

The eye was formed by the light for the light
—*Goethe*

Nothing escapes the role of intimacy
—*Thomas Berry*

We come full circle, like the snake biting its tail, the alchemical ouroboros. It seemed appropriate to end with a modern poem that addresses our contemporary situation beside the transition from an 'old' to a 'new' earth that is so much our journey now, personally, politically, ecologically.

The form of the poem was suggested by the late Cantos of Ezra Pound and the experimental cut up/fold in technique of William Burroughs and Brion Gysin and contains a number of contemporary references including people who are part of this vital and inescapable movement. There is no turning back.

503

I N THE END...
 the beginning that is
continually evolving

    this experiment of Earth

*First first time nothing no been be only dasso God He one. God
He been make heaven and ground.*

She in his depths...

    and in this green song

A man walks by a river...on the path he has chosen

—left hand, left field—

...out of spirit

    into matter

ether into earth

    Saturn, Sun and Old Moon behind it

    Creation, the Beginning

    MADE NEW AGAIN

poised forever in its ever-present mystery

that is the
first time seen first moment First Day
in anything—

forever seen as if for the first time...

Warmth radiating in the direction of light
                              light into space

and humanity, only plant-like in potential
ether-dreamed
                    in their reverie

He been make heaven for put Angels there and also we people if
we been stop good for ground.

...having to leave the sun   as we would
one day have to leave the Garden

but first
this Moment born
full of Your Presence, present

gifted pure   as intended
minus all our interference
                              see it

stripped back intact
to its essence

and good   so good   we have forgotten *how* (good)

but in every first time we can remember

The Dangerous Book

as it was in the Beginning

                       and still is

                Genesis-generated...

A descent from the periphery of the planet

                            imagine

spirit incarnating   idea-vision   virgin-origin

where inside and outside are as a seamless garment

'Show us the glory in the grey'

                     you pray—

...the river now, passing the dark mouth of a tunnel
starting to gather momentum   drawn forward

             as if by a magnet

the first and last Great Auk

And in division

                the lines of Creation

                        like staves

on an unlined page

        THE FIRMAMENT

like a dome, they thought   on day 2   dividing the waters

—part rising up as vapour
                              part flowing down—

in reality, *tohu bohu*   all mixed up   like a soup

elemental and wild
                    like birth itself

...the river accelerating, sucked forward, sliding to a sheer drop
that is waterfall—
                   plummeting!

As he stands/hovers/ poised
in the eye of a cormorant

to dive
        —this leap of faith, guided

beyond control—

to find his healing

...'in the service of love, we follow the wild energies...'

that created
             and that make us

fruitful and fecund
                    from the Father's substance

the Mother's essence

God   Love
the Land
          ...dry land, appearing

Earth born out of water
                          as we are
(womb-water)

*For number three day God He been talk say 'Make all water for
ground i de join for one place and dry ground i de come out'*

And on it, within it
                          this miracle of life creating
              seeds
seminal
              as the earth itself

SOMETHING ENTIRELY NEW

as these forever springtime buds appearing revealing
leaves unfurling
                    viriditas
                                the green fuse

the group soul of plants
                          imagine

virgin forest all around him

508

green as the day
and beyond, the sea...

*For number three day God he been talk again say 'Make grass
and jamajama and stick I de grow for ground.' And onetime so i
been be.*

where nothing can be false to itself

but made for this place
as the sole of a foot
is for the ground it steps on

in truth
                not made to be separate

—any more than our eyes are from what they see—

sun moon and stars
                        this harmony

in tune with time and space   unmeasured   dreamt

these vast circadian rhythms
                        of day and night

we are not detached from
                        until we believe we can be

and then...
            dis-ease comes into being

that is our departure
                from divine order

that is thinking I can live my own life regardless
I can do my own thing
              —like Lucifer—
                      with impunity

believing we are free
              of our terrestial bodies

to amuse abuse objectify
              and now

we're paying the price
              that is poison

that is the cancer we are
              inside and out

with the earth our mirror...

Planet Poison
              the Anti-Christ
                    of (profit-driven) disconnection

the prophets of today say/shall be our undoing

Oh Adam return
              Adam, return now

to where you left Eve behind you,
as you swan ahead

now she is
(like this swan alone
in the inky river blackness)
                    this suffering earth
                                grief

we insistently transcend...

'How on earth have we managed it
          that we no longer live in a universe?'

               dreaming of outer space

colonising dead planets
                  in our fantasy

seriously insane
            above and below

fracking our way
            to impotence
                  prostrate

human/humus/humility
             the only answer

to the cry of
        ECOCIDE

to the nameless hurricane

                Henry, Imogen

that has no ego...

the disaster the belief that it is *ours*
and not the Garden we're here to guard

the ancient numbing fear

                unhealed

the resentment at having to survive (without gratitude) that makes
us hate our mother place

                'No love of the earth,' you exclaimed

as we comfort eat above

                drought, fire, flood

Your anger become GAIA

                like a (Munch) scream

what does it mean, what does it take
to turn the tanker round?

Titanic dissolution

                of our narcissistic fantasy

and the war that is always

                doomed to failure

the realisation

Genesis Coda

'that we are just another creature

with iron in our blood...' (as you say it, Fiona)

now the land is calling us
                              as the sky is

calling us back

on this fifth day our senses were born

cosmic rays streamed from above...
                                        the earth, the water
                        seeded
teeming with life
                        which means

'we are the People of the Earth,' as you sing it

                        pilgrims
        on this pilgrim star

come back to the Kingdom
                              as it was made to be

the shift
                that is the eye of the needle

voluntary simplicity
                        'How much do I really need?'

beside our refusal to live without

what is polluting the planet

sea of glass   become sea of plastic
land of hope   become landfill—

sarvodaya

       swaraj

           swadeshi

Now: see how it rises,
this Cathedral of Creation
with its dreaming spires

           and vaulted ceilings

in the vertical—

A fairytale castle with honeycomb towers,
glowing at night

        like the inside of a stone lantern...

      'insects for door knockers

tortoises supporting columns,

        leaves joined together as doorways

climbing vines on the walls of rooms,

        dragons looking at you...'

and the cupola
             with its crystal to come

a sun-hole of heaven
             radiantly clear

And that we were the crown
             created

not out of nothing
             but (like Gaudi—) out of God's own

endless glory
             you return to

        —like a bride to the May—

and as we may be
             miraculously forgiven

prodigal sons & daughters

where it is never too late
             for the dream
        the dawn

baptism that is immersion
in an orchestra of birdsong,
our heads thrust under
by the hands of life
             and fire

*

The Dangerous Book

Christ our epiphany
rex et regina
in every man woman
that is the Kingdom
here now and always
through all dimensions...

guided back into the heart of humanity

not away from it

ever again

by the monster that is ego—

the dragon slain

our Great Work

to cross this Rubicon

to heal the disconnection

Adam and Eve come back to the gate

preceded by all the animals

we humiliate

until we see them

as we are

in one great chain of being

as the soul of our sixth day sense

Are we ready to be born now,
yes, born again?

In the New Life forever inviting us

And on the seventh day
                              inside any other day

Rest
          and Being
                    blessed
                              to meditate

to be inside
          all that is being made

                    in the company of angels
                    the living and the dead

where we are the vessels
and You forever the wine

the Passion Alive
that calls us friends

*

*

*

NOTES

EPIGRAPHS: *The Cantos* (originally published by TS Eliot) from Faber & Faber, *Intimate Journals* by Lion Publishing, and Geoffrey Hill in *Mercian Hymns* (Penguin).

Rudolf Steiner from Christianity as Mystical Fact and Occult Mysteries of Antiquity (lecture, 1908: Rudolf Steiner Press, 1961) and Rowan Williams from his book *Silent Action—engagements with Thomas Merton* (SPCK, 2011).

My main text of reference was *The Bible Designed to Be Read as Literature* (Folio Society, 1957) and *The Jerusalem Bible* (1966)—with reference also to Tyndale's originals, and to the King James version, which retains a huge percentage of his work.

We encourage you to refer to the original Old Testament stories summarised in the poems.

SAMUEL: 'Pretender'—the opening phrase here is from James Joyce.

THE SONG OF SONGS: 'Reading Between the Lines' (note in full)

The Song of Songs is about the aches and joys of union and separation. The post-rationalisation for some Christians is that it is about Christ's love for the Church. It isn't. It's one of the first great love poems known in any language, and it evidently owes its origin to an actual, sensual relationship. The poem is very sexual (there are at least two references to oral sex in it) and part of its genius is in its blending and extending of sexuality with the natural world. This is what makes it beautiful as well as believably real.

That beauty is insistent in the high lyrical quality and pulse of the poetry, underscored by the free verse nature of Hebrew poetry itself with its capacity for improvisation, which is closest to the rhythms of actual speech. It is what we also find in the greatest of the Psalms (for example Psalm 22: 'Oh my God, my God, why have you forsaken me?').

The Song of Songs is also a psychological drama, which is how I have arranged it. It enacts a relationship between a woman and a man at an archetypal as well as personal level. Solomon, who as we know had many (many) women, falls in love—and is out of his depth—with this woman. She is a bit too special, and too real, and that is scary.

Solomon 'awakens' her, but is also afraid of being overwhelmed by her, and so 'disappears.' And then he reappears, while she is left alternately bereft and then is rekindled with hope again. The poem, fragmentary as it is, tells the story quite clearly. In many ways, too, it re-enacts the Greek mythopoeic story of Eros and Psyche.

One traditional idea is that this is about a wedding (the Folio Society edition describes it as a 'fragmentary wedding idyll'), but I would argue that it is about an affair, and that Solomon's protestation of marriage is disingenuous. He loves her in his own way but he is not about to marry her.

You may wonder how many other women he has said this or

something similar to. Indeed in the original he even repeats himself.

Another interesting thing for us today is that the Shulamite is clearly African; she's not an Israelite. Solomon was known to have had many liaisons with women from other tribes and cultures and this is part of the drama, drawing on what would have been public awareness—everybody knew. Symbolically it emphasises some of the differences between men and women, which is a subtext here.

In the contemporary language of attachment theory, Solomon is classically *avoidant* while she is *anxious*. At the same time, in this brief and brilliantly economical dramatic poem, there is a distinct *movement* in which she finally returns to herself and her 'vineyard,' while Solomon seems more preoccupied with financial worldly gain. She actually changes; she becomes stronger and more self-contained. There is an alchemy at work here.

At the same time, right at the close, when he calls to her again: what happens? She responds; and the cycle seems to begin all over again. We can read the poem as a circular drama as well. It begins when they are lovers, and that's where it ends. *For love is stronger than death.*

WISDOM: 'In the greatest number of the wise lies the world's salvation' is taken from Proverbs.

EPIGRAPHS (NEW TESTAMENT): Rudolf Steiner from *Christianity as Mystical Fact and Occult Mysteries of Antiquity* (lecture, 1908: Rudolf Steiner Press, 1961), CG Jung from *An Answer to Job* (Routledge & Kegan Paul, 1956), *Slow Train Coming* from CBS, and Rowan Williams from his book *Silent Action—engagements with Thomas Merton* (SPCK, 2011).

Magdalene: this poem would not have been possible without Cynthia Bourgeault's brilliant *The Meaning of Mary Magdalene* (Shambhala, 2012).

Genesis Coda: Thomas Berry from *The Great Work* (Bell Tower, New York, 1999).

Genesis Coda references: The Pidgin English quotations are from an edition of Dr. Frederick Justus Knecht's *Child's Bible History* (British Cameroons, 1934).

Rudolf Steiner's lectures on Genesis around 1910-1912 suggest a fascinating way of looking at the evolution of our planet and its previous conditions.

'The last Great Auk' (Fogo Island, Newfoundland) is taken from Kevin Durrant's *The Earth Will Teach You* (Wide Margin, Gloucester, 2014).

'Show us the glory in the grey' is from George MacLeod of Iona.

Viriditas is from Hildegard von Bingen (1098-1179), later appearing (as if by osmosis) in Dylan Thomas' 'The force that through the green fuse/drives the flower.' It is the concept of the green energy (sap) rising as it does each Spring. The life force.

J. Philip Newell's *The Book of Creation—the practice of Celtic spirituality* (Canterbury Press, 1999), which comments on the seven days of Creation, was also a significant inspiration ('in the service of love, we follow the wild energies').

For my brief anatomy of Planet Poison (and beyond), Thomas Berry's *The Great Work* (Bell Tower, NY, 1999) was required reading, alongside Andreas Moritz's *Cancer Is Not A Disease* (Ener-chi Wellness Press, USA, 2005).

Ecocide is a term coined by international lawyer Polly Higgins and her project Mission Lifeforce.

'Oh Adam return' quotes from my own *Improvisations* (Stride, 1994).

'We are the People of the Earth' is the title of a song by Stroud-based singer and poet Jehanne Mehta, with her trio *Earthwards*.

There are various trinities (as variations on the Trinity) in the poem, beginning with God/Love/the Land, taken from the Revd. Peter Owen Jones.

Sarvodaya (care of the earth), *swaraj* (personal change) and *swadeshi* (local economy) are Hindu concepts in Satish Kumar's *Soil, Soul, Society* (Leaping Hare Press, 2013).

The 'Cathedral of Creation' is Gaudi's dream-like Sagrada Familia in Barcelona, symbolically unfinished at the time of his death.

The concept of 'immersion' was also suggested by Peter Owen Jones. The final line of *The Dangerous Book* recalls how Jesus, with his enlightened understanding of intimacy, said to his disciples that he no longer called them servants, because a servant does not know his or her employer's business . 'Instead, I have called you friends, for everything that I learned from my Father I have made known to you' (John 15:15)

—J.R.

*

ACKNOWLEDGEMENTS

My main and most significant thanks are to my friend and collaborator Martin Palmer who supported and mentored me through this entire process, stage by stage. My compositions followed these discussions at his home south of Bath.

I am also very grateful to Deborah Loveday for making the crypt at All Saints church in Uplands, Stroud available, where half the Old Testament and all of the New Testament was written.

Julia Cousins for her gift of financial support at a critical time allowed me the time to complete the work. Thank you, Julia.

Many thanks to Ranchor Prime for (as ever) his excellent design and forbearance.

Thanks to Susan Mears and her agency team for staying with it; and Mike French for doing invaluable final proofing.

Others who contributed conversation, inspiration and support: Andrew Harvey, Will Shaman, Irina Kuzminsky, Angela Warren, Victoria Finlay, Hugh Richards, Cynthia Bourgeault, Caroline Waterlow, Revd. Simon Howell and Peter Owen Jones.

Psychic Poetry: a manifesto
The White Poem (with photographs by Carole Bruce)
The Great Return: books 1–5
Strange Days
Tantrika: love songs of the Sixth Dalai Lama
Kingdom of the Edge: selected poems 1980–1998
After Rumi
Out of Time: selected poems 1998–2007
Anamnesis: the remembering of soul
Places of Truth: journeys into sacred wilderness
Gita: a dialogue of love and freedom
Agistri Notebook
Monuments
Dreams Down Under: celebrating Australia
Pilgrimage: a journey to Love Island

Angels of Fire: radical poetry in the 1980s (with Sylvia Paskin
& Jeremy Silver)
Transformation: the poetry of spiritual consciousness
Earth Ascending: an anthology of living poetry
Into the Further Reaches: contemporary poets on the spiritual
journey
Soul of the Earth: the Awen anthology of eco-spiritual poetry
(with Anthony Nanson)
Diamond Cutters: visionary poets in America, Britain &
Oceania (with Andrew Harvey)

The Poet in You (9 month poetry course)
Alchemy: the art of transformation
Crucible of Love: the alchemy of passionate relationships

BY JAY RAMSAY WITH MARTIN PALMER

Tao Te Ching
I Ching: the shamanic oracle of change
Kuan Yin: the 100 quatrains
The Book of Chuang Tzu
The Jesus Sutras
The Most Venerable Book—Shi Jing
The Three Kingdoms

OTHER BOOKS FROM FITZROVIA PRESS

THE EIGHT ELEMENTS
My Journey Through Life's Mysteries
By Ranchor Prime

'A magnificent and profound work.' Martin Palmer

A journey through nature inspired by deep empathy with the planet and with our human predicament in these troubled times of global environmental and spiritual crisis.

Ancient wisdom saw nature as made of eight elements: Earth, Water, Fire, Air, Ether, Mind, Wisdom and Ego. These elements, ranging from physical to subtle, from visible to invisible, were the substance of this world and the dress that each being wore in their earthly incarnations.

Ranchor Prime shares his personal realisations based on a lifetime of yoga and ecology.

Each chapter includes guided meditations. The book has 12 line drawings by the author.

paperback 240 pages with 12 line drawings
ISBN 978-0-9570722-1-3

£9.99